W9-DDC-329

GOLD IN AZURE

GOLD

ONE THOUSAND YEARS

IN AZURE

OF RUSSIAN ARCHITECTURE

Text and photographs by
William Craft Brumfield

DAVID R. GODINE, PUBLISHER, INC.

First published in 1983 by
David R. Godine, Publisher, Inc.
306 Dartmouth Street
Boston, Massachusetts 02116

Copyright © 1983 by William Craft Brumfield

All rights reserved. No part of this book may be used or reproduced in
any manner whatsoever without written permission except in the case of
brief quotations embodied in critical articles or reviews.

Grateful acknowledgment is made to the following for permission to reprint
previously published material:

CAMBRIDGE UNIVERSITY PRESS: An excerpt from *Mandelstam* by Clarence
Brown (1973).
CHARLES SCRIBNER'S SONS: An excerpt from *The Diary of a Writer:
F. M. Dostoievsky*, translated and annotated by Boris Brason.
Copyright © 1949 by Charles Scribner's Sons.
HARVARD UNIVERSITY PRESS: An excerpt from *Of the Russe Commonwealth*
by Giles Fletcher (facsimile edition with variants, 1966).
THE MIT PRESS: An excerpt from *Russia: Architecture for World Revolution*
by El Lissitzky, originally published in German in 1930. English translation
copyright © 1970 by the MIT Press.
PENGUIN BOOKS LTD.: An excerpt from Richard Krautheimer: *Early Christian
and Byzantine Architecture* (Pelican History of Art, revised edition, 1975)
p. 360. Copyright © by Richard Krautheimer, 1965, 1975.
An excerpt from Hugh Honour: *Neo-Classicism* (Penguin Books, 1968) p. 18.
Copyright © by Hugh Honour, 1968. Reprinted by permission of Penguin Books
Ltd.
ELSEVIER-DUTTON PUBLISHING CO., INC.: An excerpt from *Medieval Russia's
Epics, Chronicles, and Tales*, edited by Serge A. Zenkovsky.
Copyright © 1963 by Serge A. Zenkovsky. Reprinted by permission of
E. P. Dutton, Publishers.
LIBRARY OF CONGRESS: The Admiralty and its environs (front endpaper) and
the Anichkov Palace on the Nevsky Prospekt (back endpaper), both from drawings
by Mikhail Makhaev.

The map of St. Petersburg is reprinted from *La Russie* by Karl Baedeker, Leipzig,
1897 (2nd edition).

Library of Congress Cataloging in Publication Data

Brumfield, William C., 1944–
   Gold in azure.

   Bibliography: p.
   Includes index.
   1. Architecture—Soviet Union.   2. Church architec-
ture—Soviet Union.   I. Title.
NA1181.B7   720'.947   81-47320
ISBN 0-87923-436-9   AACR2

To the memory of Arthur E. Craft

Church of Saint Nicholas in Khamovniki. Moscow. 1672–82.

And the canopy of the Church of Saint John at Kholm
was decorated with stars of gold in azure.

— Medieval Russian chronicle

Church of the Dormition from Kuritsko. 1595.

CONTENTS

ACKNOWLEDGMENTS

In the course of writing and photographing the material for this book, I have drawn on the support of many organizations and individuals. My various stays in the Soviet Union were sponsored by the International Research and Exchanges Board and, most recently, by the American Council of Teachers of Russian. At Harvard University I am indebted to: Leverett House and its masters, Kenneth and Carolyn Andrews, for hospitality of Russian proportions; Donald Fanger, of the Slavic Department, and John Bethell, editor of *Harvard Magazine*, for advice at a critical moment; John Booth, at Carpenter Center, for his assistance in matters photographic; the Russian Research Center and its director, Adam Ulam, for a congenial working environment. The staffs of Houghton and Widener libraries (Harvard), and the Library of Congress kindly provided photographs of eighteenth-century Russian engravings in their collections. I would also like to thank Dan Davidson, of Bryn Mawr College, for his support during my recent year in the Soviet Union. Roger Conover and S. Frederick Starr read the manuscript and offered many helpful suggestions.

In Moscow, the Ministry of Culture introduced me to the All-Union Scientific Research Institute of Art History, whose staff generously aided my work. I am particularly indebted to the division of medieval Russian art, directed by Olga Ilinichna Podobedova. The State Architectural Museum also provided many services. In Novgorod, I am indebted to Lyudmila Ivanovna Petrova, curator of the Historical Architectural Museum; to Valentina Mikhailovna Kovaleva, director of the museum's architectural section; and to Grigory Mikhailovich Shtender, directing architect of the Novgorod Architectural Restoration Workshop. I am very grateful to Wallace W. Littell, counselor for Press and Cultural Affairs at the American Embassy, Moscow, and to Pamela Kiehl, program assistant in the Embassy's Cultural Section. And finally, to Rita and Alexander Haifetz, friends in Moscow.

At David R. Godine, Publisher—a world unto itself—my first debt is to David Godine, whose faith in this book will, I hope, be rewarded.

And to Judy Hu, project coordinator, who protected the film and kept things moving between Moscow and Cambridge; to Hilary D. Horton, copy editor, who did so much more than edit; to Rich Hendel and Jean LeGwin, whose design brought order to chaos; to Susanna Kaysen, proofreader, for her unfailing good humor; and to Isabella Dubow, editor, for her determined pursuit of clarity and precision in the manuscript. And to the other Godine staffers and freelancers, who helped in so many ways. Bless them all.

Cambridge
July 1981

AUThOR'S NOTE

The photographs in this book are the result of three stays in the Soviet Union—in the summer of 1970 and the academic years 1971–72 and 1979–80. Most were taken with a medium-format camera. The selection of material was determined largely by a desire to remain within the major developments of Russian architecture, to deal with the art of the capitals (Kiev, Vladimir, Novgorod, Moscow, and Saint Petersburg). There are obvious omissions, most notably the magnificent sixteenth- and seventeenth-century churches of Rostov and Yaroslavl. Yet for all their splendor, these monuments are an elaboration of ideas that had been stated previously in the churches and monasteries of Moscow; to squeeze them into the Moscow chapter would have been inadequate, and to devote a separate chapter to them would have gone beyond the already considerable compass of this book. There are other omissions, in particular the cathedral at Yurev-Polskoy and the eleventh- and twelfth-century churches at Staraya Ladoga: I was not allowed to travel to these places. Weather prevented the obligatory trip to Kizhi.

The system of transliteration used herein is taken from J. Thomas Shaw, *The Transliteration of Modern Russian for English Language Publications* (Madison: University of Wisconsin Press, 1967). I have tried to adhere to his System I, but there are variations, dictated by common usage, and I take responsibility for them. The same usage also determines the choice of Russian or Western form for the names of rulers and church fathers: for example, *Ivan* the Great, but *Peter* the Great.

An inconsistency of another sort appears in the nomenclature of churches dedicated to Mary. An exact translation of the Russian words *Bogomater*, or *Bogoroditsa* is 'Mother of God,' but in most cases the Western term 'Virgin' reads more easily, and I have used it.

There has been considerable difference of opinion in the dating of many old Russian monuments. I have used the dates contained in *Istoriya russkoy arkhitektury*, edited by N. I. Brunov et al. (Moscow, 1956), except where these dates have been corrected by more recent research.

Cathedral of the Smolensk Mother of God. Moscow. 1524–25.

GOLD IN AZURE

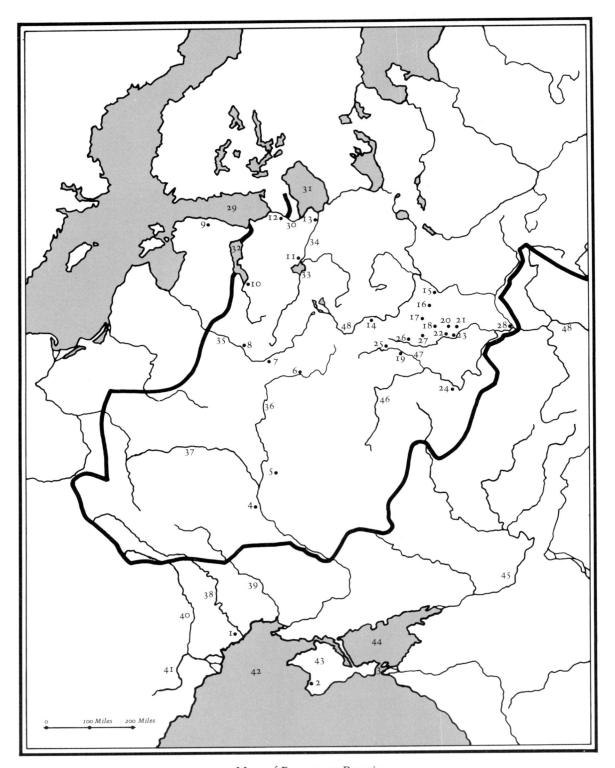

Map of European Russia

PROLOGUE

The study of Russian architecture has occupied a tenuous position in the West: suspended between art history and Russian studies, it remains largely unclaimed by specialists in either area. There is, to be sure, an increasing interest, reflected in the number and quality of English-language publications that have appeared in this field during the past decades. Post-Revolutionary modernist architecture, in particular, has recently been the subject of careful scrutiny in this country, as well as in Europe; and one anticipates more work on this long-neglected period, as the Western public is exposed to major exhibitions of modernist Russian art. In addition, there are various competent surveys of Russian art before the Revolution, and numerous albums that display the glories of medieval Russia, of Moscow, and of imperial Petersburg. Yet notwithstanding this rapid increase in publications—scholarly as well as general—few Western art historians would propose that Russia has made a significant contribution to the tradition of European architecture, or that Russian architecture represents more than a provincial elaboration of ideas taken from Byzantium, or from Italy, France, and any number of other European countries.

Indeed, there has been considerable support for this view within Russia. Mikhail Krasovsky, in the conclusion to his pioneering work of 1915 on the relation between Byzantine architecture and that of Kievan Rus (eleventh through thirteenth centuries), asserted that 'the Greeks who came to us could hardly have been outstanding masters, who, of course, would have had plenty of work at home. Most likely, they were ordinary talents, who could find work and good earnings only from undiscriminating barbarians. . . .'[1] Krasovsky has overstated the case, for many of the surviving monuments of Kiev, Novgorod, and Vladimir show considerable ingenuity in structure and form, even though they might lack certain of the compositional subtleties of Balkan and Armenian churches.

Unfortunately, we know nothing about these early Greek masters or their Russian disciples, and can only make tentative, frequently disputed, guesses about their manner of working. Did the builders of the large cathedrals in Kiev and Novgorod design according to a carefully considered system of proportions, or did the pronounced vertical thrust of these structures—unusual for middle-Byzantine architecture—result from modifications introduced by local patrons? From the medieval chronicles we can assume an exchange of architectural ideas among the widely dispersed cultural centers of Kievan Rus. And certain technical features provide additional evidence: the unusual plan and brickwork of an early-thirteenth-century Novgorod church (Saint Paraskeva-Pyatnitsa) suggest the hand of masons from Smolensk, where a similar plan was common. (Frequent invasions have spared very little of the churches of Smolensk; here, as elsewhere, the history of early Russian architecture often depends on the labors of the archæologist.)

Yet even when we define the development of an architecture inherited from Byzantium, and adapted in various regional styles, there remain substantial questions concerning the provenance of certain elements in medieval Russian architecture. What, for example, are the sources of the apparently Romanesque motifs and elaborate limestone carving on the exterior of Vladimir churches in the twelfth century? As Krasovsky and others have noted, the Greeks were not the only foreigners to build among the eastern Slavs before the Mongol invasion of 1239–40. Medieval sources refer to *nemtsy*, or foreigners from Western Europe, but we have no biographical information on any architect working in Russia until the end of the fifteenth century, when Ivan III imported Italian engineers and architects to rebuild the Kremlin. And even thereafter, the curricula vitæ of Russian architects before the eighteenth century are, at best, scanty.

The very isolation—cultural, political, religious—that separated Russia from Western art and technology (and since the seventeenth century has inspired massive efforts to catch up) has also obscured our perception of what has happened there. But one fact is clear: since the fifteenth century, the Russians have repeatedly invited Western architects to build projects glorifying the state and the church. Ivan III (the Great), protector of the Orthodox Church after Constantinople's fall, wished to rebuild the Cathedral of the Dormition in the Kremlin as a symbol of the authority of his state and bishops; when Russian architects proved unequal to the task, he imported the Italian Aristotele Fioravanti. Peter the Great wished to build a city that in both practical and symbolic terms would serve as his approach to the West, for which purpose he lured architects and engineers from half a dozen European countries. These are only the most dramatic examples of a practice that continued in Russia until the 1920s, when Le Corbusier was asked to design a large administrative building in the center of Moscow.

But whether the order came from tsar or commissar, no other European country has been so consistently dependent on initiative 'from above' in the development of its architecture. Although merchants and trade associations commissioned a number of distinguished churches in

1. *The Senate (left, 1829–34) and the Laval Mansion (right, circa 1800). Quay of the Red Fleet (formerly English Quay), Leningrad.*

Novgorod and Pskov during the fourteenth and fifteenth centuries, and although Moscow is surrounded by the elegant eighteenth-century estate mansions of the upper nobility, almost every major monument in Russia after the Mongol invasion was built in praise of or for the comfort of the tsars and the highest levels of the Orthodox hierarchy. (It must also be noted that until the end of the seventeenth century, churches made up the great majority of masonry structures in Russia.) Only in the latter half of the nineteenth century did commerce and industry begin to assume direction in matters architectural, and, typically, Russian critics of this period complained of the lack of a unifying architectural idea. (To be sure, similar complaints could be heard elsewhere in Europe.) The age of unifying ideas returned with the return of centralized authority in planning; but after a promising experiment in modernist architecture, the reassertion of control from above assumed grotesque proportions, unmitigated by the earlier imperial desire to assimilate the Western culture.

As a consequence of this peculiarly limited form of patronage, Russian architecture seems to have evolved in a series of jolts, as old forms inherited from Byzantium and developed in the idiosyncratic ways of cultural inbreeding were superseded by or grafted onto new forms from western Europe. From an art-historical point of view, such processes are difficult to classify.

One approach to the difficulty—steering a course between dismissal of native origins and full-blown nationalism—appears in the concept of 'rusticalization,' elaborated by the Russian art historian Boris Vipper (of Austrian descent). He notes:

> Rusticalization of artistic forms occurs when the traditions and elements of style pass over from one nation to another whose culture is at an inferior level of development or from one stratum of society to another. Forms are then simplified and generalized, typical qualities are emphasized, and spatial contrasts are replaced by surface rhythm. Yet, although such a process certainly implies a deformation, even a distortion of the historical style, it can never be called a decline. Impact on historical styles creates in the store of provincial art a certain repertoire of methods and motifs, which in their turn, by amalgamating with the age-old traditions of folk crafts, gradually form a kind of national artistic dialect. This is not yet style, but it forms, so to speak, the potentiality of an original independent style. . . . A tiny spark arising from a certain tension of national self-consciousness is sufficient for the local provincial dialect to reach the stage of a complete and independent language.[2]

Vipper's concept applies most conveniently to the baroque and mannerist architecture of eastern Europe during the seventeenth and eighteenth centuries; but a more general interpretation of the principle might just as easily apply to the churches of Kiev, Vladimir, and Novgorod, with their simple but expressive plasticity. As Russia recovered from the destruction of the Mongol invasion, Moscow's rulers attempted to model their cathedrals on the structural clarity characteristic of the Vladimir churches—and did so splendidly through the services of two Italian architects, who adapted Russian forms to the quattrocento.

But by the middle of the sixteenth century, Russian architecture again veered sharply to the idiosyncratic, in a series of tower churches built in Muscovy during the reigns of Basil III and Ivan the Terrible. Despite the apparent complexity of cathedrals such as Saint Basil's, the churches of this period show a tendency to tectonic simplification: the main structure enclosed less space and frequently dispensed with interior piers. By the seventeenth century, this form was entrenched, but its simplicity was masked by mannered decoration and by the picturesque distribution of subsidiary structures (bell towers, exterior galleries) around the central mass of the church. Many of these details were borrowed from Western sources, but their interpretation can only be called rustic.

Whatever its virtues in explaining the curious process of architectural assimilation in Russia, the usefulness of 'rusticalization' ends with the development of the late baroque. Nothing in Russian architecture of the eighteenth century matches the spatial complexity of the central-European baroque; and yet the best works of Bartolomeo Rastrelli and Savva Chevakinsky proclaim that Russia had indeed found its 'complete and independent language.' By the beginning of the nineteenth century, neoclassical architects in Petersburg and Moscow had designed projects as impressive as any structure of the same period in France (where most of these architects had studied). A century later, Russian architectural theory and design would again merge with that of Europe, as Russian artists and architects propounded some of the most advanced ideas of the modernist era.

All of this will be examined in the following pages; but the book will not attempt to demonstrate the existence of a Russian Sistine Chapel or Ely Cathedral—anyone familiar with monuments in Russia and the West will recognize obvious differences in technology and the range of artistic expression. Rather, the book is a record of the evolution of an architectural tradition that spans a millennium, from tenth-century Kiev to twentieth-century Moscow. Churches, palaces, fortress towers, workers' clubs, architecture as an expression of ritual and ideology—all are subsumed in a peculiarly Russian mixture of foreign borrowings and native idiom.

Much has been destroyed in the invasions and political upheavals that mark Russian history. More frequently, perhaps, ignorance and neglect (in the nineteenth as well as the twentieth century) have led to the loss of frescoes, icons, and churches deemed of no value. But the buildings that remain allow us to trace—and judge—this facet of a great culture.

I. KIEV AND CHERNIGOV:
THE BEGINNINGS

And gaze upon thy city, radiant in its splendour,
upon churches flourishing, upon Christianity
increasing, gaze upon thy city, illuminated with
holy icons, brilliant, surrounded with fragrant
darkness, filled with hosannas and divine song.

—ILARION, 'Oration to Prince Vladimir'

When Metropolitan Ilarion of Kiev composed his encomium to Vladimir (at some point between 1037 and 1050), he might indeed have marveled at the flourishing of the grand prince's city, whose towers, palaces, and churches had risen within a brief period, beginning in the latter part of the tenth century. For monumental architecture began among the Eastern Slavs with the coalescence of a Kievan state dominating the Dnieper River trade route (from the 'Varangians to the Greeks,' from the Baltic to the Black Sea), and with the acceptance of Orthodox Christianity after Vladimir's baptism in 988.

There has been much dispute over the circumstances by which all this occurred—and, in particular, over the role assigned to certain Norse adventurers in the formation of a cohesive political unit. One of the earliest Russian sources, *The Primary Chronicle*, states that in 860–62 the inhabitants of Novgorod, on the upper reaches of the trade network, summoned a Varangian, or Viking, leader named Rurik and his two brothers to 'come and rule over them.'[1] The reasons for this summons are unclear, the historicity of Rurik is uncertain, and the validity of the source, written some two centuries later, is unsubstantiated. Nonetheless, Rurik is considered to be the founder of Russia's first dynasty, the Rurikovich line, which lasted until 1598.

Kiev came into prominence in 882, according to the chronicles, when Prince Oleg of Novgorod undertook a successful campaign against the settlement, found its central location on the trade route favorable, and in effect established the capital of an emerging Slavic state, to be known as Kievan Rus. We know of Kiev's earliest princes, Oleg and Igor, from both Russian and Byzantine sources, for the Slavs frequently made raids against the Byzantine Empire, for spoils and to gain a more advantageous trading position. Hard-pressed by the Arabs to the south and the Bulgarians to the northwest, Byzantium concluded a number of agreements with the Russians, but cultural contacts remained minimal—at least until Princess Olga, widow of Igor, journeyed to

2. *Church of Saint Andrew. Kiev.*
1747–67. Architect: Bartolomeo Rastrelli, with the assistance of Ivan Michurin.

Byzantium with her retinue in 957. Olga is celebrated in Russian legend for the calculated and horrific revenge she exacted on the murderers of her husband; but she was also the first Kievan ruler to accept Christianity (for which she was later canonized by the Orthodox Church).

Nonetheless, relations with the Eastern rite remained undefined. The patriarch in Constantinople resisted any assertion of autonomy on the part of a Russian church, and a pagan revival during the reign of Olga's son Svyatoslav (964–72) threatened what limited gains had been made by the church. After Svyatoslav's death (following a campaign against Byzantium in 972), tension between his three sons erupted into warfare, resolved in 978 in favor of Prince Vladimir of Novgorod and his Viking auxiliaries. For the first ten years of his reign (c. 980–1015) Vladimir continued the policies of his predecessors in waging war with the nomadic tribes to the east, in defining a boundary with Poland, and in strengthening the authority of Kiev over other Russian cities. The question of ties with Byzantium, and the concomitant struggle between paganism and Christianity, remained unsettled until 988, when Vladimir carried out one of the most decisive acts in Russian history—the establishment of Orthodox Christianity as the official religion of Kiev.

Vladimir's motives for accepting Christianity were no doubt largely pragmatic. In the early years of his reign he had continued the attempt of his father, Svyatoslav, to reaffirm the worship of pagan deities, and apparently went so far as to gather them into a sort of pantheon— indicative of his desire to create a cohesive religious structure. Paganism could not, however, provide the sophisticated cultural and ideological apparatus that Vladimir desired for his increasingly complicated state. Familiar with Judaism, Islam, and Christianity (both Roman and Eastern), the grand prince decided in favor of Eastern Christianity— a logical choice in view of Kiev's commercial and political ties with Byzantium, and the large number of people within his realm who had already converted to Christianity. Contemporary accounts also note the positive impression made on Russian envoys to Constantinople by the elaborate Orthodox ritual and by Byzantium's magnificent achievement in the arts.

The final maneuvering centered on Vladimir's attempt to marry the sister of the Byzantine emperor Basil II, in return for Russian assistance in suppressing a revolt in Asia Minor. Although the circumstances are unclear, Basil seems to have reneged (his sister, Anne, may have had little desire to marry a barbarian with several wives), in retaliation for which Vladimir laid siege to the Black Sea port of Kherson. As Kherson submitted, so did Basil, who again agreed to the marriage, on condition that Vladimir accept the Orthodox faith—which he did, in 988. Despite the paucity of historical detail, we can infer from this course of events that the Russian's acceptance of Christianity was a diplomatic game, with considerable stakes for both Kiev and Byzantium: while Basil converted a troublesome neighbor into an ally, Vladimir acquired the cultural and social luster of the Byzantine court and church.

The first Kievan clerics were Greeks (many from Kherson), and the Kievan metropolitan was chosen in Constantinople. Yet the rituals and church literature were translated into Slavonic, in order to facilitate propagation of the new religion and to overcome the resistance to Christianity that lingered for several decades in many parts of Kievan Rus, particularly in the north. This melding of the Slavic and the Byzantine applies as well to the development of Russian church architecture from its beginnings: wooden churches, which could be rapidly assembled by a people thoroughly skilled in the use of the ax, must in some cases have achieved great complexity (chronicles speak of early churches with thirteen domes).[2] But the more substantial architectural presence that would signal Kiev's political and cultural status could come only in the form of stone and brick, of mosaics and frescoes produced by Greek and Balkan masters. Although Russian architects and craftsmen quickly learned the necessary skills for masonry construction and its decoration, the conception continued to derive from Byzantium.[3]

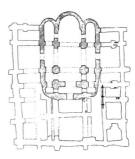

3. *Church of the Tithe. Kiev. 989–996. Plan reconstructed by Mikhail Karger.*

Unfortunately, almost nothing remains of Kiev's first major monument—the Church of the Tithe (the Desyatinnaya), built between 989 and 996 by Prince Vladimir, in honor of the Virgin, and supported by a tenth of his revenues. Destroyed by a fire in 1017 and reconsecrated in 1039, the church was looted in 1177 and 1203 by neighboring Russian princes, and finally destroyed in 1240 during the siege of Kiev by the Mongol armies of Khan Batu. There are different versions as to the cause of the structure's collapse: as one of the last bastions of the Kievans, it came under the assault of Mongol battering rams, and may have been further weakened by the survivors' attempt to tunnel out. Nonetheless, part of the eastern walls remained standing until the nineteenth century, when, in 1825, church authorities decided to erect a new cathedral on the site. Rejecting the idea of incorporating the old walls into the new, they leveled what stood down to the foundations and constructed a hideous 'neo-Byzantine' church (architect, Vasily Stasov); it was razed in 1935.

From twentieth-century excavations, however, we have a plausible, if incomplete, notion of the original church's plan; and while there is no way of determining with any accuracy the church's appearance, fragments of mosaics, frescoes, and marble ornaments give some sense of its decoration.[4] The walls were probably composed of alternating layers of stone and flat brick (*plinthos*) in a mortar of lime and crushed brick. What has remained of the foundations provides a prototype for the plan of Russia's masonry churches—the so-called cross-domed design. Composed of at least three, and sometimes five or more, aisles laid along an east-west axis, the design is characterized by a widening of the central aisle, whose width is reflected in a north-south, or transept, aisle—thus delineating a cross within a quadrilateral.[5] The space at which the arms of the cross intersect is marked by four piers that support the central cupola, elevated on a cylinder, or drum. With the addition of two or more aisles in the west, space could be obtained for a narthex, but the core of the plan consisted of the inscribed cross and the central cupola, whose interior contained a representation of Christ as Pantocrator. The eastern wall was marked by at least one apse, frequently by three (containing the prothesis and diaconicon), and in very rare instances, such as Kiev's Cathedral of Saint Sophia, by

4. *Cathedral of Saint Sophia. Kiev.*
1037(?)–50s(?). The view from
the east conveys something of the
cathedral's original appearance, con-
siderably altered since the eleventh
century. Plaster has been stripped
from portions of the five apses to
reveal the opus mixtum *(stone and*
flat brick) construction, inherited
from Byzantine architecture.

five. For all its simplicity, the cross-domed plan not only suited the complicated movement of the Orthodox service, but also achieved a metaphor of centrality; for each church, whose walls depicted the work of God on earth and in heaven, could symbolize to its congregation the center of the universe, observed by an image of the Savior at its highest, central point.

Kiev in Glory: The Reign of Yaroslav the Wise

With the establishment of the Orthodox Church in Russia, Vladimir had linked his state both politically and culturally with the Eastern empire, no matter how extensive his and his successors' contacts with the West. Indeed, what could have been gained in the tenth and eleventh centuries from the West?—backward when measured against Byzantium, under attack from militant Islam, and fragmented compared with the great territory of the new eastern Slavic state. Yet the rapid expansion of Kievan Rus contained the seeds of its own fragmentation, which began to take place even before the death of Vladimir, in 1015. That year his son Yaroslav, prince of Novgorod, refused to render tribute to Kiev, and upon Vladimir's death, during preparations for a campaign against the recalcitrant, the Kievan throne quickly became the prize in a free-for-all among the old prince's many sons. Svyatopolk—'damned Svyatopolk,' as he is known in the chronicles—managed to kill three of his brothers, two of whom, Boris and Gleb, accepted death at the hands of Svyatopolk's minions rather than enter the fray. For their piety and refusal to meet violence with violence, they were canonized in 1015 as the first Russian martyrs.

In 1016 the main struggle emerged between Yaroslav and Svyatopolk, and it continued until 1019, when Yaroslav defeated Svyatopolk and his nomadic allies, the Turkic Pechenegs, near the walls of Kiev. On the site of this battle, Yaroslav was to raise his Cathedral of Saint Sophia, inspired by the Hagia Sophia in Constantinople. But some eighteen years were first to elapse, as Yaroslav contended with further challenges to his power—the most serious being delivered by his brother Mstislav, prince of Chernigov and another of early Russia's architectural patrons. During this continual feudal strife, apparently very little was built in Kiev: a small wooden church with five cupolas that served as a mausoleum for Saints Boris and Gleb, and possibly (there are no remains) a wooden church dedicated to Saint Sophia.[6]

With the eventual consolidation of power, in 1036, Yaroslav—who as a young prince had refused to give tribute to Kiev—could at last continue the work in that city begun by his father, whose original plan was now considerably expanded, including a new wall and three large gates (fragments of one, the 'Golden Gates,' survive). But the great and lasting achievement of Yaroslav's reign is the Cathedral of Saint Sophia, which dominated his city as the Church of the Tithe had dominated Vladimir's. The cathedral was a monument not only to the ascendancy of Yaroslav, now called 'the Wise' (owing to his judicial wisdom), but also to the increasing prestige of the Russian

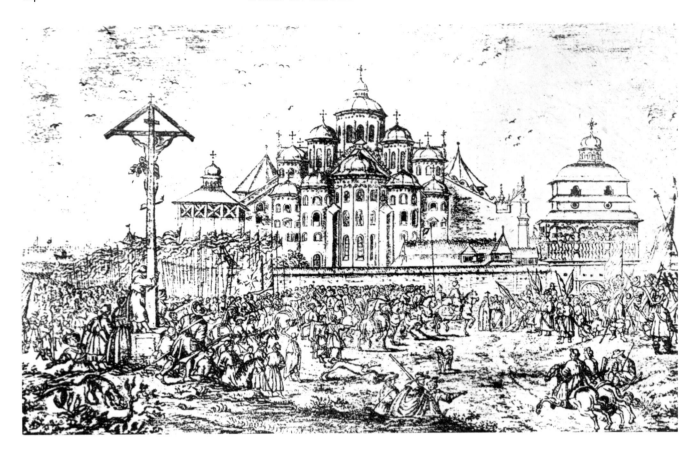

5. *Cathedral of Saint Sophia. Drawing by A. Westerfeld, a German mercenary in the army of Prince Radziwill. Made during the Polish occupation of Kiev (1651), the view shows the cathedral after its restoration by Peter Mogila, in the 1630s–40s. At this time the exterior of Saint Sophia retained an eleventh-century silhouette; its current baroque panoply dates from the turn of the eighteenth century, in a restoration supported by Mazepa (the Ukrainian hetman) and Peter the Great. Shchusev State Historical Architectural Museum, Moscow.*

Church, whose metropolitanate, created in 1037, was to be seated at Saint Sophia's for the next two centuries.

Although the exterior of the cathedral has been modified by reconstruction in the seventeenth and eighteenth centuries (it had fallen into ruin after the Mongol occupation in 1240), excavations in the 1930s and the study of possible variant designs have furnished what is now considered a definitive version of the original composition. In its basic parts, the plan of Kiev's Saint Sophia conforms to the cross-domed model; but its complexity and scale exceeded that of the Church of the Tithe—and of almost all subsequent Russian Orthodox churches. Of its five aisles, each of which culminates in an apse, the central aisle is twice the width of those flanking—a proportion that also characterized the transept along the building's north-south axis. The main cupola, focal point of the exterior, is elevated on a high drum over the center of the cross and surrounded by twelve cupolas, arranged in descending order, to create a pyramidal silhouette.

The origins of this plenitude of domes are obscure: as noted above, the chronicles refer to wooden churches with thirteen 'tops,' but no clear derivation has been established. Whatever their provenance, the cupolas—or, more precisely, their drums—serve both a practical and an æsthetic purpose as the primary source of natural light for the cathedral's interior. The thick walls, enclosed by two exterior arcaded galleries, allow almost no light from the outside, and what little enters from the windows under the vaulting is obscured by interior choir galleries along the northern and southern walls.[7] The effect is

6. *Cathedral of Saint Sophia. Transverse section, with a schematic drawing of the mosaics and frescoes surrounding the altar.*

magnificent: on entering the cathedral one sees—or is plunged into—a dimly lit space, which yields to a brilliant display of color under the central dome. The light that illuminates the area before the altar reveals not only piers and walls covered with eleventh-century frescoes (well preserved, in view of the cathedral's frequent despoliation), but also the only extensive mosaics to have survived from the Kievan period in Russian architecture, the tenth to the twelfth centuries.[8]

From the medallion of the Pantocrator in the center of the main cupola, a hundred feet above the floor, to the great Virgin orant within the central apse—blue robe on a gold background—the mosaics of Saint Sophia display what for Byzantium would be an archaic, provincial style; but the Greek masters who executed both the mosaics and the frescoes succeeded in transmitting—with vigor and occasionally with grace—the Byzantine fusion of religious art and architectural space.

In contrast to the lavish decoration of its interior, the exterior of the Cathedral of Saint Sophia demonstrates an austerity characteristic of Byzantine church architecture during the tenth and eleventh centuries. The walls, constructed by a technique known as *opus mixtum* (alternating courses of stone and flat brick—or *plinthos*—in a mortar of lime and crushed brick), are almost devoid of decoration, with the exception of niches, pilasters, and various ornamental patterns in brick—most frequently, the meander. Although parts of the facade were probably decorated with frescoes, and carved marble capitals provided a more elaborate form of architectural ornament, little else distracted the eye from the structural mass of the church, rising in

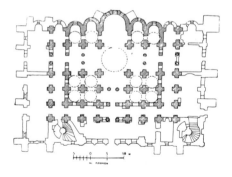

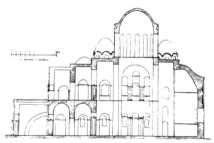

7. *Cathedral of Saint Sophia. Longitudinal section, plan. (From the construction by Kresalsky, Volkov, and Aseev.)*

pyramidal form to the central cupola. The pink masonry walls were later covered with white stucco, but even their original, more colorful appearance was restrained in relation to the interior. This contrast between an austere facade and a profusely decorated interior continued to predominate in the Russian church until the sixteenth century—the monolithic austerity separating the church from its surrounding structures, usually of wood, and the profusion conveying the worshipers to the inner world of the Church and its saints.

The Monastery Churches

During the reign of Yaroslav the Wise (1019–54) Kiev experienced its greatest prosperity. A vast trading network and numerous political alliances—frequently sealed by marriage among the ruling families—extended not only into Byzantium and present-day Poland, Germany, and Czechoslovakia, but also into western Europe and Scandinavia. One of Yaroslav's daughters, Anne, was given in marriage to the French king Henry I, for whom she served as an administrative assistant, signing documents for her illiterate spouse; another, Elizabeth, married the Viking Harold, renowned for his military exploits in Sicily and Italy and later to become king (Harold III) of Norway; and Yaroslav himself was wedded to the daughter of Denmark's King Olaf Sitricson.

After Yaroslav's death, in 1054, an uncertain principle of succession, combined with the distribution of lands among his five sons, once again threatened the fragile unity of the Kievan state. A period of cooperation among the three elder brothers, controlling most of the territory, collapsed under the pressure of the feudal infighting, attacks by the nomadic Polovtsi (a Turkic group occupying the southeastern Steppes), and popular discontent, which in 1068 led to rioting in Kiev. The struggle that developed at this point between Kiev's prince, Izyaslav, and his brothers continued for another generation without resolution: no prince wished the demise of Kievan Rus, and yet none was willing to surrender autonomy to the nominal capital.

The church was unsuccessful in its attempt to mediate among the various parties (it condemned Izyaslav for his Roman Catholic, Polonophile tendencies, and condemned his brothers for usurping the place of the eldest); but it did benefit from the largess of the various claimants to the Kievan throne, who tendered land and valuables to the city's churches and its growing number of monasteries. Of these institutions, the first, the richest, and for several centuries the primary Russian Orthodox monastery was the Kiev-Pechersky ('Cave') Monastery, founded in the middle of the eleventh century as a retreat near Kiev. The monastery quickly assumed a leading role not only in the affairs of the church, but also in the development of a literary tradition in Kiev. From the eleventh through the thirteenth centuries, its monks compiled the chronicles that provide most of the written information we have about Kievan Rus.[9]

As the monastery's holdings and wealth increased, the first small wooden church was replaced by the Cathedral of the Dormition, begun

8. *Cathedral of Saint Sophia. Central apse, with uncovered* opus mixtum *wall.*

9. *Cathedral of Saint Cyril, Kirillovsky Monastery. Kiev. Mid-twelfth century, with seventeenth-century alterations.* [OPPOSITE]

10. *Cathedral of the Dormition,*
Monastery of the Caves. Kiev.
1073–78. In ruins after the Mongol
Batu's sack of Kiev, in 1240, the
cathedral was restored in 1470,
renovated by Peter Mogila in the
1640s, and renovated by Mazepa
during the 1690s, at which time it
was given a baroque exterior. During
the occupation of Kiev in 1941, an
explosion destroyed all but portions
of the east wall and a baroque chapel
at the southeast corner. [RIGHT]

11. *Cathedral of the Dormition. Ruins*
of the eleventh-century opus mixtum
brickwork.

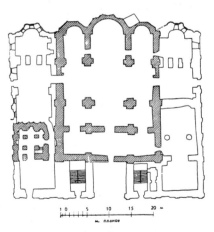

12. *Cathedral of the Dormition.*
Reconstructed plan (after Dmitry
Morgilevsky). The plan displays the
simplified design (three aisles)
adopted in large monastery churches
in the latter part of the eleventh
century.

in 1073 and completed only in 1089. (Considerable time was allowed for the masonry walls of Kiev's large churches to settle and thoroughly dry before the interior was decorated.) Although the cathedral was sacked by the Mongols in 1240 and rebuilt in the fifteenth century, much of its original core survived until its demolition during the occupation of Kiev in 1941. The remnants—a chapel in the southeast corner, portions of the eastern walls, and the foundations—have been preserved, and there are plans to rebuild the church, whose ruins themselves are monumental: a brickwork of shattered piers ascending to a nonexistent vault.

In contrast to the major churches constructed during the reigns of Vladimir and Yaroslav—with their complex plans of aisles and exterior galleries, rising through tiers of cupolas to a central dome—the monastery Cathedral of the Dormition represents both a simplification of design and a pronounced development of the vertical that was to become one of the distinctive features of Russian church architecture.[10] Although by no means small, the cathedral is modest in plan—three aisles and a narthex—as well as in its exterior (there are no flanking galleries and initially there was only one cupola); as a result, there is no distraction from the perception of its height. Alterations in the fifteenth, seventeenth, and eighteenth centuries

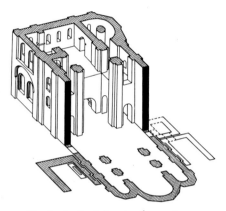

13. *Cathedral of the Archangel Michael, Vydubetsky Monastery. Kiev. 1070–88. The walls of the west part of the cathedral are currently undergoing restoration to their eleventh-century form. Situated on a bluff over the Dnieper River, the eastern part of this unusually elongated church collapsed from erosion at some point between the thirteenth and sixteenth centuries; the remaining portion was restored in the seventeenth century.*

14. *Cathedral of the Archangel Michael. Reconstruction by M. K. Karger. The collapsed eastern portion is outlined at the foundation level.*

obscured the original appearance, but its principle can be observed in other churches built soon thereafter, particularly in Novgorod, for example the Cathedral of Saint George.

Throughout the latter half of the eleventh century and the first part of the twelfth, a number of major churches were built in Kiev—most of them now destroyed or greatly altered. By and large, they were monastery cathedrals, and all conformed to the simplified plan adopted in the Dormition Cathedral. Among those that have survived, at least in fragments and at least until recent times, are: the Cathedral of the Archangel Michael at Vydubetsky Monastery (1070–88; the eastern part of the church collapsed owing to the erosion of the riverbank on which it was situated);[11] the Church of the Savior at Berestovo, part of the Court Monastery of the Savior (late eleventh century; only the western part survived destruction by the Mongols); the Cathedral of the Archangel Michael, subsequently part of the Michael Golden-Domed Monastery (late eleventh century; demolished in 1935–36); and the Church of Saint Cyril at the Kirillovsky Monastery (mid-

15. *Cathedral of the Archangel Michael. Detail from the north facade.*

16. *Ensemble of the Near and Distant Caves, Monastery of the Caves. Kiev. Left foreground: Church of the Elevation of the Cross. 1700. Background: Church of the Nativity of the Virgin, 1696; the bell tower of the Distant Caves, 1754–61, architect: Ivan Grigorovich-Barsky.*

17. *Church of the Savior at Berestovo. Kiev. 1113(?)–25. Sacked by the Mongols in 1240 and restored in the seventeenth century by Peter Mogila, the church has retained only the west walls (the narthex) of the original structure. As the court church of Vladimir Monomakh, the Church of the Savior contained the tombs of Vladimir's family, including his son Yuri Dolgoruky, Prince of Suzdalia, Grand Prince of Kiev (from 1149 to 1157), and founder of Moscow.* [LEFT]

18. *Church of the Savior at Berestovo. The remaining twelfth-century walls—here viewed from the northwest—provide the first example in Kiev of brick construction (as opposed to* opus mixtum*). The technique is known as submerged row: alternate courses of flat brick are recessed within a pink mortar of limestone and crushed brick. The decorative patterns (a meander frieze, crosses, recessed niches) are common in Byzantine architecture of this period.*

twelfth century, very approximately; relatively intact). A technical development over this period was the increasing use of brick, rather than the *opus mixtum* technique, for the construction of the walls. The Savior at Berestovo is one of the earliest examples of a church whose walls are entirely of *plinthos*, although it follows the earlier *opus mixtum* method of submerging every other brick course within the mortar.[12]

Kiev in Desolation

By the middle of the twelfth century, building in Kiev had declined with a further deterioration in the city's political position, now threatened by the rise of Vladimir-Suzdal. Indeed, Vladimir Monomakh, last effective prince in Kiev (1113–25), ruled there not by hereditary right,

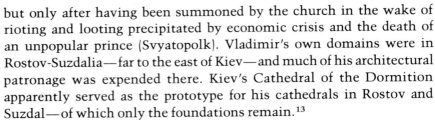

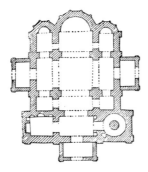

19. Church of the Savior at Berestovo. Reconstructed plan (after M. K. Karger). The narthex was wider than the main structure and evidently included a baptistry in the north section. The southwest corner contained a staircase to the gallery.

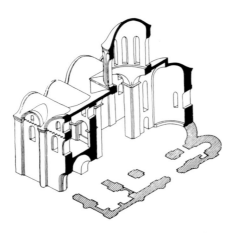

20. Church of Saint Cyril, Kirillovsky Monastery. Kiev. Mid-twelfth century. Reconstruction by Yury Aseev. In plan the church is typical of the larger monasteries: three aisles, a narthex, and a gallery. The zakomary, or gable arches, followed the contours of the vaulting—until a seventeenth-century rebuilding.

21. Church of Saint Cyril. North wall. Built entirely of brick, the walls are among the earliest to have been covered in stucco (three to four millimeters thick, of a pink hue). [RIGHT]

but only after having been summoned by the church in the wake of rioting and looting precipitated by economic crisis and the death of an unpopular prince (Svyatopolk). Vladimir's own domains were in Rostov-Suzdalia—far to the east of Kiev—and much of his architectural patronage was expended there. Kiev's Cathedral of the Dormition apparently served as the prototype for his cathedrals in Rostov and Suzdal—of which only the foundations remain.[13]

With the passing of Monomakh, in 1125, the struggle for Kiev between princes whose power base lay elsewhere finally destroyed the notion of this city as the center of a unified state. Novgorod, busily at trade with the West and colonization in the north, pursued its own course, while the eastern principality of Vladimir-Suzdal supplanted Kiev's dominance in central Russia. To be sure, Monomakh's succesor in Suzdalia, Yury the Long-Armed (Dolgoruky), strove for the throne in Kiev and finally gained it, shortly before his death, in 1157. But his son Andrey had no desire to rule there, and sacked the city in 1169. Looted again in 1203, Kiev was reduced to an insignificant position

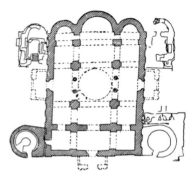

22. *Cathedral of the Transfiguration of the Savior. Chernigov. 1031–50s(?). Begun by Prince Mstislav of Chernigov and completed, after his death, in 1036, by his brother Yaroslav the Wise. The church was sacked by the Mongols in 1239, when most of its interior was destroyed. During a restoration in the seventeenth century an upper story and a conical steeple were added to the north tower, which contained a staircase to the choir; a similar tower was added on the south corner. The roof originally followed the line of the vaulting.* [LEFT]

23. *Cathedral of the Transfiguration of the Savior. In plan the cathedral is an unusual combination of the cross-domed and basilica designs: pairs of columns placed between the central piers obstruct the transverse aisle and create an elongated nave. From the exterior, however, the building preserves the appearance of a cross-domed church, with a central drum and cupola, and four lesser cupolas— much lowered—placed at the corner bays.*

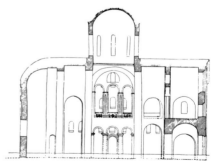

24. *Cathedral of the Transfiguration of the Savior. Section.*

among Russia's warring principalities, all of which, with the exception of Novgorod, then fell before the Mongol invasion of 1239–40.

Desolate, depopulated (a contemporary account notes that barely two hundred people survived in the city after the Mongol conquest), Kiev would gradually regain a semblance of order, but the circumstances that had once allowed it to rule from Poland to the Volga were not to be re-created. As Muscovy expanded in the east, Kiev came under the domination first of Lithuania, and then of Poland (after the Union of Lublin, in 1569), both Roman Catholic. Only in the seventeenth century, after prolonged and vicious warfare between Poland and Cossacks from the Dnieper region, did Kiev and much of the Ukraine unite with Russia (in 1654). During this period many of its ruined churches were repaired or rebuilt, under the energetic direction of Metropolitan Peter Mogila—who fostered an intellectual renaissance in the city and provided Moscow with a conduit for Western culture. Major architectural projects included the restoration of the Cathedral of Saint Sophia and the rebuilding of the great Monastery of the Caves. Indeed, in their zeal to create a new Kiev, patrons rebuilt eleventh- and twelfth-century churches in a seventeenth-century style that properly belongs to the development of a separate, Ukrainian culture among the Slavs of the Dnieper River basin.[14]

The 'Ukrainian baroque'—a rather loose term—is not devoid of its own impressive monuments, such as the Churches of Saint George at Vydubetsky Monastery (1696–1701) and of Saint Catherine in Cher-

25. Cathedral of the Transfiguration of the Savior. A baroque parvis obscures the cathedral's original portal, but bands of stucco have been removed to reveal the surface of the walls, built in the opus mixtum technique. The walls, decorated with brick patterns, were not intended to be stuccoed.

nigov (1715). Their unusual cruciform structure (different from the cuboid, cross-domed design of earlier Orthodox churches in the area), and their free interpretation of classical orders in the pilasters and cornice suggest a closer resemblance to Polish architecture of the period than to Russian. By the middle of the eighteenth century Ukrainian churches conformed to the Mannerism of the late Baroque, as practiced by Bartolomeo Rastrelli, Andrey Kvasov, and Ivan Grigorovich-Barsky (see chapter five). The Cathedral of the Nativity of the Virgin at Kozelets and the Church of Saint Andrew in Kiev are particularly notable examples of this style. But let us return to the eleventh century.

26. *Cathedral of Saints Boris and Gleb. Chernigov. Late twelfth century. One of several monuments in Kievan Rus devoted to the martyred princes, the church was incorporated into a Dominican convent between 1628 and 1649, the last years of Polish domination in the eastern Ukraine. Despite subsequent alterations and damage during the Second World War, enough of the original walls remained to make possible a reconstruction. Its exterior is one of the most fully restored from the pre-Mongol period. It is an excellent example of twelfth-century Kievan architecture, similar in design to the Church of Saint Cyril at the Kirillovsky Monastery.* [LEFT]

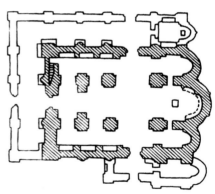

27. *Cathedral of Saints Boris and Gleb. Plan.*

28. *Cathedral of Saints Boris and Gleb. As at the Church of Saint Cyril in Kiev, the walls were of stuccoed brick, with no decorative patterns. In this case the stucco was scored to resemble blocks of stone—a detail ignored in the reconstruction.* [LEFT]

29. *Church of Elijah, Ilinsky Monastery. Chernigov. Early twelfth century. One of the smallest of the extant Kievan monuments, the church served a monastery founded in 1069 by Antony of the Caves—founder also of the Kievan Cave Monastery (1051) and one of the most revered of Russian eremites. The modest structure was expanded and given its present baroque decoration in the seventeenth century. An underground complex, now partially restored, contains three other churches.* [RIGHT]

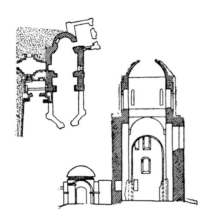

30. *Church of Elijah. Section and plan of the original structure.*

Chernigov

Although the early history of the architecture of the eastern Slavs is dominated by Kiev (at least before the twelfth century), there were numerous other cities in Rus capable of undertaking construction on the grand scale: Smolensk, Polotsk, Chernigov, Rostov, Suzdal, Vladimir, Novgorod. Frequent wars and subsequent periods of neglect have destroyed almost all of the eleventh-, twelfth-, and thirteenth-century churches in most of these cities. The exceptions—Novgorod and Vladimir—were located on the periphery of the Kievan state, and developed an architectural style that will be examined in later chapters. There is, however, one city in the area surrounding Kiev whose monuments have by some accident survived. To be sure, Chernigov never

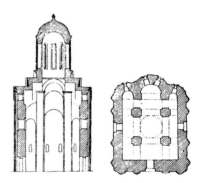

31. *Pyatnitsa Church. Chernigov. Early thirteenth century. After bomb damage in 1943, the church was stripped of various baroque accretions and restored on the basis of surviving portions of the original walls. The ornamental brickwork (open, in contrast to the Byzantine brick-and-mortar inlay of earlier churches) is an early example of the type of decoration to be elaborated in Novgorod and Pskov.* [LEFT]

32. *Pyatnitsa Church. Section, plan. The church's compact plan and stepped vaulting create a vertical thrust that recurs, in various permutations, throughout medieval Russian church architecture. There is no narthex, nor is there the exterior gallery common in Vladimir churches of the same period and essentially the same design. In the Vladimir stone churches the gallery was a means of reaching the choir level within the central structure; here, the flexibility of brick allowed the choir staircase to be placed within the walls (on the northwest corner), thus leaving the compressed vertical lines unobstructed.*

33. *Pyatnitsa Church. Detail.* [LEFT]

34. *Cathedral of the Transfiguration of the Savior. Chernigov. 1030s–50s (?).*

35. *Cathedral of Saints Boris and Gleb.*
Chernigov. Late twelfth century.

36. *Church of Saint George, Vydubetsky Monastery. Kiev. 1696–1701.
Bell tower, 1727–33.*

37. *Church of Saint Catherine. Cher-nigov. Completed in 1715. Built to commemorate the heroism of Cher-nigov's Cossacks in the storm of the Turkish fortress of Azov (1696), the church is an excellent example of 'Ukrainian baroque.' Its symmetrical centered plan—typical of the period—* *consists of four half octagons attached to a central tower, crowned with an octagonal drum and cupola. Rather than being placed on the diagonal, as is usual in a cross-inscribed Ortho-dox church, the minor cupolas here are at the points of the compass.*

38. *Refectory Church of the Savior,*
Vydubetsky Monastery. 1696–1701.

achieved the cultural level of Kiev, but its churches are excellent
examples of eleventh- and twelfth-century architecture, and on the
whole they are better preserved—at least structurally—than those of
the capital.

An admirable example of this preservation is the Cathedral of the Transfiguration of the Savior, commissioned in 1031 by Prince Mstislav and
thus (if we assume that Kiev's Saint Sophia was begun in 1037) the
oldest surviving church in Russia. A chronicle notes that by the time of
Mstislav's sudden death (while hunting), in 1036, the cathedral walls
had attained a height that could be 'reached by a man sitting on a horse.'
But there is no further information on its completion. The plan is
similar to that of Vladimir's Church of the Tithe—cross-domed, three-
aisled—yet the sharp delineation of its central aisle, separated from
the transept by arched columns, creates a perception of depth unusual
for the Russian church and reminiscent of the basilica. After the
Mongol invasion in 1240, very little was left of the original interior,
whose mosaics, frescoes, and marble characterized a style still largely
dependent on Greek masters and their materials.[15]

After the death of Mstislav, Chernigov remained without a prince
until 1054 and the accession of Svyatoslav (son of Yaroslav the Wise),

39. *Pyatnitsa Church. Chernigov.*
Early thirteenth century. [OPPOSITE]

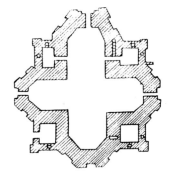

40. *Church of Saint Catherine. Plan.*

41. *Church of the Nativity of the Virgin. Kozelets. 1751–63. Attributed to Bartolomeo Rastrelli, Andrey Kvasov, and Ivan Grigorovich-Barsky. Late baroque in the Ukraine.*

who founded two monasteries—Yeletsky and Ilinsky—and whose descendants built a number of churches that have survived to the present. The Cathedral of Saints Boris and Gleb (latter part of the twelfth century), situated next to the Cathedral of the Transfiguration and initially connected to it by a palace, is one of the very few monuments of that period to have been restored to something like its original appearance. The simple exterior, similar to contemporary Novgorod churches, is divided into four bays, culminating in the semicircular *zakomary* (surmounts corresponding to the barrel vaulting) universal in Russian church architecture from the eleventh through the thirteenth centuries. Among the few decorations to have been preserved are limestone basket capitals—possibly of Byzantine provenance—displaying various fanciful animals in a web of rinceaux. (The capitals now visible on the attached columns of the exterior are rough copies of the originals, on exhibit within the church.)[16]

42. *Bell tower, Church of the Nativity of the Virgin. Kozelets. 1766–70.*

The simplicity exemplified by the exterior of the Cathedral of Saints Boris and Gleb characterizes the design of the Russian church for some three centuries. But there is one monument—to conclude our brief survey of Chernigov—that foreshadows the daring experiments of Moscow's tower churches of the sixteenth century. Although the Pyatnitsa Church, constructed at the turn of the thirteenth century, is quite modest in its dimensions—a small cube, whose four interior piers support the single drum and cupola—the resolution of the facade and the three tiers of *zakomary* create a vertical thrust curiously similar to that of the Church of the Ascension at Kolomenskoe (1532, near Moscow). The similarity is manifest in the way in which structural features, particularly the recessed vaulting arches, are designed so as to reveal an æsthetic as well as architectonic purpose, and in the use of brick detail to emphasize the building's plasticity. There is not a shred of evidence to suggest influence or continuity in any specific sense between these two monuments, so distant from each other in every respect; and yet there is a broader affinity that speaks of medieval Russian architecture's remarkable expression of the vertical.

By the time of the construction of the Pyatnitsa church, however, Kievan Rus no longer existed. For two hundred years Kiev had served as a point for the assimilation and development of the Byzantine architectural legacy, but by the twelfth century other cities, to the north and east, were to extend the legacy in ways quite unknown to Kiev.

2. NOVGOROD AND PSKOV:

CITIES OF COMMERCE

That same year [1156] the overseas merchants built
the Church of Good Friday on the market place.
　—NOVGOROD FIRST CHRONICLE

Novgorod is by a fortunate set of circumstances the great repository of medieval Russian art, with more than fifty churches and monasteries extending from the eleventh through the seventeenth centuries. The recipient of Byzantine architectural forms via Kiev, the city rapidly developed an indigenous architectural style in churches commissioned by its princes during the twelfth century, as well as in the 'commercial' and neighborhood churches of the fourteenth and fifteenth centuries. Even with the surrender of its independence to Moscow, in the late 1400s, Novgorod sustained a vital creative tradition in its adaptation of a new, 'Muscovite' style in the sixteenth and seventeenth centuries—a tradition that ceased only in the 1700s, as the city lost its strategic importance and sank into an almost total stagnation.

Medieval chronicles first mention Novgorod in connection with events between 860 and 862, when the local Slavs summoned the Varangian Rurik to assume control of their affairs—no simple task, apparently.[1] And when the Rurikovichi transferred their power to Kiev, at the end of the ninth century, Novgorod continued to exercise control over a vast area of northern Russia. In 989, a year after the Kievan grand prince Vladimir had adopted Orthodox Christianity as his and his subjects' religion, Novgorod was visited by Vladimir's ecclesiastical emissary, Bishop Joachim of Kherson (a city on the Black Sea). In his energetic imposition of Christianity on Novgorod, the bishop overturned pagan idols into the river Volkhov and commissioned the first stone church (named, appropriately, in honor of Saints Joachim and Anne; it is not extant), as well as a wooden Church of Saint Sophia, with thirteen 'tops,' or domes.

The political history of Novgorod was far from calm, for the city not only frequently challenged its leaders, including Rurik, but also participated in the princely feuds that wracked the Kievan state until its conquest by the Mongols, in 1240. Nevertheless, Novgorod prospered during the eleventh and twelfth centuries as part of the great Dnieper

43. *Cathedral of Saint Sophia.*
Novgorod. 1045–52. Apse.

trade route from the Baltic to the Black Sea. The extent of its commercial activity created a relatively large group of literate citizens, independent of Kiev and of Kiev's representative in Novgorod, the grand prince (usually the brother or son of the grand prince in Kiev).

At the beginning of the twelfth century, the assembly of citizens, or *veche*, had asserted its importance in the government of this city of merchants, and by 1117 the *veche*, summoned by a great bell, assumed the responsibility of electing a *posadnik* to direct the city's business. Novgorod's status as a republic was finally established in 1136, when Prince Vsevolod was told by the citizens: 'We do not want thee. Go whither thou wilt.' Henceforth the Novgorod prince was retained as a military leader with strictly limited privileges, while effective power lay with a merchant oligarchy and the archbishop. Novgorodians spoke of owing allegiance only to their city, 'Lord Novgorod the Great.'

During the twelfth century this city of 30,000 inhabitants, with a trading network extending from the Baltic to the Urals, was among the most advanced in eastern Europe: the streets were paved with wooden blocks, literacy was widespread, commercial transactions were recorded on birchbark, and an extensive water system was developed. In their chronicles, the monasteries compiled a comprehensive account of the city's history, with frequent references to the building and alteration of churches, and from these sources, as well as from archæological research, we know more about the life and art of Novgorod than of any other medieval Russian city.[2]

The achievement of Novgorod's medieval architecture is based primarily on a resourceful adaptation to local conditions of Byzantine and Kievan prototypes, as illustrated in the choice of building materials. The architects who worked in Novgorod did not have a source of high-quality surface stone, such as the white limestone used in twelfth-century churches of the Vladimir area. Rather, they devised a method of placing blocks of rough-hewn gray limestone of various sizes within a cement composed of crushed brick and lime, which imparted to the facade a pink hue similar to that of early Kievan churches, though coarser in texture. The use of brick was limited in most cases to ornamentation on the facade, the detailing of window and door arches, and the pilaster strips (or lesenes) dividing the exterior.[3] Stucco was originally applied only in the interior, which was then covered with frescoes painted by local and foreign masters (from Greece and the Balkans). All too few of these remarkable paintings have survived; many of them were destroyed in the Second World War, others by overpainting in earlier centuries. It is only through prewar photographs that we have some idea of the stunning contrast between the lavish interior and the stark exterior of churches such as the Savior on the River Nereditsa.[4]

It is gratifying to note that recent Soviet restorations have occasionally removed the whitewashed stucco that over the years had been applied to the exteriors of churches. Not only does the natural wall surface reveal the ingenuity with which Novgorod's medieval masons constructed and decorated their churches, but also the original rough texture creates a striking visual effect, particularly when illuminated by soft light. Given that all significant modifications in the history of a very old building are architecturally of interest, there is no one period to which a building can 'ideally' be restored. In fact, Novgorod's churches were so frequently rebuilt or substantially altered that in some cases it is impossible to re-create the original appearance of a structure. But the careful study of these buildings (or, after the Second World War, a study of their ruins) has provided a means of regaining, at least in part, the vision of Novgorod's early architects.

Architecture of the Eleventh and Twelfth Centuries: The Era of the Prince

The oldest surviving and the most imposing monument in the city is the Cathedral of Saint Sophia (1045–52). Built by Novgorod's Grand Prince Vladimir, it draws its inspiration from the Kievan cathedral of the same name, erected a decade earlier by Vladimir's father, Prince Yaroslav the Wise. And in its name as well as its size the younger cathedral provides an indication of the political and cultural importance of Novgorod in the eleventh century—a city that would rival

44. Cathedral of Saint Sophia. Novgorod. 1045–52. Built by Vladimir of Novgorod, son of Yaroslav the Wise, the Novgorod cathedral is simpler in plan than its Kievan predecessor, but notable for the vertical emphasis that culminates in the cluster of five domes; a sixth is placed at the southwest (left) corner, over a stairwell leading to the choir galleries. Seat of the Novgorod archbishopric, the cathedral served as a political and religious center during the existence of the Novgorod republic (twelfth to fifteenth centuries).

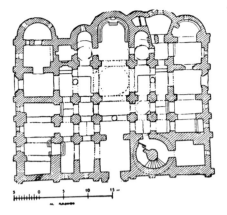

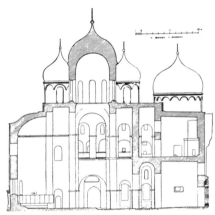

45. *Cathedral of Saint Sophia.*
Section, plan. The date of construc-
tion of the galleries attached to the
nucleus of the cathedral is unclear.
The current view holds that although
they may not have been in the
original plan, their first story was
probably built during the cathedral's
construction, to serve as a buttress. A
second story was added at the turn of
the twelfth century.

Kiev and emulate Byzantium, whence came so many of Novgorod's architects and painters.

As in Kiev, the plan of Saint Sophia is spacious (five aisles), with a surrounding gallery and a multi-domed summit rising to the great central cupola (at that time sheathed in lead); and the walls were originally without stucco. Their construction, however, differed from the technique applied in Kiev: instead of the layers of brick, or of brick and stone, the builders of Novgorod's Saint Sophia used the method described above—undressed blocks of limestone set in a mortar of lime and crushed brick.

The interior of the Novgorod cathedral lacks the splendid mosaic decoration that distinguished Yaroslav's great monument; and the floor plan is reduced both in size and in complexity.[5] But the most distinctive feature of Saint Sophia in Novgorod is its height, which, in conjunction with a more compact central plan, lends a pronounced emphasis to the church's vertical lines. This effect has been some-what diminished by additions to the central structure and by the accumulation of soil at the base of the church. (Most of Novgorod's eleventh-century churches have been similarly affected. As the build-ings settled and floods deposited new layers of soil, the floor level would be raised and rebuilt, and the walls altered to accommodate a higher entry—in some cases approaching the original second story.) Nevertheless, the Cathedral of Saint Sophia towers over Novgorod's fortress as yet another example of vertical emphasis in the develop-ment of medieval Russian church architecture.

Although no subsequent church in Novgorod rivals the Cathedral of Saint Sophia in the grandeur of its conception, the twelfth century saw a continuation of major projects initiated by the city's princes. As their hold on the citadel loosened, Novgorod's rulers initiated, in

46. *Cathedral of Saint Sophia.*
West facade. [RIGHT]

47. *Cathedral of Saint Sophia. Sigtuna Doors. Stolen by Novgorod forces from the Varangian fortress of Sigtuna in 1117, these bronze doors were produced in a foundry in Magdeburg (Germany) during the 1050s, and modified upon their arrival in Russia. They depict a centaur, saints, bishops, and scenes from the Bible.* [LEFT]

48. *Cathedral of Saint Sophia. Detail. Rough-cut limestone in a mortar reinforced with crushed brick.*

other parts of the city, the construction of large masonry churches, in an attempt to maintain a show of architectural force. Some of these structures have been destroyed and most have been modified, but four of them, built between 1113 and 1130, provide evidence of a style characteristic of the princely church: the Cathedral of Saint Nicholas in Yaroslav's Court (1113), the Church of the Nativity of the Virgin at Antoniev Monastery (1117), the Cathedral of Saint George at Yurev Monastery (1119), and the Church of Saint John in Petryatin Court (1127–30).[6] Each is a simplification of the multi-aisled plan at Saint Sophia: the number of aisles has been reduced to three, divided by six piers supporting the vaulting. The inscribed-cross plan has been re-

49. *Cathedral of the Nativity of the Virgin, Monastery of Saint Antony, Novgorod, 1117–19. The cathedral has a large cupola over the crossing and two cupolas placed asymmetrically over the southwest corner and the northwest tower; the tower provides access to the choir. The monastery was established by Antony the Roman, apparently a foreigner who found his calling as a monk in Novgorod.* [RIGHT]

50. *Cathedral of Saint Nicholas at Yaroslav's Court, Novgorod. 1113–36. Reconstruction by Grigory Shtender. The cathedral was erected by Mstislav, son of Saint Vladimir, as the second of the city's cathedrals. Its plan follows the simplified form (three aisles) prevalent in Kievan churches as of the latter part of the eleventh century. Currently under restoration.*

tained, slightly elongated with an additional bay on the west end, and the east—or altar—end is completed by a triple apse, usually rising the full height of the sanctuary wall. The low-pitched roof typically follows the contours of the interior vaulting—a feature obliterated by later, hipped roofs. In each case the interior division into bays is reflected on the exterior by pilasters that divide the austere facade into arched segments.

Of this group the most interesting is the Cathedral of Saint George, conceived in 1119 by Prince Vsevolod as part of the Yurev Monastery (endowed by the prince's court) and built by a certain Master Peter, one of the few medieval Russian architects whose name has been recorded. The plan of the cathedral is rectangular (with an additional bay on the west end), but from the southwest the structure appears to be a massive cube—an impression produced by the construction of a stair tower as an extension of the west facade. Only from the northeast does one see the tower, leading to an upper gallery for women and the prince's family, as a rectangular projection from the sanctuary. With

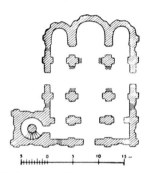

51. *Cathedral of Saint George, Yurev Monastery. Novgorod. 1119–30. View from the southeast. Erected by Prince Vsevolod, son of Mstislav, the cathedral resembles that at Saint Antony's Monastery, and it has been proposed that one architect designed both; in a rare identification, the Novgorod chronicle names Saint George's architect as 'Master Peter.' As with other Novgorod monuments of this period, the roofline would have originally followed the contours of the vaulting, here outlined by the arches of each bay.*

52. *Cathedral of Saint George. Plan.*

this additional bay on the west facade, corresponding to the rectangular extension of the sanctuary, Master Peter imposed an overall symmetry on the building, while retaining an economy in its construction. The asymmetrical division of the facade serves to vary the rhythm of a massive blind arcade, as well as to emphasize the cathedral's dominant structural feature—the great dome over the crossing, whose arms are projected onto the major arches of the facade.

Although the detailing of the exterior is restrained, the narrow arched windows and double-recessed niches complement the rhythm of the facade arches, whose indented extrados repeats the indentation of the windows and portal. The walls originally culminated in *zakomary* corresponding to the contours of the vaulting. On the roof are three cupolas in a nicely calculated asymmetrical arrangement: the largest over the crossing, the middle over the stair tower, and the smallest situated at the southwest corner. The present domes, in a shape known as 'the helmet,' probably replaced the low, hemispherical domes prevalent in Kievan Rus during the eleventh and twelfth cen-

53. *Cathedral of Saint George, Yurev Monastery. Novgorod. 1119–30. South view.*

54. *Cathedral of Saint George, Yurev Monastery. Central drum and crossing, with nineteenth-century paintings.*

55. *Cathedral of Saint George. View from the northeast. The square tower contains a staircase leading to the choir and the cathedral's only surviving twelfth-century frescoes. The niches that appear to rise from the ground were originally well above it; they indicate the church's great height.*

turies. (The development of the Russian onion-shaped dome, or *lukovitsa*, is thought to have occurred during the fourteenth century in Novgorod, but there is no clear agreement on its origin.) In a final decorative touch, the two drums supporting the larger cupolas repeat the arched-window motif of the facade, while the largest and smallest drums are crowned with a wave pattern expressed in a dogtooth brick design. All three domes have scalloped niches. In contrast to the restrained exterior decoration, the interior was covered with bold frescoes and contained icons from the prince's workshop. Novgorod's princes were to continue to commission churches during the twelfth century, yet no other monument—either in the twelfth century or thereafter—quite rivals Master Peter's cathedral.

The instability of the position of Novgorod's grand princes during the twelfth century led to a decrease in both the number and the size of new churches. The last princely church—the Transfiguration of the Savior on the Nereditsa, commissioned by Yaroslav Vladimirovich in 1198 and constructed in three and a half months—is in fact a harbinger of the simplified cube form that would define the dominant pattern in Russian church architecture for the next three centuries. Although the Church of the Savior was destroyed by artillery fire

56. *Church of Saint John in Petryatin Court. Novgorod. 1127–30, rebuilt in the fifteenth century. One of the many churches in the mercantile quarter of the city, Saint John's was commissioned by Prince Vsevolod and given to the corporation of merchants specializing in the lucrative wax trade; thereafter it served as a center for the arbitration of commercial disputes. In the 1450s Archbishop Evfimy, a staunch opponent of Muscovite expansionism, razed the dilapidated old church and commissioned a reproduction in the same style, reminiscent of Novgorod's twelfth-century glory.* [LEFT]

57. *Church of Saints Peter and Paul on Sinichya Hill. Novgorod. 1185–92. A neighborhood church commissioned by local residents, this is the only example in Novgorod of the recessed-row technique of brick masonry. It is therefore assumed that masons from western Russia—perhaps Smolensk—erected the building. As at certain other churches on the outskirts of Novgorod, the cemetery is still used, although the church is not.* [LEFT]

58. *Church of Saints Peter and Paul on Sinichya Hill. Detail.*

59. *Church of the Annunciation at Myachino. Novgorod. 1179. Interior, with twelfth-century frescoes.*

60. *Church of the Transfiguration*
of the Savior on the Nereditsa.
Novgorod. 1198. East view.

61. *Church of Thomas the Apostle at Myachino. Novgorod. 1195–96; rebuilt in the fifteenth century. Another of Novgorod's archaic reproductions from the fifteenth century, the church was long thought to be a twelfth-century structure, although the ornamental brickwork is characteristic of a later period. More recent study has shown that nothing remains of the original structure. Minimally restored to its fifteenth-century appearance, the church has a corrugated roof and bird-cage cupola.*

62. *Church of Thomas the Apostle. North facade.*

during the Second World War, it has been possible to reconstruct the building—parts of whose walls remained standing—on the basis of careful research and the results of a restoration in 1904. The church's frescoes, however, once the most complete and best preserved from early-medieval Russia, were irreparably damaged.[7]

The roofline, defined by gable arches (*zakomary*), conforms to the construction techniques applied in earlier large twelfth-century churches, and the three apses have been retained, although the flanking apses are diminished. But the number of bays along the length of the church has been reduced from four to three, thus creating a compact cuboid form dominated by a single cupola. With the exception of an arched brick cornice on the cupola drum, the exterior is entirely devoid of ornamentation. The rough, irregular line of the walls, however, lends the church a peculiar sculpted texture.

The Development of an Urban Style

With the declining importance of Novgorod's princes, both as political leaders and as patrons of architecture, the primary role in the building of churches was assumed by merchant families or corporations, and by neighborhood associations of artisans and tradespeople. The transition in sponsorship did not occur abruptly, nor was it signaled by a radically innovative architectural design; but the appearance of a plan that provides the structural model for a new Novgorod style can be dated from about the turn of the thirteenth century.

In 1207—less than a decade after the construction of the Savior on the Nereditsa—a group of merchants who controlled Novgorod's foreign trade commissioned a stone church in honor of Saint Paraskeva-Pyatnitsa, revered in Novgorod as the patron of trade. It was not the first church in her honor and on this site: in 1156 the same corporation had built a wooden church, which was replaced by yet another Saint Paraskeva in 1191. The masonry structure erected at the beginning of the thirteenth century was substantially altered in the fourteenth and sixteenth centuries, but extensive research of what has remained of the original walls and vaulting arches has provided the plan for a partial reconstruction.[8]

The Church of Saint Paraskeva represents an elaboration of the simple cuboid plan developed during the latter part of the twelfth century, with four piers, a single cupola, and three apses. The plan at Saint Paraskeva is still cross-inscribed; but the arms of the cross are now marked in the north, south, and west by three large covered porches, whereas the eastern wall consists of a rectangular projection, containing the two side chapels, and a greatly extended central apse. The derivation of this design—unique in Novogorod—has been traced to Smolensk, whose architects and masons apparently built the church, or at least began it.[9]

But in terms of its influence on Novgorodian architecture, the most notable feature of the design is the shape of the roof and its effect on the appearance of the facade: instead of a series of low arches placed on the

63. *Church of the Savior on the Nereditsa. Novgorod. 1198. Rebuilt after its destruction during the Second World War, the Savior is the last church commissioned by Novgorod's princes. Modest in its proportions and irregular in the measurements and construction of its walls, the building epitomizes the combination of an austere exterior and a richly decorated interior. Until their destruction during the war, the frescoes (1199) were among the best preserved and most extensive in medieval European art.* [RIGHT]

64. *Church of the Savior on the Nereditsa. Plan, section.*

same level (as in the Church of the Savior on the Nereditsa), the facade assumes a trefoil shape with a large central arch, corresponding to the barrel vaulting over the arms of the cross. The central arch leads downward to halved arches, which are placed over the quadrant vaults at the corners of the church. The trefoil pattern, with its emphatic vertical line, was to remain a distinctive feature of church architecture in Novgorod until the city's decline, in the sixteenth century.

Saint Paraskeva is one of the few monuments to survive from the thirteenth century, which seems to have been a period of general unrest in Novgorod. The chronicles make frequent references to fire, flood, and famine, as well as to feuds among the townspeople, with the city's right bank, or 'trading side,' pitted against the Saint Sophia side. The brawls often culminated on the Volkhov bridge, where the object apparently was to beat and throw into the river as many of one's opponents as possible. During the more violent scrimmages each side would destroy its part of the bridge. Occasionally the crowd's wrath was directed against an unpopular archbishop or prince, as, for

65. *Church of Saint Paraskeva-Pyatnitsa in the Marketplace. Novgorod. 1207, with extensive modifications in the fourteenth and sixteenth centuries. Endowed by merchants who specialized in foreign* *trade, the church honors the patron of commerce and housekeeping. Its unusual design, reconstructed by Grigory Shtender in the 1960s, is thought to have derived from Smolensk. Although the present roof obscures the original* *gables, the church is one of the earliest examples in Novgorod of the sloping trefoil roofline. In this respect it resembles its namesake in Chernigov (see Figure 38).*

66. *Church of the Nativity of the Virgin at Peryn. Novgorod. Early thirteenth century. The name Peryn derives from the Slavic pagan deity Perun, worshiped on this site before Novgorod's first bishop tossed the idol into the nearby Volkhov River. A church and monastery were founded shortly thereafter, but the present structure was built some two centuries later.*

67. *Church of Saint Paraskeva-Pyatnitsa. Plan, reconstruction by Shtender.*

example, in 1225, when the people drove Archbishop Arseny from town, 'beating him almost unto death.'

But Novgorod soon found itself threatened by a far more serious crisis. In 1238 the Mongols, having begun their conquest of the Kievan state, advanced to within sixty miles of Novgorod. Although at this point they turned back, because the terrain was unsuited to cavalry operations, the following years brought invasions by the Swedes, from the north, and the Teutonic Knights, from the west—both intent on colonizing the area. In a series of decisive campaigns directed by Prince Alexander Nevsky ('of the Neva'), Novgorod and its allies checked both invasions (the Swedes in 1240 near the Neva River, the Teutonic

Knights in 1242 at Lake Pepius, in the 'Battle on the Ice'), for which victories Alexander was canonized by the Orthodox Church and became a symbol of Russian military valor. Nevertheless, he was unable to throw off the 'Tatar Yoke.' In 1259 a delegation of Mongols, with their wives and retainers, entered the city to take a census for taxation, with the threat of a punitive expedition if their demands were not met; when the enraged mob threatened to kill them, Alexander wisely counseled submission to the Mongols and payment of their tax. Thus, Novgorod, although later to be sacked and depopulated by Moscow's grand princes, under Alexander's leadership was spared the devastation that had covered so much of Russia.

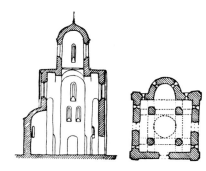

68. *Church of the Nativity of the Virgin. Section, plan.*

69. *Church of the Savior at Kovalyova. Novgorod. 1345. Northeast view. Like the Church of the Savior on the Nereditsa, this church on the western approach to Novgorod was destroyed during the Second World War; it contained beautiful frescoes. In this recent restoration the masons have indicated the height of the ruins with a jagged gash. The central plan of the church is square, but its appearance is cluttered by a mélange of porches and chambers, one of which, the south chamber, served as a burial vault for the family of Ontsifor Zhabin, the church's benefactor.*

The Fourteenth Century: Architectural Revival

As political and military relations with the Mongols stabilized, Novgorod again experienced an era of prosperity, which was reflected in the number of new churches commissioned by the city's merchants. The most notable among them are the Church of Saint Theodore Stratilates on the Brook (1360–61) and the Church of the Transfiguration of the Savior on Elijah Street (1374). Both churches display intersecting gabled roofs along the axes of the vaulting, but the restored roof of Saint Theodore Stratilates is closer to its original design, whose vaulting contours are repeated in the trefoil facade. As is the case with many churches from this period, the roof of the Church of the Transfiguration was modified during the sixteenth century to an eight-sloped hipped roof, which facilitated the application of sheet metal; it was also thought that a single plane would shed snow and ice more easily than a contoured design, although apparently this is not so.[10]

70. Church of Saint Theodore Stratilates on the Brook. Novgorod. 1360–61. Founded by Novgorod's posadnik, or mayor, the church is one of a number that represent the resurgence of the city's architecture during the latter part of the fourteenth century. Its square plan and trefoil gables are similar to those developed much earlier at Peryn, but the church's size and decoration display the new wealth that came with the city's emergence from the threat of Mongol domination. The remaining frescoes, damaged by whitewash in the nineteenth century, are now being restored.

71. Church of Saints Peter and Paul at Slavno. Novgorod. 1367. [OPPOSITE]

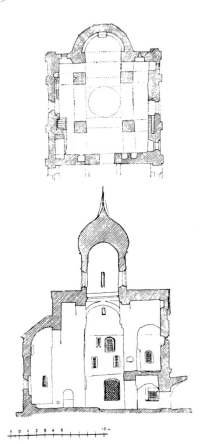

72. *Church of Saint Theodore Strati-*
lates on the Brook. Section, plan.

73. *Church of the Transfiguration of*
the Savior on Ilin (Elijah) Street.
Novgorod. 1374. View from the
southeast. Endowed by the commu-
nity on Ilin Street, this church—
within and without—is the most
richly decorated in Novgorod. The
array of crosses, of curved and toothed
decorations, emphasizes the plasticity
of the walls (which originally con-
cluded in trefoil gables). The center of
the interior and the side chambers
are decorated with frescoes by
Theophanes the Greek. The difference
in the number of curves on the east
and west panels of this facade indi-
cates that the 'square' plan is slightly
extended in the west. The arcading
and niches on the apse are similar
to those at the Church of Saint
Theodore Stratilates.

The trefoil facade of Saint Theodore is slightly extended to the west, in order to reconcile the basic cuboid plan with the need to provide space for the congregation in the western part of the church. The extension is evident in the north and south (longitudinal) facades: the central panel culminates in a trefoil crown and the east panels contain a halved trefoil, whereas the western bays of the facades display the curves of a halved pentafoil. The facades are further marked by a deeply recessed portal and two rows of windows placed in a one-two-one arrangement. The upper part of the central panel contains an elaborate cross beneath a single window niche.

The motion of the decorative pattern is repeated in the church's single apse, which is divided by a series of pilasters that in turn are linked by two series of arches above each of the rows of windows. The lower series is articulated in the sawtooth pattern (repeated on the

cornice and drum) and spans the entire distance between the pilasters, while the upper group contains a secondary series of short pilasters framing paired windows and creating an arcade within an arcade. It seems likely that this use of blind arcading on the apse is derived from Western, perhaps German, sources, although a similar pattern had appeared in Vladimir during the twelfth century. As the facade moves from curve to arch, the form follows its own rhythm, marked by narrow windows with eyebrow arches and a scalloped-wave cornice.

The Church of the Transfiguration of the Savior on Elijah Street, commissioned in 1374 by a merchant family, displays this decorative exuberance to the point of saturation. The pattern and motifs are essentially those seen at Saint Theodore, but their application reveals a fanciful and more complex attempt to emphasize the building's vertical lines. This is particularly noticeable in the distribution and

74. Church of the Transfiguration of the Savior. West facade. The brick arch indicates the position of an earlier vestibule.

75. *Church of the Transfiguration of the Savior on Elijah Street. Novgorod. 1374. Southeast view.*

76. *Church of Saint John the Divine in Radokovitsi (on the Vitka). Novgorod. 1383–84.*

77. *Church of the Transfiguration of the Savior. South facade.*

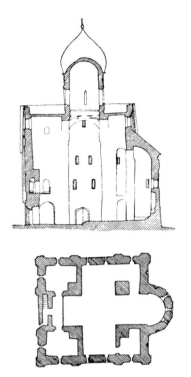

78. *Church of the Transfiguration of the Savior. Section, plan.*

framing of the windows on the side facades, where the simple one-two-one row of Saint Theodore has been replaced by larger groupings in the central panel.

From the deeply recessed portal the panel rises to a group of three narrow windows separated by blind niches. The central window is longer than the other two, and the entire group is capped with a pentafoil arch, thereby creating a pattern that echoes the division of the facade as a whole. Above this ensemble is an elaborate grouping of windows and niches—circular and rectangular—surmounted by a trefoil arch leading upward to the final burst of detail: a patriarchal cross, in relief, a single window, and a deocrative brick band, all culminating in yet another trefoil arch. In an appropriate summary, the cupola drum displays a profusion of eyebrow arches over the win-

79. *Church of the Nativity of the Virgin in Mikhalitsa. Novgorod. 1379.*

dows, a band of scalloped indentations, a band of hollow brickwork, and a wave cornice.

The plan of the Transfiguration of the Savior offers little deviation from that of Saint Theodore—the same four-pillared arrangement with the slight bias to the west, reflected on the exterior panels. As was usual for the churches of that period, the corner bays, east and west, were enclosed on the choir level to form small chambers, with access from the choir or, by an open staircase, from the ground floor (occasionally the staircase would be placed within the walls). At the Church of the Transfiguration of the Savior, these modest spaces, as well as the main part of the church, contain some of Russia's most deeply moving frescoes, painted by Theophanes the Greek.[11] In subsequent developments the modular plan of Novgorod's fourteenth-century churches continued to be widely used, but in a somewhat simplified manner, as in the Church of Saint John the Apostle (1383). Isolated decorative motifs show an obvious continuity with the Churches of Saint Theodore and of the Transfiguration, but they are used much more sparingly—particularly on the drum and the apse.

The construction of churches in Novgorod during the fifteenth and sixteenth centuries offered few original developments in either plan

80. *Church of Saints Peter and Paul in Kozhevniki. Novgorod. 1406.* [OPPOSITE]

81. *Church of Saint Dmitry of Salonika. Novgorod. 1381–83, rebuilt in 1463.* [RIGHT]

82. *Church of Saints Peter and Paul in Kozhevniki. Novgorod. 1406. Detail (see also Figure 80).*

or decoration, although a number of these buildings were quite large by Novgorod's standards. Local architects had evolved a structural unit that could be repeated easily but provided little scope for elaboration, apart from the application of certain well-established decorative patterns. A fine example is the Church of Saints Peter and Paul in Kozhevniki (1406), one of the best-restored monuments in Novgorod, with its wooden-shingled 'barrel' roof (*bochka*) and unstuccoed walls in red shell stone.[12] During the 1500s Moscow's influence on Novgorod extended to architecture as well as to politics, yet the local tradition remained vital—if not particularly innovative—for another century.[13]

The fourteenth century was the last period of Novgorod's commercial and political dominance in the northwest. As the tenacious princes of Muscovy began their campaign of aggrandizement through military, political, and religious means, Novgorod remained preoccupied with its European trade. The city's refusal to participate in Russia's first successful campaign against the Mongols (in 1380, with Russian forces under the command of Prince Dmitry of Moscow) signified its in-

83. *Church of Saint John the Compassionate in Myachino. Novgorod.*
1422.

84. *Church of Saint Vlasy on Volos Street. Novgorod. 1407. The popular mixture of pagan and Christian beliefs in the north of Russia is exemplified by the dedication of a church to Saint Vlasy, whose role as protector of cattle was assumed from the pagan god Volos.*

85. *Church of the Twelve Apostles by the Gully. Novgorod. 1454.*

86. *Church of Saint Simeon at Zverin Monastery. Novgorod. 1467. Here, as in many of Novgorod's churches of this period, the ground floor served as a storeroom for the merchants who sponsored the church.*

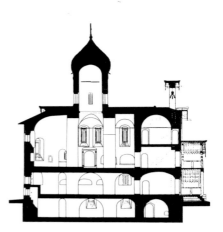

87. *Church of the Women Bearing Myrrh. Novgorod. 1510. Commissioned by a Muscovite merchant, Ivan Syrkov, the church is one of the first to be built in Novgorod after the city's subjugation by Ivan III (the Great). It was used primarily as a storehouse and as a state treasury by Ivan IV (the Terrible).*

creasing isolation from the center of power in Russia. In resisting Moscow's domination in the fifteenth century, Novgorod's oligarchy even considered allying itself with its Roman Catholic neighbors (Lithuania in particular). But Moscow prevailed. By 1479 the Muscovite grand prince Ivan III ('the Great') had reduced the city to a part of Muscovy (the great *veche* bell, symbol of Novgorod's independence, was carted away), and in 1570 the city was sacked by Ivan IV ('the Terrible'), the last great ruler in a dynasty that had begun, seven hundred years earlier, in Novgorod.

During the Time of Troubles—which at the beginning of the seventeenth century threatened the very existence of Muscovy—Novgorod was captured by (or rather, betrayed to) the Swedes; and although it quickly expelled its captors, the city took no important part in the development of the modern Russian state. By the nineteenth century Novgorod had been so diminished that the Russian political agitator Alexander Herzen, in exile there between 1841 and 1842, could write: 'Novgorod, poor and deprived of every convenience, is unbearably boring. It is a large barracks, packed with soldiers, and a small office, packed with bureaucrats. . . . In Novgorod any careless word can lead to catastrophe; Petersburg has taught the former republic how to inform.'[14]

88. *Church of the Women Bearing Myrrh. Reconstruction by T. Gladenko of the original form. The lower levels were used for storage.*

89. *Church of Saint Clement. Novgorod. 1520. Built by the Muscovite merchant Vasily Tarakonov, one of a number of merchants sent to the city to replace Novgorodians who had been deported by Ivan III at the end of the fifteenth century.*

Herzen, involved as he was with political reform, understandably had little eye for medieval architecture. And indeed it was precisely the stagnation he describes that served to perform one very great function: it preserved Novgorod's artistic legacy from an economic expansion that could have proved—as it did elsewhere in nineteenth-century Russia—more destructive than any of the excesses of Ivan the Terrible.

Pskov

In the vast, sparsely settled territory of northern Russia, Novgorod's cultural dominance remained unchallenged until the fifteenth century. There was, however, one other city within the domain of 'Lord Nov-

*90. Ensemble at the Vyazhishche
Monastery. Near Novgorod.
Seventeenth century.*

91. *Church of the Trinity in the Holy
Spirit Monastery. Novgorod. 1557.
A refectory church that combines
elements of Russian wooden architecture—particularly in the roof—
with Muscovite decorative motifs.*

gorod' that could claim an indigenous artistic style of considerable
vitality. Located some 120 miles to the southwest of Novgorod, at the
confluence of the Pskov and Velikaya rivers, the city of Pskov began,
probably during the tenth century, as a trading settlement, prospering
as part of the Kiev-Novgorod network. Pskov's social and cultural
institutions developed parallel to those of Novgorod, with a *veche*, or
citizens' assembly, that is thought to have been more democratic than
Novgorod's (where a wealthier religious and merchant elite usually
maintained control). Pskov never rivaled Novgorod as a commercial
center, yet the self-reliant spirit of Pskov's citizens—who declared
their independence from Novgorod in 1348—soon told in the turbu-
lent history of their city.

92. *Church of the Apostle Philip on Nutnaya Street. Novgorod. 1526. Contemporary Novgorod's one active church, built by merchants from Novgorod and Moscow.*

93. *Church of Saints Boris and Gleb in Plotniki. Novgorod. 1536. The pentacupolar roof, not used in Novgorod since the twelfth century, returned in this collaboration between Muscovite and Novgorodian merchants.*

94. *Refectory Church of Saint John
the Divine, Vyazhishche Monastery.
1698.*

95. *Cathedral of Saint Nicholas,
Vyazhishche Monastery. 1685.*
[OPPOSITE]

96. *Cathedral of the Transfiguration of the Savior, Mirozhsky Monastery. Pskov. 1156, with additions in the sixteenth and seventeenth centuries.* [RIGHT]

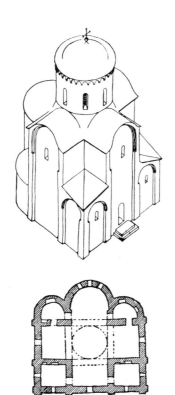

97. *Cathedral of the Transfiguration of the Savior, Mirozhsky Monastery. Section, plan, reconstruction by Yury Spegalsky.*

Although Pskov was one of the few early Russian cities to develop a style of secular architecture, here, as elsewhere, the major resources were allotted to the construction of churches. In the middle of the twelfth century stone was first used, for the Cathedral of the Transfiguration at the Mirozhsky Monastery, established by Archbishop Nifont of Novgorod. The design of the cathedral has been traced to Byzantine prototypes in Asia Minor (perhaps by way of Kherson)—a simple cruciform plan, with low corner bays and one large cupola situated on the four interior piers.[15] Shortly after its construction the cathedral was considerably modified, as it continued to be in later periods, but the central structure, with its twelfth-century frescoes, has been preserved and is now undergoing restoration.[16]

The Cathedral of the Transfiguration is the only Pskov monument extant from the twelfth century, and little survives from the thirteenth and fourteenth centuries. Not only did Pskov build fewer and smaller churches than Novgorod, but in addition its position as a western outpost placed it in the line of foreign invasion, particularly from the Teutonic Knights, who captured the city in 1240 and remained there until being routed by Alexander Nevsky in 1242.

With the resumption of a stable economy in the fourteenth and fifteenth centuries, Pskov, like Novgorod, witnessed the construction of numerous churches, sponsored by merchants and neighborhood organizations. Most of these churches were quite small and strictly functional (many contained strong rooms on the lower levels for the protection of valuables), and not intended as enduring monuments. Of the twenty-two built during the first half of the fifteenth century, only one is still standing: the Church of Saint Basil on the Hillock (1413).

Saint Basil's, built on the site of an earlier church of the same name, underwent extensive modification in the seventeenth century, but its

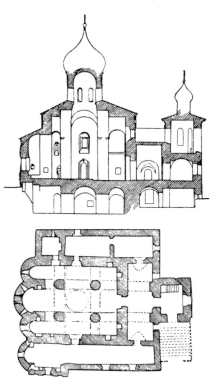

98. *Church of Saint Basil on the Hillock. Pskov. 1413, with alterations in the seventeenth and nineteenth centuries.* [LEFT]

99. *Church of Saint Basil on the Hillock. Plan, section.*

basic design provides a model for church architecture in Pskov during the next two centuries. The simple four-piered arrangement, augmented by surrounding galleries, chapels, and a bell gable over the west facade, is dominated by a single cupola and drum, raised over the vaulting by a system of corbeled arches (among medieval Russian cities Pskov was particularly inventive in the use of the corbeled arch). The only decoration—on the cupola drum and the apses—consists of ornamental bands fashioned from blocks of limestone.[17]

Subsequent churches in Pskov conform to the pattern of Saint Basil's, with certain modifications. These include the adoption of a trefoil facade, the development of complex eight- and sixteen-sloped roofs (only one of which survives, at Meletovo, near Pskov), and the transformation of the bell gable into a large, free-standing structure (*zvonnitsa*), supporting an open row of arches from which the bells were suspended; the Novgorod citadel contains a large *zvonnitsa*, but only in Pskov were bell gables used so extensively and with such impressive effect as part of the church ensemble. The uneven limestone surface of both church and tower would have been covered—lightly—in plaster and whitewash of a delicate sandy color. In their best work, it must be said that Pskov architects mastered the virtue of simplicity.[18]

In the late fourteenth and the fifteenth century, artists and architects from both Novgorod and Pskov contributed importantly to the development of new artistic forms during the rise of a centralized Russian state dominated by Moscow. In 1474 architects from Pskov were consulted about the construction of the Cathedral of the Assumption in the Moscow Kremlin, and ten years later another team was commissioned to build the Cathedral of the Annunciation, also in the Kremlin. Al-

101. *Church of the Nativity and Intercession of the Virgin. Pskov. Sixteenth century (?).*

100. *Church of Saint George on the Slope. Pskov. 1494.* [OPPOSITE]

102. Church of the Epiphany across the Pskov. Pskov. 1496.

though at the beginning of the sixteenth century Pskov, like Novgorod surrendered its ancient freedoms to Moscow, the smaller, more remote city was spared the punitive expeditions inflicted upon Novgorod, and Pskov's acceptance of Muscovite rule, in 1510, did not signify the end of its role in Russian history, as did Novgorod's capitulation.

It was, indeed, a monk from Pskov who formulated the doctrine of Moscow as the 'Third Rome.' In a letter of 1511, Philotheus of the Eleazar Monastery proclaimed to Tsar Vasily III: 'Two Romes have fallen [Rome and Constantinople], a third [Moscow] stands, a fourth there shall not be.'[19] The clergy of Novgorod and Pskov may well have favored Moscow's suzerainty as a means of preserving the 'true' Orthodox faith and combating heretical tendencies imported from the West through these two most cosmopolitan, democratic centers in Russia. Henceforth, Pskov was to serve as a defensive outpost on Muscovy's western march.

In this role Pskov achieved its finest hour in 1581, at a time when the military and political fortunes of Ivan the Terrible were at their nadir. Beset by enemies from the south (the Crimean Tatars) and entangled in a protracted war in Livonia, Muscovy faced an invasion by King Stephen Báthory, ruler of Hungary, Lithuania, and Poland. Pskov remained the only barrier in the west—and it held. The role of the clergy, with its warrior-monks (members of the military aristocracy

103. *Church of Saints Kozma and Demyan by the Bridge. Pskov. 1507.* [LEFT]

104. *Church of Saints Kozma and Demyan by the Bridge. Reconstruction.*

105. *Church of Saint Nicholas on the Dry Spot. Pskov. 1371, reconstructed 1535–37.* [LEFT]

106. Church of Saint Anastasia of the Smiths. Pskov. Sixteenth century.

who had taken monastic vows) and the symbols of the Orthodox faith—the icon and the Church—in rousing the people to a defense against the Roman Catholic 'infidels' is conveyed in an ornate military story written shortly after the siege, entitled *The Tale of Stephen Báthory's Campaign against Pskov*.

The account fashions a web of images around the protection of the Holy Virgin: the height of battle occurs on the feast day of the Birth of the Virgin (September 8). The Tower of the Intercession of the Virgin, captured by the invaders, has become the point of desperate struggle, during which the defenders seek protection from an icon of the Virgin, brought from the Cathedral of the Trinity (founded in the twelfth century, rebuilt in 1682). Explicit comparison is made to another icon of Mary, *The Vladimir Mother of God*, reputed to have deterred Tamerlane from an assault on Moscow in 1395. At the climax of the battle:

> The Poles and Lithuanians were fiercely fighting against the Russians in the breaches of the wall and in the Tower of the Intercession of the Virgin. Together with the warriors, the Russian officers and commanders were fighting, preventing the enemy from

107. *Great bell tower, Pskov Monastery of the Caves. Near Pskov. Sixteenth and seventeenth centuries.*

108. *Tower of the Intercession of the Virgin. Pskov. Sixteenth century. A key point in the defense of the city against Stephen Báthory (1581). Western travelers in the seventeenth century were surprised at the primitive appearance of Pskov's fortifications, but the structures served their purpose.*

109. *Walls of the Pskov Cave (Crypt) Monastery. Pechory, near Pskov. 1553–65. Constructed during the reign of Ivan the Terrible as part of a defensive system against the Livonian Order.*

breaking through into Pskov. And when the church procession moved from the cathedral with the icons, at the head of the procession, black-robed heralds rushed on their steeds; they were no soldiers, but the warriors of Christ. Among them were the cellarer of the Crypt Monastery, whose name was Arseny Khvostov; the treasurer of the Monastery of the Birth of the Holy Virgin in Snetogorsk, Jonah Naumov; and the abbot, Mantiry, who was known to everyone in Pskov. All three of these monks were aristocrats by birth and, before becoming monks, had been great warriors. Seeing the bloody battle, they rushed to the breach, and, for the sake of God and their holy faith, called out in strong voices. And it seemed as if these voices were coming from the icons. They called to the commanders and to the whole Christian army: 'Be not afraid. Let us stand firm. Let us charge against the Polish and Lithuanian forces. The Holy Virgin has come to our aid with all her mercy and protection, and with all the saints.'[20]

Today Pskov is a backwater with some 100,000 inhabitants; but its fortress walls—now restored—and its churches and monasteries evoke an earlier greatness. Unable to preserve its independence before Moscow, Pskov served as the origin for the doctrine of Muscovite absolutism; and its architects, builders of simple, sturdy churches, were to construct the most elaborate of Moscow's fifteenth- and sixteenth-century monuments.[21]

110. *Church of the Intercession of the
Virgin on the Nerl. Bogolyubovo
(near Vladimir).* 1165.

3. VLADIMIR AND SUZDAL:
THE GLORY OF WHITE STONE

*And in that year [1160] the Church of the Holy
Mother of God was completed in Vladimir by the
devout and beloved of God Prince Andrey; and he
decorated it with wondrously many ikons, and
precious stones without number, and holy vessels,
and covered it with gold, for by his faith and devotion
to the Holy Mother, God brought him masters from
all lands. . . .*

—LAURENTIAN CHRONICLE,
   on the Cathedral of the Dormition

While Novgorod and Pskov pursued their commercial destinies in the
west and the authority of Kiev eroded under the impact of incessant
princely feuds, a third center of power arose in Russia, to the northeast,
in the upper reaches of the Volga River and its tributaries. The lands of
Suzdalia were settled as early as the first century by Finno-Ugric tribes,
and by the tenth century Slavs from the west had begun to colonize
the area, rich in forests and tillable land. During the eleventh century
Kievan princes extended their authority over Suzdalia (in 1024 Yaroslav
the Wise, builder of the Cathedral of Saint Sophia in Kiev, suppressed
a rebellion in Suzdalia, incited by pagan wizards).[1] At the beginning
of the following century the new town of Suzdal was fortified and
acquired its own prince.

Suzdal was soon overshadowed, however, by the fortress of Vladimir,
established in 1108 a few miles south of Suzdal, on the Klyazma River.
Its founder, Vladimir Monomakh, grandson of Yaroslav the Wise and
grand prince in Kiev from 1113, was the last of Kiev's great rulers. His
death in 1125 led to competition for succession to the throne at Kiev
among his numerous sons, including the heir to Suzdalia, Yury the
Long-Armed (Dolgoruky). Yury finally gained Kiev shortly before his
death, in 1157, but during the protracted struggle he built much in
Vladimir, center of his principality, and established a number of settlements in Suzdalia—among them a small fortified post called Moscow,
after the river on which it was located.

Although the white-limestone palace and church commissioned by
Yury Dolgoruky in Vladimir are not extant, two of his churches—
at Kideksha and Pereslavl-Zalessky—provide early examples of an
architectural style that would soon lead to an extraordinary series
of monuments, beautifully conceived and executed. The church at
Kideksha has been severely altered, but the Cathedral of the Trans-

*III. Church of Saints Boris and Gleb
at Kideksha. Near Suzdal. 1152. West
facade. The earliest limestone church
extant in the Vladimir-Suzdal region.
A rebuilding in the seventeenth century destroyed the original vaults,
roofline, and cupola (with drum).
Limestone blocks from the twelfth-
century church are visible at the base
of the seventeenth-century covered
entrance.* [RIGHT]

*112. Church of Saints Boris and Gleb
at Kideksha. Elevation (reconstruction), plan.*

figuration of the Savior at Pereslavl-Zalessky (1152–57) has retained
most of its original structure.[2] Lacking the harmony of proportions
that characterizes later churches built by Yury's sons, the cathedral
nonetheless demonstrated the assimilation of a technique essential to
the further development of Vladimir architecture: the cutting and application of limestone ashlar as a primary structural material. (Suzdalia
is the only area before the rise of Moscow to have used dressed stone
for the exterior of its churches.) The walls, of limestone facing and
rubble core, are without decoration, except for an ornamental frieze
on the apse and drum; but when compared with the bare, 'molded'
appearance of Novgorod's twelfth-century churches, the lines of this
cathedral display greater precision and clarity—a contrast derived
from the qualities of the different building materials.

The Cathedral of the Transfiguration at Perslavl-Zalessky provides
the basic design for all but one of Suzdalia's major twelfth-century
churches: a cross-domed plan, with a triple apse and four piers support-

113. Church of Saints Boris and Gleb at Kideksha. South view. [LEFT]

114. Church of Saints Boris and Gleb at Kideksha. Apsidal structure (lowered in the seventeenth century).

ing a single cupola. Within a year of the completion of this cathedral, Yury's son Andrey Bogolyubsky had commissioned the Cathedral of the Dormition, the first of the great churches in Vladimir.

Andrey Bogolyubsky

Andrey has entered Russian history as a controversial figure, feared by those who supported the power of Kiev and Novgorod, but venerated in his own, eastern principality of Vladimir. In 1155, against his father's wishes, he left Kiev for Vladimir, the city he considered his own; and for the rest of his reign he ruthlessly and with great tenacity pursued a policy of aggrandizement at the expense of Kiev and Novgorod. His intention was not to rule from a capital in the south, but to transfer power to Vladimir; in this he was largely successful. His sack of Kiev in 1169—some seventy years before its devastation by the Mongols—might roughly be compared to the taking of Constantinople by the

Crusaders in 1204. Kiev, its churches despoiled and much of its population deported, continued to exist, but its military and political strength had collapsed. As part of the same campaign, Andrey's forces marched on Novgorod, and although his army was repulsed—in a battle commemorated in Novgorod's chronicle and icons—Andrey succeeded in blocking the city's grain supply from the south, so that Novgorod, like Kiev, was forced to accept his candidate for grand prince.[3] In effect, Andrey had established his authority over Russia, not from Kiev but from Vladimir.

It seems to be axiomatic in the history of Russian architecture that the expansion or establishment of political power is inevitably accompanied by intensive building activity on the part of a ruler who wishes to impress with his structures, particularly churches. In addition, one is tempted to conclude that the more bloodthirsty and driven the prince, or tsar, or emperor, the greater is his architectural legacy (Andrey, Ivan the Great, Ivan the Terrible, Peter the Great). Exceptions immediately come to mind, but it is beyond question that Andrey Bogolyubsky, despoiler of Kiev, is one of the great patrons of Russian architecture. Even though only a fraction of what he built has survived, that is more than sufficient to support the claim. His first church, the Cathedral of the Dormition in Vladimir (1158–60), conformed to the elongated, six-pier plan typical of Novgorod's large churches of the same period, and it displayed, on a very limited scale, the high-relief carvings in limestone so distinctive in later Vladimir architecture.[4] However, the structure was substantially enlarged after partial destruction by fire in 1185, and the cathedral as it now exists belongs more properly to the reign of Andrey's brother Vsevolod III.

The one church from Andrey's reign that has survived in something like its original form, the Church of the Intercession on the River Nerl, is probably the most perfect thing created by medieval Russian architecture. Located a short distance from Vladimir, near Andrey's palace at Bogolyubovo, the church honors the holy festival of the Intercession of the Virgin, established by Andrey independent of Kievan and Byzantine religious authorities. The church's plan follows the traditional cross-domed design, with four piers, a single dome, and a tripartite facade culminating in *zakomary*. Yet subtle modifications in design and articulation create an unprecedented sense of harmony in the building's proportions.

This mastery over material and form is expressed most clearly in the unknown architect's understanding of the vertical principle in the design of the Russian cruciform church. The architect was aided by Andrey's choice of site—and a very unlikely one, on low, marshy ground near the confluence of the Klyazma and Nerl rivers. (The Klyazma has since shifted course, leaving a small oxbow lake on two sides of the church.) On this unpromising location, exposed to spring floods as high as twelve feet, the builders fashioned an artificial hill, paved with stone, that not only protects the church from high water and provides a buttress for the deep foundation walls (sixteen feet), but also serves as the first stage of the visual ascent.

115. Cathedral of the Transfiguration of the Savior. Pereslavl-Zalessky. 1152–57. Northwest view. Originally the cathedral had exterior galleries leading to the choir level (upper tier, on the west); the cupola was of a lower, hemispherical shape, but the structure is otherwise well preserved. [OPPOSITE]

116. Cathedral of the Transfiguration of the Savior. Section, plan.

117. Cathedral of the Transfiguration of the Savior. Interior.

118. *Cathedral of the Transfiguration of the Savior. Decorative cornice on the apse.*

On this well-engineered and durable foundation, the structure rises in two tiers: a lower story of thick walls, culminating in an arcade band; and the upper-facade panels, sharply recessed within the three bays of each wall. The vertical thrust, defined by the proportions of the building, is reinforced by the receding surface of the walls, and by a slight calculated lean inward, which creates a foreshortening effect. Continuity between the two levels is maintained by pilasters, accentuated by attached columns ascending from plinth to *zakomary*. This rhythm, established by the arched bays, is repeated in the arcade strip and in the narrow stepped windows of the upper tier. The ascent is completed by the slender drum, whose eight recessed windows echo those of the walls.

The vertical lines of the Church of the Intercession are determined by an unusual proportional system among the facade bays. A simple method of expressing the proportions is provided by the number of arches, in the blind arcade, contained within each bay: on the north and south facades the numbers (counting from the east) are three, six, and five; on the west facade, four, six, and four. Each of the three facades (north, south, and west) contains fourteen arches of equal width and each central bay—the extension of the axes of the church—contains six arches.

The complexity of the arrangement arises from the spacing of the side bays along the north and south facades. The need to extend the west end of the church in order to accommodate the congregation was usually accomplished (in Novgorod, for example) by adding another bay (as in Master Peter's Cathedral of Saint George), or simply by lengthening the west bay. By contrast, the Church of the Intercession obtains the additional space in the west by shifting the central crossing slightly to the east—as indicated by the number of arches in the east and west bays (three to five). The final, graceful touch is provided by

119. *Church of the Intercession on the Nerl. Reconstruction, by Nikolay Voronin, of the original form, with exterior gallery.*

120. *Church of the Intercession on the Nerl. Near Bogolyubovo. 1165. Section, with diagram by Nikolay Voronin of the artificial hill and foundation.* [RIGHT]

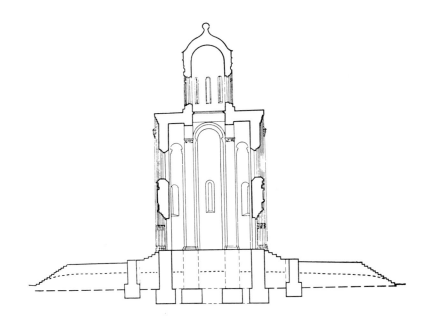

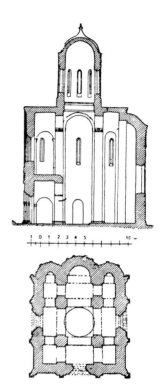

121. *Church of the Intercession on the Nerl. Apse.* [LEFT]

122. *Church of the Intercession on the Nerl. Section, plan.*

the apses, which rise to the archivolt of the *zakomary* and display the same sense of proportion that characterizes the central structure.

The elegance of the design brings to a culmination the architectural principles first stated in the simpler churches from the reign of Yury Dolgoruky, with their two-tiered structure, sharply molded facades, splayed window niches, and so forth. Its sculptural decoration may also have had precedents in Suzdalia, but the Church of the Intercession is the earliest surviving monument to display an iconographic message in stone.[5] The white limestone quarried along the Volga provided a durable material suitable for carving, yet apart from the arcade frieze at Pereslavl-Zalessky, the sculptural possibilities of stone had not been exploited before the building of the Cathedral of the Dormition in Vladimir, which contained a few carved figures and columns. The rapid development of this form of exterior ornamen-

123. *Church of the Intercession on the Nerl. West portal.*

tation at Andrey's Bogolyubovo churches (the palace church—not extant—and the Church of the Intercession, both completed by 1165) suggests supervision by a foreign master, familiar with the Romanesque style in central Europe.

The variety of carvings can be divided into two general categories: the highly stylized foliated patterns on the archivolts of the portals and on the capitals of the engaged columns, and the bestial and human figures on the facades. The dominant element in the latter group is a high-relief carving of King David, placed in each of the central *zakomary*. Enthroned, with the right hand raised in blessing and the left holding the Psalter, David is flanked by two birds and two lions, signifying both submission and protection. The prominence allotted David suggests various interpretations: as God's anointed, the king of

124. *Stair tower at the palace of Andrey Bogolyubsky. Bogolyubovo (near Vladimir). 1158–65. This stair tower, presumably the site of Andrey's murder, is the only remaining part of the palace compound at Bogolyuobovo.*

Judah, he represents the warrior-leader who defeated his enemies and united the various factions within his kingdom—deeds Andrey no doubt wished to compare to his own frequent campaigns against other Russian princes, as well as against such external enemies as the Volga Bulgars. Built to commemorate a victory over the Bulgars, the church testifies to the power of divine intercession so frequently invoked in the Psalms.

More precisely, however, the name of the church honors the intercession of the Virgin Mary, whose protection is extended to the people of Vladimir and their just, God-fearing ruler. No representation of Mary appears on the Church of the Intercession, but the concept of feminine protection is expressed in the twenty high-relief masks of young women, placed slightly below the *zakomary*. Striking in their stylized primitive form, the masks suggest not only the exaltation of the feminine in Orthodox religious art, but also the indigenous celebration of fertility and the reverence for the Russian earth as a female being. (It has been noted that the Feast of the Intercession of the Virgin—October 1—occurs at a time of the year, after the harvest, when marriages were traditionally made. The Christian holiday may

125. *Stair tower at the palace of*
Andrey Bogolyubsky.

well have superseded an ancient ceremony devoted to a pagan goddess.)[6]

A variety of forms proliferated on the consoles supporting the columns of the arcade band—pig snouts, lion faces, leopards, griffins, and other chimeras. Of course, when the church was originally built, much of this fantasy was obscured by a gallery placed against the lower tier of the west, south, and north facades.[7] (Accepted practice apparently dictated that each structural unit be decorated separately, probably by different teams of craftsmen.) Although some purists insist that the loss of the gallery poses a serious obstacle to our appreciation of the design—and the loss is certainly regrettable from a historical and archæological point of view—the æsthete will quietly enjoy the unobstructed view of a serene and graceful form.

The Church of the Intercession represents only one part of the architectural ensemble Andrey constructed at the village of Bogolyubovo, although very little of the ensemble remains today. His residence,

126. *Cathedral and passage to Andrey Bogolyubsky's palace. Reconstruction by Nikolay Voronin.* [LEFT]

127. *Palace cathedral, Bogolyubovo. Reconstruction by Nikolay Voronin.*

fortified with stone walls, included the Church of the Nativity of the Virgin, whose lavish decoration was noted by a contemporary chronicler: 'He adorned it with a luster that could not be looked upon, for all the church was of gold. . . . He adorned it with precious icons, with gold and valuable stones, with a priceless pearl of great size, with various ornaments of jasper, and many precious things with carved patterns.'[8]

It was at this residence, in the summer of 1174, that Andrey met his death, at the hands of conspirators exasperated by his strong temper and autocratic rule. According to a contemporary account, the assassins rushed his chambers one night, surrounded the unarmed prince, and flailed away—with some difficulty, for they were drunk and he, despite his age, was still quite vigorous. Having overcome his resistance and hacked at his body, they left the prince for dead, only later to hear groans from a staircase in the gallery connecting palace and church. With lighted candle, trembling, they followed the trail of blood, found the wounded prince, cut off his right hand, and threw him into the courtyard, where he lay 'for the dogs' while his palace was ransacked.[9] Many of the local inhabitants, indifferent to their ruler's fate, took part in the pillage. Two days later a Kievan recovered the corpse and placed it on the parvis of Andrey's Church of the Nativity of the Virgin; not until six days after the murder did a delegation from Vladimir retrieve the body for proper burial in the city. What remained of Andrey's palace was converted into a monastery in the thirteenth century, and in 1702 he was canonized.

In endeavoring to unite the Russian lands around a new center of power in the northeast, Andrey had clearly been aware of the symbolic use of architecture. He intended his churches to rival those at Kiev, and is recorded as saying: 'I wish to build just such a church as that one with the golden gates [in Kiev], that it may be a remembrance to my land.'[10] This church, the Nativity of the Virgin, attached to his palace in Bogolyubovo, survived the Mongol devastation of Suzdalia in 1238, only to collapse in 1723 through the ineptitude of an abbot

128. *Cathedral of the Dormition.*
Vladimir. 1158–60; rebuilt and
expanded in 1185–89. East view.

who, in an attempt to enlarge the windows, disturbed the finely calculated balance of the walls. (In design, the church closely resembled the Intercession on the Nerl, which was itself nearly razed by another abbot, who wanted the stone for the Bogolyubovo monastery: the contractor refused the job—too little money.) All that now remains of Andrey's compound is the foundation of the church, several carved ornaments, and the palace tower where Andrey received martyrdom.

Vsevolod III

With Andrey's death, rule of the principality passed to his brother Vsevolod III (or Vsevolod the Big Nest, by virtue of the great number of his male progeny). Vsevolod proved as energetic and knowledgeable a patron of architecture as his predecessor, whose Cathedral of the Dormition he rebuilt after the fire of 1185. In an ingenious design, Vsevolod's architects retained the walls of the earlier structure, weak-

129. *Cathedral of the Dormition. Vladimir. 1158–60, enlarged in 1185–89. South facade.*

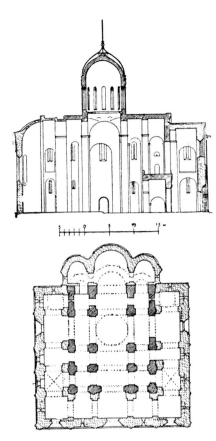

130. *Cathedral of the Dormition.*
Section, plan. The darker piers indicate
the outline of Andrey Bogolyubsky's
original cathedral, whose walls were
incorporated into this later structure.

131. *Cathedral of the Dormition.*
Blind arcade, with carved capitals
and consoles.

ened by the fire, as the core of the building, and added another aisle on each side. As the seat of the Vladimir bishopric, the Cathedral of the Dormition exceeded in size all other churches in Suzdalia, but the carvings on its facade are meager in comparison with those of the Church of the Intercession or of Vsevolod's later Cathedral of Saint Dmitry (see below).

During the Mongol sack of Vladimir in 1238, the bishop and the family of Prince Yury (Vsevolod's son) retreated to the upper gallery of the Dormition. The Mongols placed wood against the walls and ignited it, so that those within perished; but the cathedral remained standing and at the end of the century it was repaired, when Vladimir replaced Kiev as the center of the Russian Orthodox Church. Twice again desecrated by the Mongols, in 1408 and 1410, the Cathedral of the Dormition continued to be regarded as the preeminent example of church architecture in central Russia. In the 1470s, when political and religious power had shifted to Moscow, it provided Aristotile Fioravanti with the model for his grand Cathedral of the Dormition in Moscow's Kremlin.

In contrast to the austere walls of the Cathedral of the Dormition, Vsevolod's palace cathedral, the Cathedral of Saint Dmitry, displays stone sculpture in rank profusion. Built between 1194 and 1197, the church (dedicated to Saint Demetrius of Salonika) conforms to the square cruciform design adopted in the Bogolyubovo churches, with an arcade frieze separating two tiers, the upper of which is covered in carved limestone. Although Vsevolod's sculptors undoubtedly drew on skills developed three decades earlier by Andrey's artists, there is no clear source for the extraordinary iconographic exercise on the facades of the Cathedral of Saint Dmitry. The possibility of European influence, derived from the late Romanesque in central Europe, has been suggested by some specialists, while others have noted similarities to the carved-tufa facades of Armenian churches;[11] but no reliable evi-

132. *Cathedral of Saint Dmitry.*
Vladimir. 1194–97. Northeast view.

133. *Cathedral of Saint Dmitry.*
Southwest view.

134. *Cathedral of Saint Dmitry.*
Vladimir. 1194–97. West view.

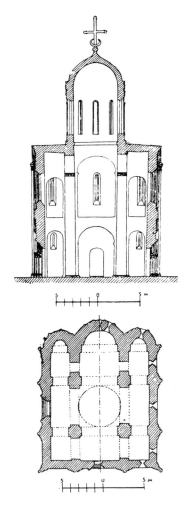

135. *Cathedral of Saint Dmitry. Section, plan.*

dence exists for any one theory of derivation. In view of the Russian receptivity to foreign architects and artisans—from Byzantium, the Balkans, central Europe, and, possibly, the Caucasus—the simplest explanation lies in a confluence of motifs and patterns from several sources, reworked to suit local tastes. However eclectic the design— indeed, because of their eclecticism—the twelfth-century churches of Suzdalia, like Saint Petersburg's baroque palaces, are inimitably *Russian*.

Of greater significance is the semantic question posed by the carvings, whose order has been preserved reasonably intact despite reconstruction and renovation over a period of eight centuries. (Like the Church of the Intercession on the Nerl, the Cathedral of Saint Dmitry was originally constructed with an exterior gallery that would have obscured much of the ornamentation of the arcade band. Again, *pace* purists,

136. *Cathedral of Saint Dmitry. South facade, arcade frieze, and upper tier.*

we must be thankful for its removal during a 'restoration' in 1832.)
That the facades contain an iconographic system is obvious, but its
meaning eludes a precise definition, despite the resourceful investi-
gations of Soviet scholars such as Georgy Vagner.[12]

Although certain of the fanciful plant and animal carvings can be
associated with motifs widespread in Indo-European folklore, their
function seems primarily decorative—the repetition of highly stylized
elements in a clearly defined pattern. The human figures, however,
have been identified in most cases, and it is now possible to propose
a reading of the facades as a depiction of the prince whose authority is
sanctioned by God, the Church, and its saints, and of the military arts
that sustain the princedom.

As in the Church of the Intercession, each of the central *zakomary* is
dominated by King David or King Solomon, the great lawgiver and
builder of the Temple in Jerusalem.[13] Beneath the king are creatures of

137. *Cathedral of Saint Dmitry.
Drum and cupola, viewed from
the west.*

138. *Cathedral of Saint Dmitry. South facade, left bay; with a relief, under the arch, of the baptism of Christ.*

139. *Cathedral of Saint Dmitry. South facade, central bay; with King David and warrior saints.*

140. *Cathedral of Saint Dmitry.*
South facade, right bay; with a relief,
under the arch, of Alexander the
Great ascending to heaven.

141. *Cathedral of Saint Dmitry. Upper tier, central bay of the west facade. King David, with lions, peacocks, archers, hunters, warrior-saints, angels.*

142. *Cathedral of Saint Dmitry. Portal, west facade.*

the earth and sky: griffins, peacocks, leopards, lions, doves, eagles, pheasants, deer, centaurs, panthers. As the ideal of the wise and just ruler, Solomon and David are complemented by mythological and historical figures (Hercules, Alexander the Great) popular in medieval Russian legend, as well as by warrior saints such as Theodore Stratilates, emblematic of the virtues of courage and sacrifice. The left *zakomara* of the north facade displays a carved group containing Vsevolod and five of his sons, the youngest of whom he holds on his knee. From Alexander to Solomon to Vsevolod, the continuity of just rule and divine sanction represented in stone at the Cathedral of Saint Dmitry bears witness to a highly developed culture shortly before its collapse under the most thorough and devastating invasion in Russian history.

143. *Cathedral of the Nativity of the Virgin. The Kremlin, Suzdal. 1222–25; rebuilt in 1530. East view.*

144. *The Kremlin, Suzdal. Thirteenth to seventeenth centuries. Northwest view.*

145. *Cathedral of Saint Dmitry.*
Interior. [RIGHT]

146. *Cathedral of Saint Dmitry.*
Archivolt detail, west portal.

147. *Cathedral of Saint Dmitry.*
North facade, left bay. The patron,
Prince Vsevolod, with five of his sons.

But one period remains before the deluge: the reign of Vsevolod's son Yury, who assumed the title of grand prince in 1212. In architectural history Yury is known primarily for his rebuilding in 1222 of the Cathedral of the Nativity of the Virgin in Suzdal, first erected in 1101 by his grandfather Vladimir Monomakh. In 1445 the upper tier of the structure collapsed, and when rebuilt yet again, in 1528, the cathedral conformed to the pentacupolar design of the large Muscovite churches of the sixteenth century. Yet much of the thirteenth-century ornamentation was preserved, particularly in the arcade frieze, and it is evident that the facades retained—in some respects advanced—the elaborate patterns of limestone carving characteristic of Vladimir architecture.[14] The style was carried to an extreme, however, by Yury's brother Svyatoslav, in the Cathedral of Saint George in Yurev-Polsky (1230–34). Founded by Yury Dolgoruky in the middle of the twelfth century, the town of Yurev-Polsky had belonged to the Vladimir principality, but with the distribution of lands among Vsevolod's sons in 1212, it became the seat of a minor principality under the rule of Svyatoslav.

148. *Cathedral of the Nativity of the Virgin. Suzdal. 1222–25, upper tier rebuilt (in brick) in 1530. South facade.* [LEFT]

149. *Cathedral of the Nativity of the Virgin. Detail, south facade.*

150. *Cathedral of the Nativity of the Virgin. Detail, south portal.*

151. *Cathedral of the Nativity of the Virgin. Detail, south portal.*

In 1230 he decided to rebuild Yury Dolgoruky's Church of Saint George (1152). Whether Svyatoslav intended to engage in architectural one-upmanship with his brother is not clear, but his cathedral ran riot with high- and low-relief carving taken to a degree exceeding anything that had appeared before it. The lower tier was covered with an intricate floral motif and the attached columns were carved, as were the ogival arches (one of their earliest appearances in Russia), the capitals, and every space in the arcade frieze. In addition to the floral patterns, the facades displayed mythological scenes, biomorphic elements, episodes from the Old and New Testaments, the figures of saints, human masks, and various fantastic beasts.

When the upper part of the church collapsed in the 1460s (a distressingly frequent event among Russian churches during the fifteenth century), Ivan III commanded that it be rebuilt. But the task of restoring

152. *Cathedral of the Transfiguration of the Savior, Spaso-Evfimy Monastery. Suzdal. 1582–94. South view, with seventeenth-century frescoes.* [OPPOSITE]

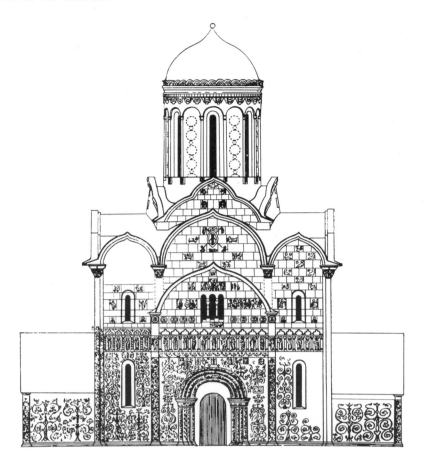

153. *Cathedral of Saint George. Yurev-Polsky. 1234. Reconstruction of west facade by G. K. Vagner.*

the walls to their original appearance proved beyond the capabilities of the Muscovite architect Vasily Yermolin, who lowered the roofline and succeeded in replacing only a few of the fragments in some logical order; the rest of the pieces were distributed haphazardly, or employed as building material in adjoining structures. Except for the decoration of the relatively intact north wall, the facades now compose a stone puzzle, dynamic in its chaos.[15]

The Mongol Conquest

'1224. The same year, for our sins, unknown tribes came whom no one exactly knows, who they are, nor whence they came, nor what their language is, nor of what race they are, nor what their faith is; but they call them Tatars. . . .'[16] Thus the Novgorod chronicle describes the first appearance of the Tatars in Russia.

Other chronicles were to give more precise information—the 'Tatars' were in fact part of the Mongol hordes of Genghis Khan—but all accounts contain the same interpretation, drawn from the lamentations of Old Testament prophets: that an unprecedented calamity had overtaken Russia as punishment for its sins. (Typically, the same explanation is given for the sack of Kiev by Andrey Bogolyubsky.)

154. *Spaso-Evfimy Monastery. Suzdal. Founded in the fourteenth century by Evfimy of Suzdal, the monastery is emblematic of the political and religious resurgence of central Russia under Moscow's grand princes. The present walls date from the end of the seventeenth century.*

After the crushing defeat of the Russian princes on the river Kalka in 1223, the Mongols returned to the eastern Steppes, where they were to reorganize following the death of Genghis Khan, in 1227, and launch another attack to the northeast. Led by Batu, a grandson of Genghis Khan, a Mongol army of some 150,000 troops struck the fragmented Russian principalities, first at Ryazan in 1237, and then at Vladimir in the winter of 1237–38. The invasion eventually carried them to Kiev (1240), then Poland and Hungary (1241); and at each stage the sequence of events was essentially the same: the capture of a town by cunning or superior force, its destruction, and the massacre of its inhabitants.

The Galician-Volhynian chronicle describes the campaign in some detail, and from this account we know that the catastrophe at Vladimir began with the defeat of Russian forces and the death of Grand Prince Yury, killed while raising another force. When the Mongols approached the city and threatened the inhabitants, in an attempt to gain surrender without a siege, Bishop Mitrofan assumed leadership (Yury's young son Vsevolod was thoroughly demoralized, according to the chronicle), and exhorted the citizens to fight, while preparing them for the martyr's crown:

> Bishop Mitrofan spoke to the multitude with tears: 'Children, let us not fear the temptation of the ungodly, let us not consider this corruptible and fleeting life, but rather let us take heed of that other life which does not pass, that life which is with the angels, and if they capture our city, and give us over to pillage, and give us unto death, I offer to you, my children, the promise that you shall receive the uncorruptible crowns from Christ our Lord.' The people of the city hearkened to these words and began to fight with greater strength. The Tatars battered the town with their wall-battering instruments; they released arrows without number. Prince Vsevolod saw that the battle waxed yet more fierce, took fright because of his youth, and went forth from the town with his small company, carrying with him many gifts and hoping to

155. *Refectory Church of the Dormition, Spaso-Evfimy Monastery. 1525.*

receive his life. Batu, like a wild beast, did not spare his youth, but ordered that he be slaughtered before him, and he slew all the town. When the bishop, with the princess and her children, fled to the church [the Cathedral of the Dormition], the godless one commanded it to be set on fire. Thus they surrendered their souls to God.[17]

With the death of Grand Khan Ugedei, Batu withdrew from Europe to the lower part of the Volga, where he established his leadership of the part of the Mongol empire known as the Golden Horde. From their capital of Old Sarai, Batu and his successors exacted tribute from Russia, conferred the title of Grand Prince on Russian leaders who were willing to submit to their rule, and made periodic raids to maintain their dominance. Russian princes were frequently required to accompany Mongol punitive expeditions against rebellious Russian cities; the ambitious princes of Moscow were particularly ruthless in this role, which helped them gain power over their fellow countrymen.

The 'Tatar Yoke,' which was not formally abrogated until 1480, led to a cultural decline in Russia paralleled in Europe only by the Dark Ages. Brilliant as they were in military organization, the Mongols had

156. *Pokrovsky (Intercession) Monastery. Suzdal. Sixteenth century.*

157. *Church of the Ascension, Alexander Monastery. Suzdal. 1695. The monastery, founded in 1240, is named for its benefactor, Alexander* *Nevsky. The present church was endowed by Natalya Naryshkina, mother of Peter the Great.*

158. *Gate Church of the Annunciation, Monastery of the Intercession. Suzdal. Early sixteenth century.*

little to offer the more highly developed Russian culture, from which they remained detached by both religion and secular custom. (Alexander Pushkin remarked: 'The Tatars were not like the Moors. Having conquered Russia, they gave her neither algebra nor Aristotle.')[18] When the process of assimilation did occur, as happened with increasing frequency in the fifteenth century, the direction was invariably toward the acceptance by the Mongols of the Russian Orthodox religion and other cultural traditions.

In the period following the Mongol domination, a modicum of organized existence returned to the devastated towns of Suzdalia, even though the principality was still exposed to frequent raids. In 1252 the title of Grand Prince of Vladimir was bestowed by the Mongols on Alexander Nevsky—prince of Novgorod and grandson of Vsevolod

159. Church of Saints Kozma and Demyan (right) and Church of Saint Andrey Bogolyubsky (left). Suzdal. 1696. In Suzdal there are a number of such paired churches, one of which—the 'warm' (heated)—would be used in winter, the other—the 'cold' (unheated)—in summer. Here, the church of Saint Andrey Bogolyubsky is the 'warm.'

III—whose policy of accommodation provided a fragile stability to the area. However, Vladimir's predominance in Russian affairs had passed. In 1328 Moscow's Grand Prince Ivan I (Kalita, or 'Moneybags') persuaded the metropolitan of the Russian church to transfer his residence from Vladimir to Moscow; and by the end of his reign Vladimir had been incorporated into the Muscovite principality.

Throughout the two centuries of harsh Mongol rule, the church had provided the most important link with the pre-conquest culture of Russia, and during the fourteenth and fifteenth centuries it continued to play a leading role in the resurgence of central Russia. Nevertheless, the economic devastation wrought by the Mongols deprived the church of the means to maintain, on even a limited scale, the architectural excellence of twelfth-century Suzdalia. In Novgorod, relatively unscathed, construction did continue in the thirteenth century, and revived considerably in the fourteenth, but in the Vladimir area no building of any consequence was erected for more than two hundred years. When certain of the more important churches of Suzdalia were restored or rebuilt in the fifteenth century, the impetus came from Moscow—Yury Dolgoruky's outpost, whose rulers were now embarked on a quest for power over the Russian lands. With their rise to preeminence, Moscow's princes developed an interest in preserving the architectural legacy of Suzdalia as an expression of the political and religious authority they fully intended to inherit. Ivan the Great's command to rebuild the decrepit (built in 1326) Cathedral of the Dormition in the Kremlin stipulated that the architects adopt the Vladimir Cathedral of the Dormition as their model—an appropriate gesture that led, under the capable direction of Fioravanti, to the creation of one of Moscow's most imposing monuments. But the Cathedral of the Dormition proved in fact to be the last of the great

160. *Church of Saints Boris and Gleb. Suzdal. 1747. Provincial architecture, in an archaic style—but a fine silhouette.*

'white-stone' (limestone) churches in the Vladimir tradition. By the sixteenth century, Moscow had developed a style very much its own, as expressed with such éclat in the Cathedral of the Intercession on Red Square (popularly known as Saint Basil's).

Suzdal: A Postscript

Contemporary Suzdal, with its clusters of churches, monasteries, and brightly painted towers, has been set aside by the Soviets as a museum of Russian architecture. Tourist accommodations are placed within old monastery walls and a restaurant in the archbishop's palace serves 'medieval' Russian fare (a reference perhaps to the quality of the meat). With the exception of fragments of the lower walls at the Cathedral of the Nativity, most of the monuments in Suzdal date from the sixteenth, seventeenth, and eighteenth centuries; although the effect is picturesque, the style is provincial in every sense of the word, with little relation to the great era of Suzdalian architecture.

By the fifteenth century, Suzdal had settled into a torpor—legendary even by Russian standards—which preserved the domains of the

162. *Holy Gates, Monastery of the*
Deposition of the Robe. Suzdal. 1688.

161. *Cathedral of the Trinity, Danilov*
Monastery. Pereslavl-Zalessky.
1530–32. Frescoes by Gury Nikitin
and Sila Savin, 1662–68. [OPPOSITE]

163. *Cathedral of Saint Fyodor, Fyodorovsky Monastery. Pereslavl-Zalessky. 1557. A votive church, built for the birth of Ivan the Terrible's son Fyodor I.*

164. *Cathedral of the Trinity, Danilov Monastery. Pereslavl-Zalessky. Cathedral, 1530–32; bell tower, 1689. A votive church endowed by Basil III on the occasion of the birth of his son, Ivan IV (the Terrible).*

wealthy monasteries from commercial or administrative encroachments. The town possessed little economic or political significance (in times of severe stagnation its churches seemed to outnumber its households), and so it served admirably for tsars (Basil III, Peter the Great) who needed a secure place of exile for inconvenient wives or political prisoners. Thus, the conditions conducive to a vital and innovative architecture were lacking, despite the high quality of the local workmanship.

There are, however, some fine things in Suzdal: the Gate Church of the Annunciation at the Convent of the Intercession, with its perfect

165. *Church of the Metropolitan Peter.*
Pereslavl-Zalessky. 1585.

distribution of portals and gallery arches; and the Spaso-Evfimy Monastery, one of the best preserved monastery ensembles in Russia. Its walls are splendid examples of the art of fortification in late-seventeenth-century Russia. The most appealing monuments in Suzdal today are the eighteenth-century wooden churches that have recently been brought from remote settlements in central Russia and reassembled as a separate architectural museum. (See Appendix A.) Here, one feels, are the ingenuity and creative spirit that lead into the great era of Muscovite architecture.

4. MOSCOW:

the GOLDEN-DOMED

When they rise in the morning, they goe commonly
in the sight of some steeple, that hath a crosse on
the toppe: and so bowing themselves towardes the
crosse, signe themselves withal on their foreheads
and brests.

—GILES FLETCHER on MOSCOW, 1591

'Come to me, brother, in Moscow.' Prince Yury Dolgoruky's laconic invitation to his ally Prince Svyatoslav of Chernigov is the earliest historical reference (1147) we have to a small outpost on the banks of the Moscow River, a part of the Vladimir-Suzdal principality. 1147 is now officially taken as the year of the city's founding; but, as the invitation implies, some form of settlement must have existed before then—probably a collection of log structures, among which would have been a compound sufficiently large to accommodate a 'hearty feast' celebrating their alliance.[1] However modest the town's appearance at the time, its position at a strategic juncture of trade routes and political boundaries was not lost on Dolgoruky, who in the course of his freewheeling princely wars succeeded in shifting the center of power in pre-Mongol Russia from Kiev to his domains in Suzdalia.

In 1156, on high ground at the confluence of the Neglinnaya and Moscow rivers, Yury built a wooden fortification placed on an earthen rampart that protected a cluster of workshops and trading rows. Over the following eight centuries very little has changed in this general arrangement: the Kremlin today occupies the site of Yury's original fortification and the city's largest department store stands slightly to the north of the oldest trading center. The infrequent references to Moscow in the early chronicles note that the town was burned in 1176 during a raid by a neighboring prince, was fought over by the sons of Vsevolod the Big Nest (of Vladimir) in the 1210s, and was destroyed in January 1238 by the Mongol armies of Batu on their way to Vladimir. This grim history in no way distinguishes Moscow from any number of other Russian towns during the twelfth and thirteenth centuries, as Kievan power collapsed and Russian princes proved incapable of uniting to meet the Mongol threat.

For the century following the Mongol invasion, Moscow—afforded some protection from Tatar raids by a barrier of forests and rivers—gradually increased its territory by a policy of collaboration with the

166. Trinity-Saint Sergius Monastery. Zagorsk. Fourteenth to eighteenth centuries.

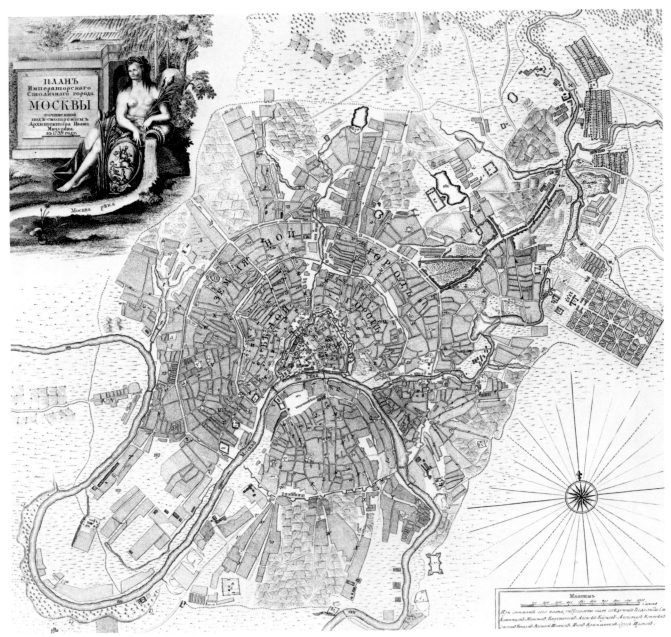

167. *Plan of Moscow, 1739. For cen-*
turies Moscow's growth was defined
by a series of concentric walls and
ramparts whose nucleus was the
Kremlin, site of the city's first known
settlement (twelfth century). By the
nineteenth century the fortifications
had lost their military value, but the
circular pattern has been maintained
by a ring expressway encompassing
340 square miles. From the fifteenth
through the seventeenth centuries,
the city's southern approaches,
exposed to attack from the Mongols
and the Crimean Tatars, were
defended by monastery-fortresses
(visible on the lower part of the map):
Novodevichy, Andreevsky, Donskoy,
Danilovsky, Simonov, Novspassky,
Andronikov. All are still standing:
with certain exceptions, this map
could serve as a guide to central
Moscow today. Houghton Library,
Harvard University.

Horde and the skillful acquisition of neighboring real estate through marriage, purchase, and inheritance. The rise was by no means steady, and humiliating submission to Mongol overlordship was an absolute precondition to local autonomy; Prince Daniil Alexandrovich, who, in 1263, at the age of two, inherited the city from his father, Alexander Nevsky, and ruled in Moscow from 1283 to 1303, was one of the first Russian princes to be given the *yarlik*, or seal of authority, by the Mongols. His city, however, was sacked by them in 1293. But the Mongol domination provided the one essential element that had been lacking in the pre-conquest disintegration of the warring Russian princedoms: an overwhelming military force that could be exploited by any prince adroit enough to gain Mongol favor. Moscow produced such a leader in Ivan I ('Kalita'), who ruled from 1325 to 1340 and is considered the first of the city's great princes.

Ivan Kalita quickly grasped the strategy of using an alien military force for internal political purposes—and quickly applied it. In 1327 he was asked to participate in the suppression of an uprising against the Mongols in the city of Tver, Moscow's main rival for power in central Russia; for his services he was invested with the title of Grand Prince by the Mongol khan, Nogay, and given the authority to collect tribute for the Horde. This position (providing his nickname, Kalita: 'Moneybags') led to the aggrandizement of Muscovy. Of equal importance to the prestige of the young city-state was the decision in 1326 of the metropolitanate of the Russian Orthodox Church to move from Vladimir to Moscow, an event of significance not only for the political and religious status of Moscow (the two could hardly be separated), but also for its architectural development.

In 1326 Ivan Kalita commissioned Moscow's first major cathedral, whose dedication to the Feast of the Dormition of the Virgin served as a symbol of the continuity between Vladimir, cultural center of pre-Mongol Russia, and its inheritor, Moscow. It should be noted, however, that the Dormition (Uspensky sobor) was not the earliest masonry structure in the Kremlin; in the 1960s archæologists uncovered there the foundations of a stone church presumably dating from the thirteenth century.[2] Although little is known of the appearance of these earliest stone churches, they undoubtedly represented a similar attempt, however modest, to revive the tradition of Vladimir architecture. But it would be some time before Moscow possessed the resources and stability to raise a monument comparable to the Vladimir cathedrals.

The results of Kalita's realpolitik came to bear during the reign of his grandson Dmitry Ivanovich, or Dmitry Donskoy ('of the Don'), who ruled as grand prince of Moscow between 1359 and 1389, and who led the combined Russian forces to their first major victory over the Horde, in 1380. In the early part of his reign Dmitry continued the work of his predecessors in expanding Moscow's political dominance (Tver finally submitted to Muscovite power in 1375) and in strengthening the city's defenses. In 1367 the wooden walls of the Kremlin were replaced with stone and extended to roughly their present length (two kilometers), while a number of fortress monasteries were established to protect the city's southern and northern approaches.

Indeed, the increasingly militant Orthodox Church played a major role in rallying Russian forces around the banner of Moscow in a crusade against the Horde. Shortly before the great battle at Kulikovo Pole ('Snipe Field'), Dmitry was exhorted by the abbot Sergius of Radonezh, his spiritual adviser, to 'concern himself with the flock entrusted to him by God and to go against the infidels.'[3] So he did, and his victory over a Mongol army led by Khan Mamai is considered one of the most significant events in Russian history.

The victory was not, however, decisive in any immediate sense. In fact, not all of Russia was united in the campaign: Novgorod refused to send its troops, and one Russian prince was actually in alliance with the Mongols. In 1382 another Mongol army, led by Tokhtamysh, besieged Moscow in Dmitry's absence, took the Kremlin by ruse, burned the city, and left with a great number of captives and many riches. Although Tokhtamysh was later routed by a rival Mongol horde, led by Tamerlane (who ravaged the Golden Horde's capital, Old Sarai, on the Volga), Moscow continued to pay tribute to the Horde for another century, and its lands continued to suffer devastating raids. (Tamerlane himself threatened Moscow, in 1395, but suddenly turned back—a retreat attributed by the Russians to the miraculous intervention of the twelfth-century Byzantine icon now known as *The Vladimir Mother of God*.) Nevertheless, the victory over Mamai demonstrated not only the extent of Russian resurgence, but also the position of Moscow as the new center of national power, based on a union of religious, political, and military interests.

During the fourteenth century—and for three centuries thereafter—Moscow remained almost entirely a wooden city, prey to fires, though capable of being quickly rebuilt. Yet as the consolidation of its strength continued, so did the building of stone churches within the Kremlin, center and symbol of the city's might. Apart from traces of foundations uncovered by archæologists and fragments of churches incorporated into later structures, nothing remains of these early attempts at masonry construction in Moscow: almost all of the Kremlin churches from this period were demolished in the course of the fifteenth century, to make way for the grander monuments that currently compose the Kremlin ensemble (the most notable being the Cathedrals of the Dormition, of the Annunciation, and of the Archangel Michael, each of which replaced a fourteenth-century stone church of the same name).

Zvenigorod

There is, in one of the outlying districts of the Moscow region (in the village of Kamenskoe), a small stone church dedicated to Saint Nicholas that is thought to date from the second half of the fourteenth century;[4] but for the earliest surviving examples of more complex architectural stone forms, one must go to Zvenigorod, located in picturesque hilly country some forty miles to the west of Moscow.

168. *Church of Saint Nicholas at Kamenskoe. Southwest of Moscow. Late fourteenth century. The church is perhaps the oldest building in the Moscow area. The village of Kamenskoe belonged to Prince Yury of Zvenigorod, whose cathedrals in the town of Zvenigorod bear some resemblance to this church. The piers are not free-standing; they are attached to the interior corners. The cornice may have originally culminated in decorative pointed zakomary—as at Zvenigorod's Cathedral of the Nativity (see Figure 174).*

169. *Church of Saint Nicholas, Kamenskoe. Apsidal structure, with a view of plinth and molding.*

Although its early history is obscure, the town probably existed as an outpost of one of the western principalities (Chernigov, most likely) during the twelfth century.[5] By the fourteenth century, written records place Zvenigorod within the domains of Moscow's princes, and in 1389 Dmitry Donskoy bequeathed the town and its lands to his fifteen-year-old son, Yury, who then presided over its brief prominence in Russian history. As had his father, Yury maintained close relations with the Holy Trinity Monastery, founded by Sergius of Radonezh and subsequently the religious center of Muscovy. By the end of the fourteenth century, Yury had amassed the resources to endow a monastery of his own in Zvenigorod, under the spiritual direction of the monk Savva, who had served as prior of the Trinity Monastery for six years after the death of Sergius (1392).

The founding of what was subsequently to be known as the Savva-Storozhevsky Monastery (after its location on Storozhi, or 'Lookout,' Hill) was complemented by Yury's efforts to develop the center of his town. At some point about the turn of the century (the exact years are unknown) he commissioned two stone cathedrals: the Dormition, which served as the court church within the city's fortress, and the Nativity of the Virgin, located in the monastery. In comparison with

170. *Cathedral of the Dormition.*
Zvenigorod. 1399(?). Commissioned
by Prince Yury of Zvenigorod, the
cathedral is one of the more success-
ful attempts to resurrect the Vladimir
tradition of limestone building. The
facades and drum are decorated with
three strips of stone carving. The
cornice was originally composed of
ogival zakomary.

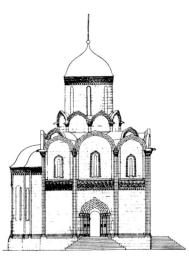

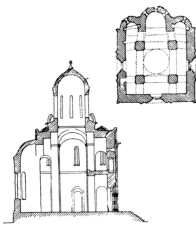

171. *Cathedral of the Dormition.*
Reconstructed north elevation,
section, plan.

the limestone churches of pre-Mongol Vladimir, Yury's cathedrals display a simple notion of design, in which the complex relation of structure and ornament characteristic of Vladimir is replaced by a few insistently repeated decorative motifs, as in the profusion of ogival arches between the cornice and cupola drum. The Cathedral of the Dormition, whose pointed arches were removed in a rebuilding of the roof, bears a greater resemblance to the Vladimir churches of Andrey Bogolyubsky, with its emphasis on verticality—enhanced by a slight tapering of the walls—than does the squatter, heavier Cathedral of the Nativity of the Virgin.

Both churches follow the plan of their Vladimir predecessors, with a central cube containing four piers, which support a single drum and

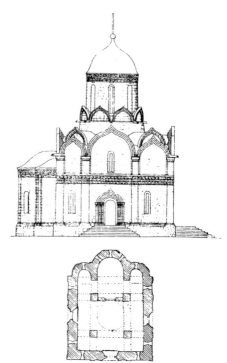

173. *Cathedral of the Nativity of the*
Virgin, Savva-Storozhevsky Monastery.
Zvenigorod. 1405(?). North elevation,
plan. (See Figure 166.)

cupola, and with three apses extending from the sanctuary's eastern
wall. Each facade is divided into three parts by slender half columns
and an ornamental band that is placed slightly above the midpoint of
the wall. And, as at Vladimir, the portals are framed by perspective
arches.

But though the debt to the older Vladimir is obvious—and to be
expected—the differences in Zvenigorod are several and in some
cases prefigure a distinctly Muscovite ornamental style that emerged
in the sixteenth and seventeenth centuries. The rounded arches and
zakomary of Vladimir have been replaced by pointed forms. The
exterior division of the walls no longer corresponds to the interior
arrangement of pier and vault. And the ornamental band, which in

174. *Cathedral of the Nativity of the Virgin, Savva-Storozhevsky Monastery. Zvenigorod. 1405 (?) North view.*

Vladimir had served to demarcate the thicker, lower part of the wall from its upper panels, now assumes a very different, inverted appearance, unrelated to the structure of the wall: the highest of the three strips composing the band overhangs the other two in what is assumed to be a device to protect the intricate limestone carving from erosion by rain. (In Vladimir churches, such as Saint Dmitry's, this purpose is served by blind arcading on the facade.) The greatest difference is in the nature of the motifs composing the strips; for instead of the profusion of mythological, Biblical, and fantastic subjects—displayed with instructive as well as decorative intent on the facades of the Vladimir churches—the ornamental strips at Zvenigorod consist of a foliate pattern repeated without variation for the length of the band.[6]

Although the destruction of Muscovy's earliest churches makes it impossible to trace the evolution of a Muscovite style derived from Vladimir, the cathedrals at Zvenigorod provide evidence of a departure from the close integration of structure and decoration, a greater freedom in the relation between interior and exterior design, and a heavier reliance on purely ornamental effects—such as *kokoshniki* (pointed arches)—with no structural purpose. The tendency to ornamentalism was to assume many forms in the development of Muscovite architecture, some trivial and others indicative of a highly imaginative, if idiosyncratic, genius. The full expression of this tendency would occur, however, only in the sixteenth century, when brick had replaced stone as the primary building material.

Yet for most of the fifteenth century Zvenigorod's limestone cathedrals provided the pattern for Muscovy's major churches, such as the Trinity Cathedral at the Holy Trinity Monastery (*lavra*).[7] Jointly endowed in 1422 by Prince Yury of Zvenigorod and Grand Prince Basil of Moscow, to contain the grave of the recently canonized Sergius of Radonezh, the cathedral suffers in comparison with the Zvenigorod churches: its decoration is more austere and the relation between the interior arrangement of space and the design of the facade is awkwardly conceived. The shift of the main crossing and cupola toward the east is not reflected by the symmetrical division of the facade—nor is it at Zvenigorod; but, in contrast to the latter, the monastery church has an off-center portal on the north facade, which reveals the disjuncture between interior and exterior.

Symmetry and balance are emphatically reaffirmed, however, at Moscow's Cathedral of the Savior. Located within the Spaso-Andronikov Monastery (named for its first prior, Andronik), the church is considered the earliest preserved monument in the city, although the year and even the decade of its construction are uncertain—a striking illustration of the dearth of information on early Muscovite architecture. At some point between 1410 and 1427 (even these dates are open to question) the church was apparently endowed by the Yermolins, among the first in a distinguished line of Muscovite merchant-patrons of architecture. The structure is by far the most ornamental to be found in Muscovy—or in all of Russia up to that time. The use of pointed *zakomary* and *kokoshniki*, culminating in the high drum and cupola, placed over the center of the structure, creates a vertical thrust

175. *Cathedral of the Savior, Spaso-Andronikov Monastery. East view.* [LEFT]

176. *Cathedral of the Savior at Spaso-Andronikov Monastery. Moscow. 1410–27(?). Northwest view.* [OPPOSITE]

that is reinforced by a lowering of the corner vaults. M. A. Ilin considers this design the prototype for Moscow's tower, or pillar, churches of the sixteenth century,[8] and though other sources could be proposed, there is little question that the Savior Cathedral prefigures much in later Moscow architecture—and in a much more specific manner than do the Zvenigorod churches.

But though the Cathedral of the Savior represents in certain aspects a departure from the tradition of Vladimir's limestone churches, it, like the other three of Muscovy's oldest surviving monuments, displays an essentially conservative, 'provincial' attempt to reaffirm an earlier and more distinguished style. None achieves the complexity of design and construction demonstrated at Vladimir, Bogolyubovo, and Yurev-Polsky. Indeed, for the history of Russian art this Muscovite

177. Trinity–Saint Sergius Monastery. Zagorsk. East view. Founded about 1345 by Sergius of Radonezh, the monastery currently contains churches from the fifteenth through the eighteenth centuries. Visible in this view (from left to right) are the Refectory and Church of Saint Sergius (1686–92); the drum and cupola of the Church of the Holy Spirit (1476); the bell tower, by Dmitry Ukhtomsky—over 280 feet in height, with 42 bells (1741–70); the Cathedral of the Dormition (1559–85); and the Church of John the Baptist over the Holy Gates (1692–99). The brick walls and towers date from the sixteenth to the eighteenth centuries.

architecture is of less importance than the possibility that Andrey Rublev, Russia's greatest medieval artist, participated in the painting of frescoes and icons at all four churches. (His work at the Holy Trinity Cathedral has survived, and it is known that he did the interior and possibly participated in the construction of the Cathedral of the Savior; unfortunately, practically nothing remains of the interior decoration in this, his last work. Certain frescoes in the Cathedral of the Dormition at Zvenigorod have been attributed to Rublev, and it is thought that his great 'Zvenigorod Row' of icons—of which three survive—was painted for the Cathedral of the Nativity of the Virgin.)

The Kremlin: Renaissance in Moscow

Muscovy's modest, though promising, recovery at the turn of the fifteenth century was interrupted at the end of the 1420s by the outbreak of a protracted struggle between the followers of ten-year-old Grand Prince Basil II of Moscow and Prince Yury of Zvenigorod. Yury refused to recognize the succession of Basil, son of Yury's older brother, Basil I, to the title Grand Prince. After Yury's death, in 1434, his sons, Dmitry Shemyaka and Basil the Squint-Eyed, continued the war, during

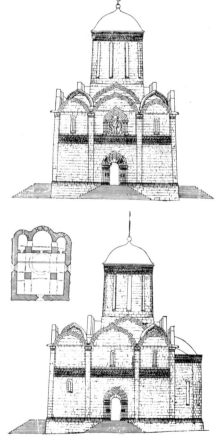

178. *Cathedral of the Trinity, Trinity–Saint Sergius Monastery. Zagorsk. 1422. Commissioned by the brothers Yury of Zvenigorod and Basil I of Moscow, this building is the last of Muscovy's early limestone churches. Its design is awkward, off balance, compared with that of the Zvenigorod churches or Moscow's Cathedral of the Savior at Andronikov Monastery. This is the original site of Andrey Rublev's most notable icon,* The Old Testament Trinity.

179. *Cathedral of the Trinity. West and south elevations, plan.*

which both Basil II and Basil the Squint-Eyed were blinded. By 1450 Moscow and the principle of direct succession had emerged triumphant.

Over a period of some fifty years, masonry construction in Muscovy was limited primarily to the strengthening of the Kremlin walls and the repair of the pre-Mongol cathedrals at Pereslavl-Zalessky and Yurev-Polsky—the latter rebuilt after its collapse by the Muscovite architect Vasily Yermolin. When new construction finally resumed, in the 1470s, under Ivan III ('the Great'), the results were initially inauspicious: an attempt to build a new Cathedral of the Dormition on the site of the earlier dilapidated structure had reached the point of vaulting when the northern and western walls collapsed. A team of master builders from Pskov, summoned to assess the situation, praised the stonework but found the mortar too weak and refused to assume further responsibility. The disaster was in fact one of the most fortu-

180. *Church of the Holy Spirit,*
Trinity–Saint Sergius Monastery.
1476. The church was built by mas-
ters from Pskov, as were many of the
churches of Ivan the Great's reign.
The placement of a bellcote under the
cupola represents an early attempt to
create a centralized tiered church.

nate events in the history of Russian architecture, for its resolution
not only introduced the Italian Renaissance into Russian art but also
led to the creation of a monument immeasurably superior to anything
that had preceded it.

Much in this sudden accession to excellence stems from the political
situation in Moscow at the middle of the fifteenth century. After the
Fall of Constantinople in 1453, Moscow proclaimed its role as the
protector of Orthodox Christianity and the successor of Byzantium.
Moscow had never accepted the Union of Florence, of 1439, a position

181. *The Kremlin, Moscow. South-east view. From left to right: the Cathedral of the Annunciation (1484–89), the Cathedral of the Archangel Michael (1505–09), the Cathedral of the Dormition (1475–79), and the Bell Tower of Ivan the Great by Bon Fryazin and others (1505–08). The upper tier and cupola were added in 1600 by Boris Godunov.*

that led to the establishment in 1443 of a Russian Orthodox Church independent of Byzantium. With the elaboration of the ecclesiastical and political concept of Moscow as the 'Third Rome,' the Muscovite grand prince asserted a claim that justified his domination of all Russia (the 'republic' of Novgorod included), signaling the emergence of a major power. Not only did Ivan III now assume the title Tsar (derived from 'Caesar'), but he also married Zoë Paleologue, niece of the last Byzantine emperor. It is she who may have suggested that Ivan turn to Italy, where she had lived in exile, for an architect capable of implementing a project intended as a further demonstration of religious and political authority.[9]

In the fall of 1474 Ivan sent Semyon Tolbuzin on an embassy to Venice, where he met and was duly impressed by the eminent Bolognese architect and engineer Aristotile Fioravanti. Tolbuzin apparently considered the major monuments of Venice, Saint Mark's included, to be the work of Fioravanti, who seems to have taken advantage of the Russian's gullibility. Fioravanti returned the compliment when, on seeing the Cathedral of the Dormition in Vladimir, he affirmed that it could well have been built by an Italian.

Upon arriving in Moscow, in the spring of 1475, Fioravanti directed

182. *Cathedral of the Dormition, the Kremlin. Moscow. 1475–79. Architect: Aristotile Fioravanti. South facade, with sixteenth-century frescoes over the portal.*

the razing of the remaining cathedral walls (Muscovites were startled to see what had taken three years to build dismantled, with the Italian's technological ingenuity, in a week), and in June he began the con-struction of a new foundation. Placed on oak piles, the foundation walls were the deepest (more than four meters) yet seen in Russia for such a structure, insuring a firm base for the limestone walls, which were unusually thin in comparison with those of earlier churches. He also established a brickworks, whose large, well-fired bricks were far stronger than those previously produced by the Muscovites, and he corrected the deficiency in mortar that had been noted by the Pskov masters. Fioravanti's thick mixture provided the firm bonding that had been known by builders in Novgorod and Vladimir but had been lost—along with much else in the art of building—during the period following the Mongol invasion.

Having initiated the construction of the cathedral and entrusted its

183. *The Kremlin Cathedrals. Moscow. Southeast view.* [OPPOSITE]

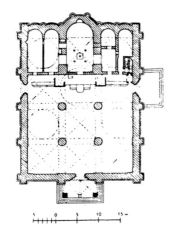

184. *Cathedral of the Dormition.
Section, plan.*

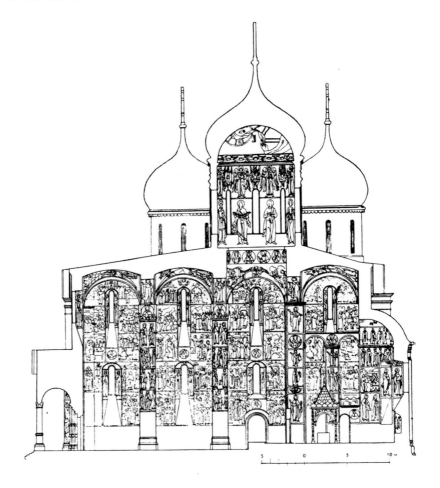

supervision to his son Andreas, Fioravanti set forth on a tour of Vladimir, as well as of other Russian cities. Like the hapless Russian architects before him, he had been commanded to use the Cathedral of the Dormition in Vladimir as the model for his project, and certain similarities between the two cathedrals are readily apparent: the pentacupolar arrangement; the *zakomary*, which effect the transition from facade to roof; the application of an arcade band along the facade, delineated to reflect the interior division of bays; and the use of perspective arches to frame the portals.

Fioravanti's plan contained, however, a number of significant deviations from the traditional cross-inscribed, barrel-vaulted pattern applied so widely in Russia's masonry churches. In part the differences derive from technological innovations that obviated the need for massive walls to support the weight of so large a structure (and Fioravanti, unlike Vladimir's architects, had no intention of obstructing the sculpted mass of his church with exterior galleries, which had provided additional support for the twelfth-century limestone walls). The lightness of Fioravanti's cathedral was made possible by the use of brick, instead of stone, for the vaulting, and by the application of iron stays for additional support—again, an innovation in both cases. On the exterior the walls were buttressed by large pilasters, dividing

185. *Bell Tower of Ivan the Great, the Kremlin. Moscow. 1505–08. Architect: Bon Fryazin and others, with upper tier and cupola added by Boris Godunov in 1600. The flanking structure is thought to have originally been the Church of the Resurrection (sixteenth century), which was converted in the seventeenth century to a bell tower of the Pskov style. It was blown up by Napoleon and then rebuilt, with modifications, in 1814–15.* [LEFT]

186. *Church of the Deposition of the Robe, the Kremlin. Moscow. 1484–85. Constructed by masters from Pskov. Brick, with a terra-cotta frieze.*

187. *Cathedral of the Dormition,*
the Kremlin. Moscow. 1475–79.
Architect: Aristotile Fioravanti.
Southeast view.

the facade into equal vertical segments, whose proportions were determined by the principle of the golden section.

Indeed, Fioravanti applied the concept of structural harmony as determined by the rules of geometry to a degree unknown in Russia. In so doing he abandoned the cross-inscribed plan, which had dictated a widening of the central axes to delineate the figure of the cross. The Cathedral of the Dormition is composed of twelve quadrilateral bays, equal in size and cross- rather than barrel-vaulted—a technique that increased the span of the brick vaults, whose light weight enabled a corresponding reduction in the size of the six interior piers, or pillars. From the interior all five cupolas appear to have the same diameter— the result of Fioravanti's replacing the cross-inscribed plan with a division into equal bays—but from the exterior the central drum and cupola are distinguished from the surrounding four cupolas by greater height and by the extension of the circumference over the spring arches of the central bay.

The sense of spaciousness created by Fioravanti's design and technical innovations was enhanced by the decision to eliminate what had been an obligatory feature in almost all masonry Russian churches up to that time: the choir gallery, or *khor*. Thus an unprecedented amount of the interior, richly decorated with frescoes and icons, was immediately visible to those entering the cathedral. From the exterior, the unity of the massive sculpted form—as if cut from one stone, according to a Russian chronicler—is preserved by a discreet resolution of the eastern wall, whose five apses (instead of the traditional three) extend slightly from the central block of the church and are partially hidden by an extension of the corner pilasters. In this way Fioravanti retained the traditional elements of Vladimir's twelfth-century cathedrals, while placing these elements in an essentially different plan.

188. *Hall of Facets (Granovitaya Palata), the Kremlin. Moscow. 1487–91. Architects: Marco and Pietro-Antonio Solari.*

189. *Cathedral of the Annunciation,*
the Kremlin. Moscow. 1484–89.
Southeast view.

Conceived as a grand and solemn space for the crowning of Russian
tsars and the investiture of metropolitans and patriarchs of the Russian
Orthodox Church, Fioravanti's Cathedral of the Dormition of the Virgin
represents a felicitous meeting of two cultures: the Russian, with its
Byzantine heritage, and the western European, as expressed in the
architectural ideals of the Italian Renaissance.[10] Indeed, the cathedral
can be seen as the culminating monument of the Vladimir tradition,
the last of the great limestone churches. Henceforth limestone would
be used primarily for the ground level and for decorative detail, but
the predominant building material would be brick, whose qualities
were to be so thoroughly exploited in later Muscovite architecture.

The extent of Fioravanti's achievement is demonstrated by a comparison of his cathedral with two other churches constructed in the
Kremlin toward the end of the fifteenth century: the Cathedral of the
Annunciation (1484–89) and the Church of the Deposition of the Robe
(1484–85). Both were built by architects from Pskov, and both represent a fusion of early-Muscovite and Pskov styles, particularly in the
decoration. The Church of the Deposition of the Robe (named for the
holiday commemorating the taking of the Virgin's robe from Palestine
to Constantinople in the fifth century) was built as the residential
church of the Russian patriarch; it is the most modest of the surviving
Kremlin churches. The decorative brickwork on the drum derives from
Pskov, as does the design of the three apses—all of the same height—
whereas the facade displays a playful, purely decorative medley of
early Muscovite forms, such as the pointed arch and the ornamental
frieze (here, in terra-cotta).

Of much the same style is the Cathedral of the Annunciation,
completed in 1489 as the court chapel of the grand prince. Its present
elaborate exterior derives in large part from the reign of Ivan the
Terrible (Ivan IV), who in the 1560s commissioned the four side
chapels and placed an additional two cupolas on the main sanctuary,
thus creating a pyramid of nine cupolas, burnished in gold. In 1472
Ivan, excommunicated for his fourth marriage, enclosed part of the
southern gallery to create a small chamber from which he could hear
the service without entering the sanctuary. The separate entrance to
his chamber from the Kremlin's square still exists, with much of its
intricate carving.

The return to the attractive though relatively unsophisticated principles of Pskovian and early Muscovite architecture demonstrated in
these two churches, and in their contemporary the Church of the
Holy Spirit at Trinity Monastery, did not signal the end of the Italian
presence at the Muscovite court. Quite the contrary. Italian architects
and engineers continued to play the dominant role in the reconstruction
of the Kremlin during the end of the fifteenth and the beginning of the
sixteenth centuries. Between 1485 and 1516 the Kremlin's limestone
walls, which had been constructed under Dmitry Donskoy in 1367,
were replaced with a series of towers connected by massive brick walls
that exemplified the Italian genius for fortification engineering, and
endowed the Kremlin with its singularly imposing appearance. (The
tent-shaped turrets that now dominate the towers were added in the

190. *Cathedral of the Archangel Michael, the Kremlin. Moscow. 1505–09. Architect: Alevisio Novy. Northwest view.* [RIGHT]

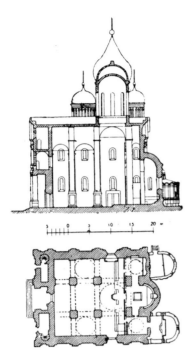

191. *Cathedral of the Archangel Michael. Section, plan.*

192. *Kremlin towers, Moscow. In the foreground: Beklemishev Tower (1487–88, Marco Fryazin); Constantine and Elena Tower (1490, Pietro-Antonio Solari); and Frolov (Spasky) Tower (1491, Pietro-Antonio Solari). During the seventeenth century the towers acquired their various turrets and steeply pitched roofs.* [OPPOSITE]

seventeenth century.) The Kremlin's walls have been compared to those of the fortress at Milan[11]—a reasonable comparison in view of the northern-Italian origins of the Kremlin's architects: Antonio Fryazin (or Antonio 'the Frankish'—the Russians apparently content to designate all foreigners as Franks), Marco Ruffo (also known as Marco Fryazin), Pietro-Antonio Solari, and Alevisio Fryazin the Elder.

Ruffo and Solari were also engaged in the construction of the Kremlin's earliest stone palace, the Granovitaya Palata, or Hall of Facets (1487–91). Intended as a large reception hall for state occasions, the Palata was decorated with a rusticated eastern facade composed of faceted limestone blocks. The original pairs of narrow windows in a late-Gothic style were replaced in 1685 with the present wider windows, framed with elaborately carved columns and capped with an equally elaborate entablature. The original steep roof has also been replaced—with one much lower—and the facade now seems to end with its sharply defined cornice. Each corner of the faceted wall is marked by a narrow column decorated with a spiral motif. The faceted appearance of the eastern wall proved to have an enduring appeal in

Russian architecture during the sixteenth and seventeenth centuries, but it was rarely again applied in stone: local architects preferred to paint the facets on their walls as gaudy trompe l'oeil.

The final stage in Ivan the Great's reconstruction of the Kremlin began in 1505, with the commissioning of the Cathedral of the Archangel Michael on the southern flank of Cathedral Square, to replace a church of that name dating from the time of Ivan Kalita (1333). Its architect, the Venetian Alevisio Novy (Alevisio 'the New,' the Russian way of distinguishing him from the 'Elder' Alevisio), had arrived in Moscow in 1504 with the embassy of Dmitry Ralev, after completing a palace for the Crimean khan at Bakhchisarai. Alevisio was soon at work on the cathedral that was to serve as the final resting place for Russia's grand princes and tsars until the time of Peter the Great, two hundred years later. This cathedral displays the most extravagantly Italianate features of the Kremlin's 'Italian period,' and yet at the same time it seems to represent a return to the more traditional forms of the Russian cross-inscribed church, particularly in comparison with

193. *Church of Saint Trifon in Naprudny. Moscow. 1492(?). Located in one of Ivan III's villages, this small church is without interior piers. Its drum is projected upward by a combination of groin and domical vaults (*kreshchaty svod*).* [RIGHT]

194. *Church of Saint Trifon in Naprudny. Section, plan.*

the plan of Fioravanti's cathedral, which from the exterior bears a much closer resemblance to the Vladimir tradition.

There is now, however, some question as to how consciously and to what extent Alevisio Novy drew on Russian tradition for the design of his cathedral. The Soviet scholar S. S. Podyapolsky has pressed cogent claim for the northern-Italian origins (ultimately deriving from Byzantium) of Alevisio's delineation of the central aisle and crossing, as well as of the articulation of the facades.[12] Podyapolsky's evidence for the Italian derivation is impressive, and he further notes that there is no precedent for the six-piered, cross-inscribed church in Muscovite architecture, whose *surviving* monuments follow a four-piered, single-cupola pattern. (The Cathedral of the Dormition is, as noted above, sui generis.) The lack of information on Alevisio's design makes a clear resolution of the question unlikely, but Podyapolsky's position provides a corrective to the opinion that Alevisio served pri-

195. *Church of the Conception of Saint Anne on the Corner. Moscow. 1530s(?). A neighborhood church in the Pskov style, it is similar in structure to the Church of Saint Trifon.*

196. *Cathedral of the Nativity of the Virgin, Rozhdestvensky Monastery. Moscow. 1501–05. The pyramidal silhouette, with pointed* zakomary *merging into* kokoshniki, *resembles that of the cathedral at Andronikov Monastery. Corbeled arches, resting on four piers, support the drum. The grey structure in the foreground is a later addition.*

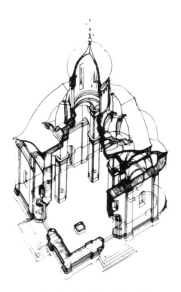

197. *Cathedral of the Nativity, Rozhdestvensky Monastery. Axonometric reconstruction. Shchusev Museum, Moscow.*

marily as a decorator, applying Italian ornaments to a Russian form. That Alevisio could have drawn from his own culture a conception so close in spirit to the great cathedrals of Kiev, Chernigov, Novgorod, and Vladimir attests, rather, to the pervasive influence of Byzantium on medieval European architecture.

The Cathedral of the Archangel Michael has undergone a number of modifications since the sixteenth century, most notably in the roof, whose original form, in black tile, followed the vaulting contours. The present sheet-metal roof, overhanging the *zakomary*, obscures the limestone pyramidal ornaments that originally crowned the arches and gives an obtrusive, weighty effect to the roofline. Nonetheless, the scallop motif—another Italian innovation that was soon to enter the repertoire of Moscow's architects—remains intact and provides an emphatic accent to the cathedral walls, which are divided with a complicated array of cornices, arches, and pilasters. The lower tier, in the form of a blind arcade rising from a clearly defined limestone base, is separated from the upper tier by a cornice resting on a series of classical capitals. The entablature of the upper tier in turn isolates the scallop-form *zakomary*, creating the effect—unprecedented in Russia—of a large square structure with a lavishly decorated roof.

Alevisio's design has been frequently criticized as an interruption of the vertical unity of the bays, a destruction of the monolithic quality inherent in the relation between the vaulting and the structure of the facades in earlier Russian churches—including the Cathedral of the Dormition. The sense of fragmentation is exaggerated by the large number of bays—five, of unequal size, on the northern and southern facades (the fifth delineates a special gallery for the use of the grand

198. *Cathedral of the Smolensk Mother of God, Novodevichy Monastery. Moscow. 1524–25.*

199. *Church of the Ascension at Kolomenskoe. Near Moscow. 1530–32.
Southeast view. Photograph taken in
1979 after whitewashing. Compare
with Figure 200, taken in 1972.*

200. *Church of the Ascension at*
Kolomenskoe. Moscow. 1530–32.
Photograph taken in 1972. Compare
with 1979 photograph, Figure 199.

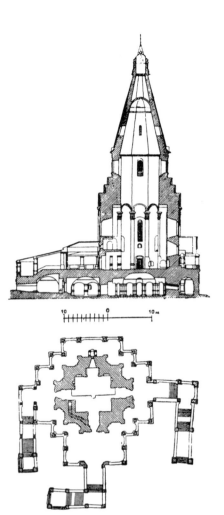

201. *Church of the Ascension, Kolomenskoe. Detail, south facade.*

202. *Church of the Ascension, Kolomenskoe. Section, plan.*

princess and her suite on the western end of the cathedral). In his defense, however, it must be said that the architect's bold use of classical elements creates a sculpted form in its own right, a form whose plasticity and exuberance provide a welcome complement to its monolithic counterpart on the opposite side of Cathedral Square.

Ivan the Great did not live to see the completion of the Cathedral of the Archangel Michael, nor of its contemporary, the bell tower named in his honor (begun by another 'Fryazin,' Bon, in 1505, and subsequently enlarged in the sixteenth and seventeenth centuries). Ivan's magnificent patronage had created an architectural ensemble that dominates the Kremlin—indeed, Moscow—to this day; and in the process he had introduced to backward Muscovy a group of architects whose sense of adventure must surely have equaled the brilliance with which they performed the role of *Kulturträger* (Fioravanti is the first Westerner known to have penetrated the far north of Russia). The reign of Ivan the Great witnessed the culmination of one great tradition, the limestone church derived from Vladimir-Suzdal, and the beginnings of another, characterized by massive brick forms decorated with motifs borrowed from the West but applied in a manner peculiarly Russian. During the half century following Ivan's death, in 1584, the techniques assimilated during his reign were to produce three of the most distinctive monuments in Muscovite architecture.

Sixteenth Century: The Ascent of Muscovite Architecture

About the beginning of the sixteenth century the number of masonry churches in Moscow increased rapidly, although wood remained by far the predominant building material. The style and scale of church construction varied considerably, from such structures as Saint Trifon's on the Pond (1490s)—one of Ivan the Great's estate chapels, built of stone and of particular interest for its use of the Pskovian technique of vaulting without the use of interior piers—to much larger cathedrals, such as the one dedicated to the Smolensk Icon of the Mother of God at Novodevichy Convent (1524–25). The latter illustrates one of a number of attempts in the sixteenth century to emulate Fioravanti's Cathedral of the Dormition, but without a thorough understanding of its structural principles.[13]

Nothing from this period, however, quite prepares one for the next of Muscovy's great monuments, the Church of the Ascension at Kolomenskoe, country retreat of the grand prince. Commissioned by Basil III in 1529 or 1530 as a votive church for the birth of an heir (Ivan IV), the Church of the Ascension continues to baffle those who seek a clear derivation. Its form—a tower composed of a square base surmounted by an octagon, from which soars the 'tent' roof with a small

203. *Church of the Ascension, Kolomenskoe. Interior of the tent-shaped tower (*shatyor).

204. Church of the Decapitation of John the Baptist at Dyakovo. Moscow. Circa 1550. [OPPOSITE]

cupola—has been compared to the traditional wooden tower churches so distinctive of Russian architecture. The assumption that these churches served as a model is supported by a contemporary chronicle's reference to the church's being constructed 'in the manner of wood' (*na derevyannoye delo*); but this probably alludes to a resemblance, not a prototype: the differences between wooden and masonry construction on this scale are simply too great.[14]

There are, of course, possible precedents, however remote their appearance from that of Basil III's church: the movement toward the tower form can be detected as early as the thirteenth century, notably in Chernigov's Paraskeva-Pyatnitsa Church, and certain aspects of the form—such as the octagonal transition with ascending *kokoshniki*—are evident in such Muscovite churches as the Cathedral at the Nativity Monastery. In addition, the brick tower had become a familiar structure in the city's architecture, both as a part of the Kremlin fortifications

205. Bell tower, Church of Saint George at Kolomenskoe. Near Moscow. Sixteenth century.

206. *Church of the Decapitation of John the Baptist at Dyakovo. West facade.* [LEFT]

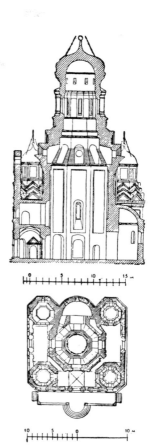

207. *Church of the Decapitation of John the Baptist at Dyakovo. Section, plan.*

and as displayed in the bell tower commissioned by Ivan the Great. From a technical point of view, Muscovy clearly possessed the resources to erect large and complex brick structures. Finally, the application of Italianate decorative motifs—particularly in the capitals and consoles of the main structure—suggests not only an affinity with the Cathedral of the Archangel Michael but also the possibility that Italian masters were directly involved in the construction of the Church of the Ascension. (Petroch the Small, in Moscow between 1528 and 1552, has been proposed as the architect.)[15]

And yet the imaginative leap implied in so distinctive a structure eludes a final explanation. Rising from a low gallery (originally without a roof), the compressed central block of the sanctuary, dominated by massive pilasters, leads to three tiers of pointed *kokoshniki*, echoed in the cornice of the octagon. From this point the 'tent' ascends (one wonders whether the builder was aware of the elaborate architectural metaphor he had created in his church)—ascends in a pyramidal shape of eight facets delineated by limestone ribs. The rise is accentuated by a rhomboid pattern, also in limestone, that narrows toward the culmination of each facet. The tower concludes with an octagonal lantern, a cupola, and the cross. The tower church will henceforth play a major role in the development of Muscovite architecture; but Basil III's church at Kolomenskoe represents the apotheosis (to return to the metaphor of ascension), the most rigorous expression of the vertical in Russian architecture.

208. *Church of the Decapitation of John the Baptist at Dyakovo. Near Moscow. 1547 or 1554. East view.* [OPPOSITE]

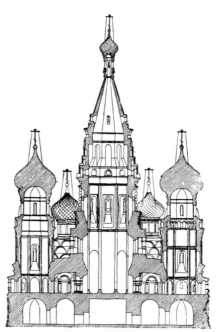

209. *Cathedral of the Intercession on the Moat, popularly called Saint Basil's. Red Square, Moscow. 1555–60. Architects: Barma and Postnik. Detail. (See Figures 211 and 212.)* [LEFT]

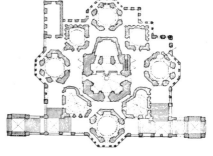

210. *Saint Basil's. Plan, elevation.*

Within two decades of the completion of the Church of the Ascension, Basil III's heir, Ivan IV ('the Terrible'), had commissioned another votive church, possibly for the birth of his son Ivan, in 1554, although the precise date of the church is unknown. Situated in the village of Dyakovo, which is separated from Kolomenskoe by a wide ravine, the Church of the Decapitation of John the Baptist is as innovative and striking in appearance as the neighboring Church of the Ascension. (The effect of both is enhanced by their location on a high bluff overlooking the Moscow River.) Although it lacks the vertical *point* provided by the 'tent' at Kolomenskoe, the Church of John the Baptist can be classified as another variant of the tower, or 'pillar,' church, whose sanctuary is compressed in the interest of obtaining a vertical silhouette.

The core of the church, resting on a square base, is composed in an

211. *Cathedral of the Intercession of the Virgin (Saint Basil's). Moscow. 1555–60. Northeast view.* [OPPOSITE]

octagonal pattern, each of whose facades is delineated not by pilasters—as at Kolomenskoe—but by large recessed panels, reminiscent of Alevisio's sculpted facades at the Cathedral of the Archangel. Above the cornice a tier of semicircular *kokoshniki* is surmounted by pediments in a transition to the great drum, whose plastic form is composed of a series of semicylinders placed on a high octagonal base. A circle of panels above the cylinders preserves the cupola from the clutter of forms beneath it. The relation of rounded and octagonal volumes of circular and pointed surfaces creates a peculiar dynamic

212. Church of the Crucifixion, Alexandrov Compound. Alexandrov. 1570s. The nucleus of this tower church dates from the beginning of the sixteenth century. During Ivan the Terrible's stay at Alexandrov, a two-story octagonal arcade—supporting decorative gables (kokoshniki) *and a tent-shaped tower* (shatyor)—*was built to surround the church.*

213. *Church of the Trinity at Khoro-shevo. Moscow. 1598. Built on an estate belonging to Boris Godunov, the church resembles the Old Cathedral at Donskoy Monastery, with tiers of* kokoshniki *rising to the central drum and cupola. (See Figure 220.)*

that is reinforced by the four side chapels, whose design echoes that of the central tower. From a structural perspective, this symmetrical arrangement of chapels around the central mass—all resting on the same base—is the most innovative feature of the Church of John the Baptist. And though its use here can be seen as an idiosyncratic variant of the pentacupolar design, the implications of this modular system were soon to be thoroughly exploited in the most renowned of Russia's architectural monuments, the Cathedral of the Intercession on the Moat, popularly called Saint Basil's (1555–60).

The fame of the building that has come to epitomize the color—and, for some, the barbarism—of Muscovite imagination rests on more than its extravagant exterior. Legends of the cruelty of Ivan the Terrible—who commissioned the cathedral as a commemoration of the taking of Kazan (1552) and is supposed to have blinded the architects to prevent a rival monument—have conspired to foster the notion of a structure devoid of restraint or reason. In fact, Barma and Postnik, masters from Pskov, created a remarkably coherent, logical plan for the cathedral.

The idea behind the design, it must be noted, represents the combi-

214. *Cathedral of the Intercession.*
Detail.

215. *Cathedral of the Intercession
(Saint Basil's). West view.*

216. *Church of the Trinity at Vyazyomy. Near Moscow. 1590s. Built on Godunov's estate at Vyazyomy, the church is of lime-stone, with brick vaults and drums and an elevated open gallery. The ground plan, a central cube with two flanking chapels, is a variation of that at Khoroshevo.*

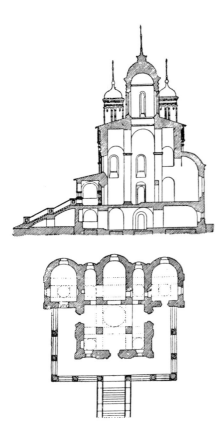

217. *Church of the Trinity at Vyazyomy. Section, plan.*

nation of violence and religious mysticism so evident in the latter part of Ivan the Terrible's reign; for the cathedral is composed of nine churches, most of which honor the saints on whose days occurred a significant event in the siege of Kazan. Thus, the northwestern chapel is dedicated to Grigory the Armenian, whose day—September 30— saw the capture of one of the main points on the city walls; while the central part, dedicated to the Feast of the Intercession of the Virgin (October 1), commemorates the beginning of the final storm of Kazan. It should also be noted that although only eight such days (including the Feast of the Intercession) were designated, the architects took the

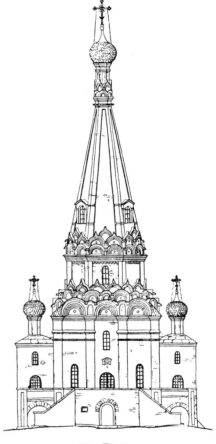

218. *Church of the Intercession at Medvedkovo. Moscow. 1620s(?). Commissioned by Prince Dmitry Pozharsky, a leader in Russia's expulsion of Polish troops during the Time of Troubles (1605–13). The* shatyor *is decorated with ceramic tiles.* [LEFT]

liberty of modifying the plan by adding a ninth church (the Entry of Christ into Jerusalem) in the interest of symmetry.

The resulting arrangement therefore displays a central tower church (the Intercession) surrounded by eight chapels, placed at the corners of two intersecting squares. The octagonal motif is repeated in the drum and tent roof of the central tower, as well as in the four octagonal chapels placed on the points of the compass. The remaining, smaller chapels consist of a cupola and round drum raised on three tiers of *kokoshniki* and placed so as to complement the cupolas of the taller chapels (lower alternating with higher, in a finely calculated use of proportion and spacing). The profusion of decorative motifs—semi-circular *kokoshniki*, sharply pointed pediments, rosettes, lancets, pilasters, recessed panels—was somewhat less vividly displayed during the sixteenth century, when the color scheme of the church was

219. *Church of the Intercession at Medvedkovo. West elevation, plan.*

220. *Old Cathedral, Donskoy Monastery. Moscow. 1593.*

221. *Church of the Trinity in Nikitniki.*
Moscow. 1628–51.

limited to red and white (white in the limestone details), and to colored tiles on the main tower. By the end of the sixteenth century, however, the original cupolas (helmet shaped) were replaced with the fanciful *lukovitsi* (onion-shaped cupolas) that exist today, with their facets, whorls, and primary colors. And during the seventeenth century much of the cathedral's surface was painted: floral motifs, particularly, were applied to the panels of the *kokoshniki*, and even the brick was painted brick red with white tracing, as it is today after a recent restoration.[16]

Saint Basil's, whose basic plan derives so clearly from a combination of the tower church at Kolomenskoe and the Church of John the Baptist at Dyakovo, represents the extreme point in decorative and structural saturation. Each commissioned as a memorial to a specific secular event, all three churches—the Ascension, John the Baptist, and Saint Basil's—are conceived in terms of monumentality, of exterior effect, with little concern for decoration of the interior as a place of worship. Tellingly, the Church of the Ascension does not even contain an apse: in the apse's place, on the exterior of the eastern facade, was an elaborately carved throne, from which the tsar could survey the broad expanse of his domains across the Moscow River.

Earlier Russian churches—at Kiev and Novgorod—had been guided by a very different approach, in which the exterior, however imposing, was austere in comparison with the celestial vision rendered in the frescoes and icons that covered the interior. (Again, it should be noted that Muscovy's modest churches from the beginning of the fifteenth century provided the setting for the greatest works in the history of Russian painting.) By contrast, the interior canopies of the three tower churches were decorated with an ornamental motif—probably floral—that would have provided no obstruction to the visual appreciation of the ascent. By the seventeenth century, Muscovy's churches began to

222. *Church of the Trinity in Nikitniki. Window detail.*

223. *Church of the Trinity in Nikitniki. West elevation, plan, section.*

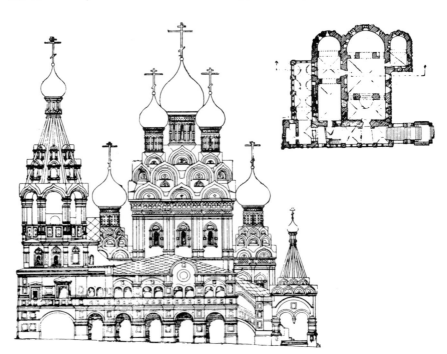

224. *Church of the Trinity in Nikit-niki. Moscow. 1628–51.*

225. *Church of the Trinity in Troitsko-Golenishchevo. Moscow. 1644–46. Similar in plan to the Church of the Intercession, Medvedkovo, with flanking chapels and a surrounding gallery.*

combine the ornamental facade with a lavishly painted interior; but however delightful the results, the scale is altogether minor in comparison with the 'pillar' churches of the mid-sixteenth century.

Seventeenth Century: Ornamentalism

After the completion of Saint Basil's, Muscovite architecture entered another period of stagnation—the result of the political and social dementia that characterized the latter part of Ivan the Terrible's reign. There have been many ingenious attempts to rationalize the chaos that ensued when Ivan, supposedly locked in a power struggle with the boyars and certain segments of the clergy, abandoned Moscow and divided his country into two parts, only one of which he claimed as

226. *Church of the Nativity of the Virgin in Putinki. Moscow. 1649–52. This is the last of Moscow's churches to use the* shatyor. *Here the function of the three 'tent' towers is purely decorative—they admit no light.*

227. *Church of the Nativity in Putinki. West elevation, plan.*

his own (the *oprichnina*). He then proceeded to make war on the other part, and in the course of a decade not only tortured and executed many of Moscow's citizens, but also launched devastating campaigns against Tver, Novgorod, and Pskov. His troops, the *oprichniki*, adept at terrorizing a defenseless population, proved incapable of repulsing Russia's external enemies, in particular the Crimean Tatars, who laid waste to much of Moscow in 1571. During this period of unrest, famine, and war, very little was built in Muscovy, apart from the tsar's compound at the village of Alexandrov, which became the center of Ivan's state within a state.[17] The reign of Ivan the Terrible must, nonetheless, be considered one of the most brilliant in Russian architectural history, largely by virtue of the churches at Dyakovo and on Red Square.

The decline was temporary, for the end of the sixteenth century witnessed a revival of church construction under the patronage of Tsar Boris Godunov (1598–1605). Godunov's estates at Khoroshevo, Besedy, and Vyazyomy provided the settings for three churches, each very different in appearance and each representative of a type prevalent at the turn of the century. The 'tent' variant of the tower church (Besedy) became firmly entrenched in the Muscovite architectural imagination—although implemented on a reduced scale in compari-

228. *Cathedral of the Twelve Apostles, the Kremlin. Moscow. 1642–55. Architect: Antip Konstantinov.*

229. *Church of the Trinity at Ostankino. Moscow. 1678–83. Architect: Pavel Potekhin. This most elaborate brickwork in Moscow is complemented by limestone details and ceramic tiles. The bell tower was added in 1832.* [OPPOSITE]

son with the Church of the Ascension. The more sober style loosely derived from Fioravanti's Cathedral of the Dormition remained a model for large pentacupolar churches (Vyazyomy). The most productive tendency, however, led toward increasingly elaborate ornamentalism, characterized by the masses of *kokoshniki* and fanciful window surrounds (*nalichniki*) applied to the church at Khoroshevo and to the Old Cathedral at Donskoy Monastery.[18]

After the interregnum—or 'Time of Troubles'—from the death of Boris Godunov to the establishment of the Romanov dynasty (in 1613), the building of churches resumed; they were still virtually the only masonry structures in Moscow. By the middle of the century, the taste for elaborate decoration seemed to admit no limits; and yet, oddly enough, the general effect of the best of these churches is one of coherence, however irresponsible the application of certain details.

230. *Church of the Archangel Michael at Arkhangelskoe. Near Moscow. 1667. The architect is thought to be Pavel Potekhin.*

231. *Church of Saint Nicholas in Khamovniki. Moscow. 1679–82. Commissioned by the weavers' guild in Khamovniki, the Church of Saint Nicholas is in the ship form, with bell tower, refectory, and main cube. The exterior detail is vividly highlighted in orange and green.*

232. *New Cathedral at Donskoy Monastery. Moscow. 1684–98. The cruciform structure of the cathedral was sharply delineated until the nineteenth century, when the corner bays were heightened, obscuring the original design. Although the decoration is restrained, the centralized plan anticipates the 'Moscow baroque' tiered churches that soon followed.*

Both the harmony and the irresponsibility are most fully demonstrated at the Church of the Trinity in Nikitniki. Endowed by the merchant Grigory Nikitnikov (whose vast wealth made him an occasional banker to the tsars), the church consists of a central cube with five cupolas and no interior piers—an indication both of its modest size and of the more flexible possibilities of brick construction. Completed in 1634, the central part of the church, which included a refectory, acquired over the next two decades two chapels (attached at the northeast and southeast) and an enclosed gallery, leading to a tent-shaped bell tower on the northwest corner. At this point the gallery turns at a right angle and descends by a covered staircase to a covered porch (southwest corner), capped by *kokoshniki* and yet another tent tower. This array of forms has led some to suggest a resemblance to wooden churches in the Russian countryside, with their covered galleries,[19] porches, and tent-shaped towers; and yet the building's design is in fact determined by and perfectly adapted to the constraints of an urban setting. When

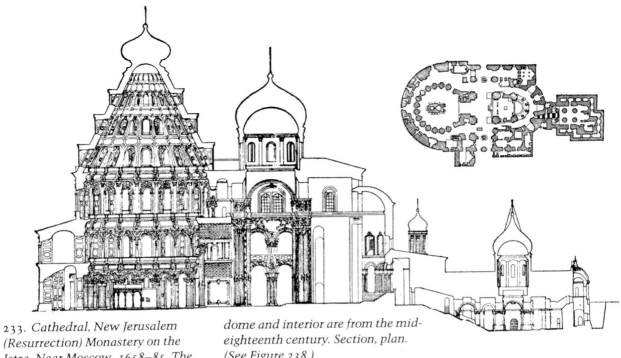

233. *Cathedral, New Jerusalem (Resurrection) Monastery on the Istra. Near Moscow. 1658–85. The* dome and interior are from the mid-eighteenth century. Section, plan. (See Figure 238.)

234. *Church of the Annunciation. Taininskoe (near Moscow). 1677. West facade, with gallery. (See Figure 244.)*

235. *New refectory, Simonov Monastery. Moscow. 1683–85. Architects: Parfen Peterov and Osip Startsev. The unusual stepped pediment, with its limestone detail, has been attributed to the influence of the Polish baroque. The design of the columns and cornice also shows an awareness of that architectural style.*

viewed from the southwest corner, the ascent from entrance to sanctuary impresses not only with the harmony of its shapes, with the balancing of various projecting chapels and galleries, but also with the clarity, the logic of its design, which effects the transition from the street, or southern, side to the main east-west axis of the Orthodox church.

The decoration of the Church of the Trinity, like its structure, evolved over several years, during which Nikitnikov was apparently able to draw on the services of the tsar's own artisans, who were then engaged in the decoration of the Kremlin's Terem Palace (1635–36). As they now exist, the facades provide an inventory of ornamental devices applied in Muscovite architecture during the seventeenth century: carved limestone *nalichniki* in Romanesque and Moorish patterns, limestone window pediments, deeply recessed decorative squares (*shirinki*), *kokoshniki* sculpted with recessed arches, limestone pendants (*girki*) within the entrance arches, attached columns, pilasters, arcading on the cupola drums, arches of every conceivable sort—all subsumed in a color pattern of red with white trim. This by no means exhausts the array, whose application must in some cases be judged capricious. Despite the fact that Russian masters had assimilated the details of Western architectural orders—particularly as interpreted in Italy—the details' context was ignored in favor of

236. *Cathedral of the Virgin of the Sign, Znamensky Monastery. Moscow. 1679–84. This is a well-restored church, with a wooden roof—not unusual for Moscow in the seventeenth century.* [RIGHT]

237. *Dulo Tower, Simonov Monastery, Moscow. 1640s, turret added in the 1670s. The last of the great monastery fortifications, the Simonov walls were an anachronism by the time of their completion; by the end of the seventeenth century walls at other monasteries (Donskoy, Novodevichy) had assumed a largely decorative character.*

238. *Cathedral, Monastery of the Resurrection on the Istra. Near Moscow. 1658–85; rebuilt in the mid-eighteenth century.* [OPPOSITE]

a purely ornamental approach, which might place a 'classical' window pediment on the same facade as a series of ogival arches.

The collision between Muscovite ornamentalism—whose evolution can be traced back as far as the Zvenigorod cathedrals—and architectural borrowings from the West was to be emphatically resolved in favor of the latter, during the eighteenth century. Before that time, however, Moscow's architects and artisans were to have ample re-

239. *Refectory and Church of the Dormition, Novodevichy Convent. Moscow. 1685–87. The restrained pattern of the window surrounds embodies a concept of architectural detail far removed from the earlier exuberance of seventeenth-century Moscow architecture. An unfortunate rebuilding in the nineteenth century destroyed the* zakomary *and five cupolas that originally crowned the church. For an idea of its intended appearance, see the similar Gate Church of the Transfiguration.*

sources to pursue the fancies so brilliantly displayed at the Church of the Trinity at Nikitniki, and also to develop a more coherent style of ornamentalism, which became known as 'Moscow baroque.'

The Moscow Baroque

Of the great estates that surrounded Moscow in the seventeenth century, most by now have been absorbed into the city's gargantuan housing projects, with only a church, an occasional manor house, or just a name to mark their former existence: Tropareva, Konkovo, Zyuzino, Troekurovo, Ostankino, Perovo, Fili, Izmailovo. Within this sprawl there are, however, oases, villages where the way of life seems to have been little touched by the twentieth century. One such village is Troitskoe-Lykovo, located at the western fringes of the city, on the banks of the Moscow River. You can get there—just barely—on a bus

240. *Gate Church of the Trans-figuration, Novodevichy Convent. Moscow. 1688.* [LEFT]

241. *Church of the Metropolitan Peter, Vysoko-Petrovsky Monastery. Moscow. 1686. This small eight-lobed church exemplifies one type of the centralized tower design that dominated Moscow architecture at the turn of the eighteenth century. Here, the painted floral decoration around the windows and portals imitates masonry decoration.*

that winds through the immensity of the new Strogino development before hitting a series of ruts that passes for a road.

By far the preferable way is to board the cutter that leaves from Serebryanny bor ('Silver Pines') Park, and make the brief crossing of the Moscow. En route you will catch sight of one of the most stunningly beautiful churches in Moscow—the Holy Trinity at Lykovo, situated at the high point of a bluff overlooking the river. One enraptured scholar has compared the church to a bride arrayed in a Russian wedding dress, admiring her reflection in the waters of the Moscow—a comparison that might be lost to Westerners, but an indication nonetheless of the effect the building has on an otherwise sober observer.[20]

The church is not large—none of the estate churches were, apart from those belonging to the tsar. It impresses, rather, by the proportions of the central tower, which rises from a cube to an octagon, to yet another octagon (with bells), to a drum (also octagonal), and finally to the golden cupola and cross. The tower is flanked on the east and west by two projections of equal size—the entrance and the apse—also ascending, in two octagonal tiers, to a cupola and cross. The architect is presumed to have been Yakov Bukhvostov, author of another of the period's most graceful churches, the Savior, on the Sheremetevs' estate at Ubory.

The Church of the Trinity is one of the best examples (certainly the most delicate) of a style that flourished from the 1680s through the 1690s, and is designated Moscow, or Naryshkin, baroque ('Naryshkin' after the boyar family that commissioned a number of the churches for its estates, including Lykovo). The style's origins can be traced from the tiered (*yarusny*) structure—octagonal forms above a central cube—which first appeared in masonry construction at the beginning of the 1680s and represents the reassertion of the vertical principle after Patriarch Nikon's condemnation in 1653 of the 'tent' (*shatyor*) as unorthodox.

242. *Bell tower and Church of the Intercession, Vysoko-Petrovsky Monastery. Moscow. 1694.*

243. *Refectory Church of Saint Sergius of Radonezh, Vysoko-Petrovsky Monastery. Moscow. Early 1690s.*

244. *Church of the Annunciation at Taininskoe. Near Moscow. 1675–77.*

245. *Church of the Resurrection at*
Kadashi. Moscow. 1687–95. Archi-
tect: Sergey Turchaninov(?). Although
its structure retains the elements of
the traditional ship form (bell tower,
trapeza, main cube), the Church of
the Resurrection displays some of the
best limestone carving of the Moscow
baroque. Its sponsors—the guild of
linen weavers attached to the tsar's
court—could well afford the magni-
ficent display. [RIGHT]

246. *Church of the Resurrection at*
Kadashi. Detail.

247. *Church of the Resurrection*
at Kadashi. East elevation and section
(by G. V. Alferova). Shchusev
Museum, Moscow.

Like its predecessor of the tent variety, the tiered church is thought
to derive from a wooden prototype, and indeed with more justification,
as examples of wooden tiered churches dating from as early as the
mid-seventeenth century have survived.[21] But here as well the similarity of the basic shape is overshadowed by the greater complexity of
the brick tiered church. For not only does the church of the Moscow-
baroque style reinterpret the central-tower structure; it also integrates
the bell tower within the main part of the church, achieving, finally, a
symmetry in which the apse is balanced by an identical projection on
the opposite end. In more complicated designs, projections were also
added on the north and south of the sanctuary, thus creating a four-
lobed pattern (at the Church of the Intercession at Fili and the Church
of the Sign at Dubrovitsy). The resulting compact form did not allow
for a large sanctuary—unnecessary in an estate church—and the

248. *Church of the Archangel Michael at Troparevo. Moscow. 1693. A particularly fine example of the ship form, with horseshoe* zakomary.

thick walls needed to support the weight of the tower placed further constraints on the size of the interior.

But apart from the structure (which shows considerable variation among the twenty or so churches displaying the style), the most distinctive feature of Moscow baroque is its adaptation of seventeenth-century ornamentalism to a pattern that has been compared to the richly carved and gilded iconostases peculiar to the latter part of the century.[22] This was no longer a simple, if lavish, application of architectural details highlighted by bright colors. The new form of ornamentation consisted, rather, of sculpted details (in limestone, for the most part) frequently borrowed from Western handbooks and distributed on the facade in a stricter, more coherent fashion than had been the case with earlier churches, such as the Trinity in Nikitniki and the Trinity at Ostankino.

249. *Church of the Dormition at the Krutitsky retreat* (podvore). *Moscow. 1667–85. As was frequently the case during this period, the subsidiary drums are purely decorative: they admit no light.*

250. *Tower and entrance gates at the Krutitsky retreat. Moscow. 1693–94. Architects: Osip Startsev and Larion Kovalev; ceramic work by Osip and Ivan Startsev. 'Paradise'—that is what contemporaries called this residence of the Metropolitan of Sarsky and Podonsky, who spared no expense in decorating it with brick, limestone, and ceramic tiles.*

Ц. ПОКРОВА
В ФИЛЯХ

Although brick remained the primary building material, the intricacy of the limestone carving used on the cornices, or for window surrounds and attached columns, and the symmetry with which these elements were placed suggest a greater sophistication on the part of Moscow's architects—and their patrons, an increasingly secularized, cosmopolitan group. In particular, the Naryshkins and Golitsyns, whose largess supported many of the Moscow-baroque churches, were closely associated with Peter the Great, and by the standards of the time they were quite 'Westernized.'

It must be noted, however, that not all monuments classified under the Moscow baroque were commissioned by the nobility, nor were they all estate churches. For example, the Church of the Resurrection in Kadashi (1687–95), situated within view of the Kremlin, served as the place of worship for a community of weavers attached to the tsar's court. And in design it displays not a central tower constructed on the tiered principle, but a more traditional 'ship' form, consisting of a bell

251. *Church of the Intercession at Fili. Moscow. 1690–93. Axonometric projection. Commissioned by the boyar Lev Naryshkin, this first of the great Moscow-baroque tower churches has four lobes extending from the central cube, each with its own cupola. All projections but the east (apsidal) one have a stone staircase descending from the gallery that encircles the church. The decoration is relatively restrained: attached columns, without carving, and cornice crests ('combs'), set off by the painted-brick facade. Shchusev Museum, Moscow.* [ABOVE]

252. *Gate Church at the Resurrection Monastery on the Istra. Near Moscow. 1694. Architect: Yakov Bukhvostov. Destroyed during the German retreat from Moscow in December 1941, the church has been rebuilt in approximately its original form. Concurrently with this project Bukhvostov, who had recently finished the monastery walls, was at work on churches in Ryazan and Ubory; his inability to meet his numerous deadlines landed him briefly in jail, for breach of contract.*

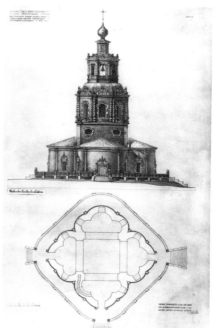

253. *Church of the Transfiguration of the Savior at Ubory. Near Moscow. 1694–97. Architect: Yakov Bukhvostov and others. Commissioned for the estate of boyar Peter Sheremetev, the Church of the Savior follows the four-lobed plan of the Church of the Intercession at Fili, but omits cupolas over the four projections. The limestone carving here is more elaborate, particularly in the columns; the cornice of each lobe may originally have been decorated with limestone crests.*

254. *Church of the Transfiguration of the Savior at Ubory. West elevation and section (by V. Podklyuchnikov). Shchusev Museum, Moscow.*

tower with a tent-shaped roof (still permitted on bell towers), a refectory, and a large pentacupolar sanctuary, all arranged on one axis. It is nonetheless considered Moscow baroque, by virtue of the superb limestone carving displayed along its cornice and on the facades. Although the appearance of the church in Kadashi has been harmed by eighteenth-century additions, and although its view is partially obstructed by a cannery, it still dominates the surrounding area, as it did almost three centuries ago, when Moscow's neighborhoods were defined by such churches.[23]

A survey of the vitality of the Moscow baroque might appropriately conclude with the Church of the Sign at Dubrovitsy—one of the Golitsyn estates, located to the south of Moscow. The church was begun in 1690, seven years before the Church of the Trinity at Lykovo, and its plan—a four-lobed base surmounted by a central tiered structure—places it among the tower churches of the period, but its appear-

255. *Church of the Trinity at Troitskoe-Lykovo. Moscow. 1698–1703. Architect: Yakov Bukhvostov(?). With only two projecting lobes (east and west), the Church of the Trinity, in contrast to the Church at Fili, permits a more sophisticated working of the facades, while retaining the symmetry of the tiered church.* [RIGHT]

256. *Bell tower of the Novodevichy Monastery. 1690.* [OPPOSITE]

ance is radically different from that of any other Moscow-baroque church. To begin with, it is constructed entirely of limestone, rusticated on the first level of the four projecting lobes. The plasticity of the curvilinear stone walls, accented by the broad steps leading to each projection, creates a sculpted effect that is reinforced by the carved details and statues that cover the church above the cornice. In the sheer luxuriance of its stonework the church can be compared only to such late Vladimir monuments as Saint Dmitry's and the cathedral at Yurev-Polsky; yet its ambience is largely Western, as is evident from the extensive use of statuary—unprecedented in Russia—and the decidedly unorthodox crown that completes the tower. (It is assumed that a group of Swiss sculptors, working in Moscow at the

257. *Church of the Trinity at Troitskoe-Lykovo. Limestone carving. South facade.* [RIGHT]

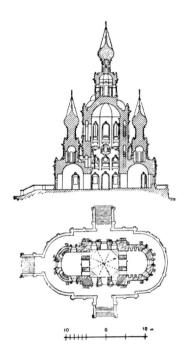

258. *Church of the Trinity at Troitskoe-Lykovo. Plan, section.*

259. *Church of the Trinity at Troitskoe-Lykovo. Crucifix above the iconostasis. The presence of a crucifix—as opposed to an icon of the Crucifixion—is rare in the Russian Orthodox Church, and in this case possibly derives from Polish influence.*

beginning of the eighteenth century, are responsible for the church's interior, which bears a resemblance to the interiors of central-European baroque churches of the late seventeenth century.) Completed in 1704, the church at Dubrovitsy represents at once an extreme variant of Muscovite ornamentalism and the quickening pace of Westernization that would turn Russian architecture from Byzantium to Rome.

Eighteenth Century

In terms of architectural achievement, of the excellence of monuments, the reign of Peter the Great (1694–1725) is far inferior to that of Ivan the Great. But in one important sense the two rulers had a similar impact on the development of Russian architecture: each employed Western architects on a large scale, which resulted in fundamental changes in both the style and the technique of building in Russia. The course of this development in eighteenth-century Russian architecture is confined mostly to the city founded by Peter—Saint Petersburg—and endowed by his successors with a series of monuments equal to the best of contemporary European architecture. But at the beginning of the century, Moscow too searched for new forms, even as it tried to retain the old.

The resulting Muscovite admixture of old and new is highly idiosyncratic, as illustrated by such churches as the Deposition of the Robe (1701), Saint John the Warrior (1709–17; supposed to have been built according to Peter's own sketches, but now attributed to Ivan Zarudny), and the Archangel Gabriel (1710–17; also by Zarudny), popularly known

260. *Church of the Trinity at Troitskoe-Lykovo. Detail, iconostasis (wood carving). Now under restoration.*

261. *Church of the Virgin of the Sign at Dubrovitsy. Near Moscow. 1690–1704.* [LEFT]

262. *Church of Saints Boris and Gleb*
at Zyuzino. Moscow. 1688—1704.

263. *Church of the Intercession of the Virgin at Fili. Moscow. 1690–93.*

as Menshikov's Tower. Commissioned by Peter's associate Alexander Menshikov, the Church of the Archangel Gabriel can be considered the last of the Moscow-baroque tower churches, conforming to the octagon-on-square plan; but its design and the decoration of its facade show the influence of Peter's Western architects, particularly in the use of classical orders and European baroque ornamentation. Much of the church's sculpted-plaster decoration has been attributed to the Italian-

264. *Church of the Virgin of the Sign at Dubrovitsy. Detail.*

265. *Church of the Virgin of the Sign at Perovo. Moscow. 1690–1705.*
[RIGHT]

 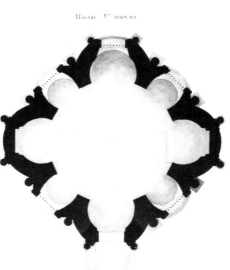

266. *Church of the Virgin of the Sign at Perovo. Section, plan. Shchusev Museum, Moscow.* [LEFT]

267. *Church of the Dormition at Pokrovka. Moscow. 1696–99; the bell tower is a later addition. One of the best examples of the Moscow baroque, the church was razed about 1930. Drawing by Giacomo Quarenghi. Shchusev Museum, Moscow.*

268. *Entrance gate at the Krutitsky Retreat. Moscow. 1693–94. Ceramic work by Osip and Ivan Startsev.*

269. *Church of the Trinity at*
Troitskoe-Lykovo. Moscow.

1698–1703. Architect: Yakov
Bukhvostov (?). North view.

270. *Church of Saint Anne at Uzkoe.*
Moscow. 1698–1704. The Muscovite
church that comes closest to the
cruciform church of the Ukrainian
baroque (see Figure 39). [RIGHT]

271. *Church of the Archangel Gabriel*
('Menshikov Tower'). Moscow.
1701–07. Architect: Ivan Zarudny(?).
Elevation.

Swiss masters who came to Russia with Domenico Trezzini, one of
the most prolific of Peter's architects. The tower's original form resembled Trezzini's tower and spire for the Cathedral of Saints Peter
and Paul, in Saint Petersburg (see chapter five).

Apart from these early Petrine monuments, very little of Moscow's
baroque architecture has survived. Peter, who forbade masonry construction in the city after 1714, concentrated all possible resources on
the building of Saint Petersburg; and even after the lifting of the ban
at the end of Peter's reign, in 1725, construction in the new capital
received priority. In 1730 Empress Anne commissioned the greatest
baroque architect working in Russia, Bartolomeo Rastrelli, to build
two large wooden palaces at her Moscow residence, Annenhof; and

272. *Church of Saint Clement. Moscow. 1762–70(?). Architect: Pietro Antonio Trezzini(?). Thought* *to have been built to a design by Pietro Antonio Trezzini (no relation to Domenico), who worked in Russia* *1726–51. Southwest view, with bell tower completed in 1758.*

during the same period Rastrelli began the reconstruction of a large stone palace within the Kremlin. But none of these structures remains.

There is, however, one architectural oddity in the Moscow area that can be partially attributed to Rastrelli: the Resurrection Cathedral at the New Jerusalem Monastery. Built between 1658 and 1685 at the order of Patriarch Nikon, the main sanctuary consisted of a large rotunda covered with a tent-shaped roof (the patriarch's own edict of 1653 notwithstanding). In 1750 Rastrelli submitted the design for a new wooden roof, to replace the original which had collapsed in 1728; during the following decade its construction was supervised by Karl Blank. Heavily damaged during World War II, the cathedral is now being restored and presents a most unusual sight, with its massive *shatyor*—ringed by three tiers of white-framed baroque windows— and its rococo interior.

273. *Church of the Archangel Gabriel (Menshikov Tower). Moscow. 1701–07. Entrance.* [OPPOSITE]

274. *Church of the Metropolitan Philip. Moscow. 1777–88. Architect: Matvey Kazakov.*

275. *Church of the Metropolitan Philip. Section, plan.*

276. *Church of the Metropolitan Philip. Interior.*

*277. Project for the Great Kremlin
Palace, Moscow River elevation.
1770s. Architect: Vasily Bazhenov.
Shchusev Museum, Moscow.*

Bazhenov in Moscow

The Muscovite flair for the eccentric in architecture received its fullest
expression through the imagination of Vasily Bazhenov (1737–99), a
native genius whose work encompasses the extremes of neoclassicism
and a unique idiom, which might be called 'Moscow gothick.' Discovered by the Muscovite architect Dmitry Ukhtomsky, Bazhenov
pursued his architectural studies at Petersburg's Imperial Academy
of the Arts, and was for three years (1755 to 1758) apprenticed to
Savva Chevakinsky, builder of Petersburg's baroque Cathedral of
Saint Nicholas (1753–62). During the early 1760s Bazhenov lived in
western Europe, where he garnered honors from the academies of Paris,
Rome, Florence, and Bologna—high recognition from the cities that
had given so much to Russian architecture.

Bazhenov's first major projects were commissioned for Petersburg,
but in 1767 he was commanded by Catherine the Great to do no less
than rebuild Moscow's Kremlin in the neoclassical style. The dimensions of his design were staggering—far larger than anything Rastrelli
had conceived: had the design been implemented, the Kremlin would
have been transformed into a system of squares and palaces, with
boulevards radiating into the city. Bazhenov's plans and a wooden
model of the Great Kremlin Palace indicate that the entire Kremlin
frontage along the Moscow River was to be reconstructed as a four-

story palace, with the lower two, service, floors rusticated and the
upper two, intended for the court proper, designed as an enclosed
colonnade of the Ionic order. Other aspects of the plan were similarly
grandiose (the Kremlin cathedrals were to be preserved within this
Ionic and Corinthian ambience), but Catherine changed her mind, and
after preliminary excavations the project was canceled, in 1775. (The
provincial cities were not so fortunate: Vladimir's cathedrals in particular suffered from Catherine's obsession with neoclassical 'rational'
architecture, imposed with little concern for the setting of older
monuments.)

Just as construction at the Kremlin had come to a halt, Catherine
turned Bazhenov's energies to another project, not quite so vast but by
no means modest: a complex of palaces, pavilions, and service buildings
at the recently acquired suburban estate of Tsaritsyno. In this sylvan
setting, marked by ravines and a small river, Catherine chose to dispense
with the neoclassical and commanded Bazhenov to create something
in the pseudo-Gothic style then fashionable in Europe. The results
could hardly have been anticipated, particularly from an architect so
thoroughly at home in the neoclassical idiom; for Bazhenov's creation
is an ingenious reinterpretation of old Muscovite elements with a thin
overlay of the 'gothick.' His materials—red brick and limestone for the
details—are entirely in the tradition of Muscovite architecture of the
sixteenth and seventeenth centuries, as are many of the decorative

278. *Church of Saint John the Warrior.
Moscow. 1709–17. Architect: Ivan
Zarudny (?). Southwest view.*
[ABOVE]

279. *Church of the Deposition of the
Robe. Moscow. 1701.* [OPPOSITE]

280. *Vasily Bazhenov's sketch for the country residence of Catherine the Great at Tsaritsyno. Near Moscow. 1780s. The Opera House and Figured Gate are at the right, the palace is in the center, and various auxiliary buildings (the Cavaliers' House, and so on) are to the left. Shchusev Museum, Moscow.* [ABOVE]

281. *Main bridge, Tsaritsyno. Architect: Vasily Bazhenov.*

motifs. His fancy, however—his genius—combined them in a way that suggests a delightful play of sources but remains, finally, idiosyncratic in the highest sense.

Alas, poor Bazhenov, the most ill-starred of Russia's great architects. Hardly had the walls been completed for most of the structures, after ten years of work, when Catherine again called a halt, commanded that the two palaces (one for her, one for her son Paul) be razed, and entrusted their rebuilding to the talented but less imaginative Matvey Kazakov. Kazakov's palace was in its turn left unfinished in 1793; Catherine had lost interest in the project. Soviet specialists are now attempting the completion of one of the larger buildings, with the aid of Bazhenov's sketches, but one must question the wisdom of their decision. There is, after all, a fine irony in the fact that this ensemble, which included among its pavilions specially designed 'gothick' ruins, should itself have become so grand and picturesque a ruin.

The last important monument in Moscow to be attributed to Ba-

282. *The Figured Gate, Tsaritsyno. Architect: Vasily Bazhenov. The Opera House, with the imperial eagle in limestone, is visible through the gate.*

283. *Main Palace, Tsaritsyno.*
1780s. Architect: Matvey Kazakov.
Kazakov's palace shell rests on the
foundations of Bazhenov's earlier
(and also uncompleted) palace.

zhenov, the Pashkov House (1784–86), marks the return to neoclassicism.[24] The two wings, with Ionic porticoes, are separated from the main structure by rusticated galleries, whose length is half that of the central facade. This distance, and its relation to the height of the wings, creates a perfectly balanced system of proportions, which unites the three elements without causing a sense of clutter. While each of the elements has sufficient space to be appreciated separately, one is always aware of their relation to the whole. Nothing in Petersburg can surpass it, and yet this impeccably detailed neoclassical palace is situated in an entirely different environment, dominated by the sixteenth-century Kremlin walls Bazhenov had intended to rebuild, in the most grandiose of neoclassical schemes.

The juxtaposition—or confrontation—of neoclassicism with Moscow's earlier architectural styles vitiated any attempt to impose the sense of large ensemble that characterizes the planning of Petersburg during the eighteenth and early nineteenth centuries. Yet varieties of neoclassicism flourished in Moscow both before and after the great fire of 1812. Although no other architect equaled Bazhenov's command of the more elaborate classical orders, works by Giacomo Quarenghi and Kazakov (Bazhenov's pupil) exemplify the vitality of the style as developed in Moscow. A survey of Kazakov's buildings demonstrates just how adaptable neoclassicism was to any monumental structure, be it church, hospital, government building, assembly hall, or university.[25]

But neoclassicism in Moscow is essentially the architecture of the palazzo, with—predictably—a Palladian cast. The rotunda, the rusti-

284. *Gate Church of the Tikhvin*
Mother of God, Donskoy Monastery.
Moscow. 1713–14. [OPPOSITE]

285. *Gate to the bakery (Khlebny Dom), Tsaritsyno. Architect: Vasily Bazhenov.*

286. *Pashkov mansion. Moscow. 1784–86. Architect: Vasily Bazhenov(?).*

287. *Yushkov mansion. Moscow.*
1793. Architect: Vasily Bazhenov.

cated ground floor, the austere facade (painted stucco), the portico columns (in white), and an occasional decorative frieze, or panel, compose the basic elements of Moscow's late classicism—less imposing than the Petersburg variant, but attractive in its homey way. The city's mansions in the style resemble country-estate houses, with a spacious court flanked by wings and a garden in back; and despite their masonry appearance, many of them are in fact wooden structures with stucco applied over wattle. Even the grand estate mansions of the Sheremetevs, the Golitsyns, and the Yusupovs at Kuskovo, Ostankino, and Arkhangelskoe maintain a certain domesticity when compared with the imperial palaces in and around Saint Petersburg. The style of the former was invariably neoclassical, with the firm sense of order and proportion that characterizes the best of Moscow's late-eighteenth-century monuments—and, incidentally, illustrates the virtuosity of the owners' serf architects, who played a major role in the construction of these palaces.[26]

During the rebuilding of the city after the Napoleonic occupation, neoclassicism continued to dominate in the works of transplanted foreigners such as the French Osip Bove and the Italian Domenico Gilardi, and of Gilardi's Russian pupil Afanasy Grigorev (born a serf).[27]

By the 1840s, however, the classical style had begun to wane, in Moscow as well as in Petersburg. As an architectural expression of the ideal of nobility—and of the nobility—that had emerged in the reign of Catherine the Great and reached its culmination under Alexander I, neoclassicism in its various phases had given rise to a remarkably coherent manner of building, whose scale and articulation conveyed dignity without pomposity. But with the advent of economic and social pressures linked with Russia's belated acceptance of the Industrial Revolution, neoclassicism proved incapable of further adaptation, at least in any creative sense. Moreover, the classical notions of harmony and reason based on universal principles (so obviously imported from western Europe) were found uncongenial to attempts, particularly pronounced in Moscow, to discover or formulate a Russian national

288. *Church of the Kazan Mother of God at Kolomenskoe. Moscow. 1649–53.* [OPPOSITE]

289. *Palace at Ostankino. Moscow. 1792–98. Architects: Francesco Camporesi, Giacomo Quarenghi, and Pavel Argunov.*

290. *Durasov mansion at Lyublino. Moscow. 1801. Architect: Ivan Yegotov(?). Four wings, connected by an Ionic colonnade, radiate from a round central hall.*

291. Stroganov mansion at Bratsevo. Moscow. End of the eighteenth century. Architect: Andrey Voronikhin. A simple, noble exercise in classicism designed for Alexander Stroganov by his former serf, Voronikhin.

292. Old Merchants' Yard (Gostinny Dvor). Moscow. 1790–1805. Architects: Giacomo Quarenghi and Matvey Kazakov.

identity. As a Muscovite architectural critic, A. V. Ikonnikov, has put it, 'The stern proportions of classicism were alien to the tastes of the Russian merchant.'[28]

Moscow Revival

With the decline of neoclassicism and its ideal of universal architectural principles dominated by the order system, Moscow rapidly succumbed to the fashion of eclecticism, a variety of styles based on a historicist conception of architecture. No one style was considered

293. *Moscow University. Designed by Matvey Kazakov (1782–93), the university was rebuilt after the Moscow fire of 1812 by Domenico Gilardi (1817–19).*

preeminent; each age in the history of architecture was worthy of emulation—Egyptian, Byzantine, Gothic, Moorish, early Renaissance. The reasons for this proliferation of styles were as varied as the styles themselves: history interpreted by Romanticism as a series of stages defining the essence of a nation made for a fascination with bygone eras, and a rising interest in the description and analysis (however imprecise) of architectural monuments of the past provided models that could be applied in contemporary architecture. To be sure, Moscow in the eighteenth century had produced examples of the Gothic and Moorish revivals, yet the predominance then of the baroque and the neoclassical was not seriously challenged.

By the 1840s, any style seemed acceptable, and students at Moscow's Court Architectural School were encouraged to experiment with a variety of periods. Some designs of the mid- and late nineteenth century attempted stylistic unity by adopting one particular historical period, while more eclectic structures borrowed freely from various periods. In either case it would be excessively generous—indeed, erroneous—to call such exercises even a pale reflection of the styles

294. *Ruins of a mansion, Petrovskoe
Alabino. Near Moscow. 1775–85.
Architect: Matvey Kazakov(?).*

they attempted to interpret. And whatever the claims of the proponents of neo-Renaissance and neo-Gothic architecture, the main purpose of eclecticism in Moscow (and Petersburg and Kiev) was to decorate facades of large buildings erected for speculative or commercial reasons, with little attention to ensemble or environment.

A comprehensive analysis of the styles employed in eclecticism (or historicism, as it is sometimes called) more properly belongs in a study of Russian architecture that focuses on 1830 to 1890. It should nevertheless be stated that within this movement the Moscow Revival is of particular interest for its attempt to apply the highly ornate decorative devices of seventeenth-century Muscovite architecture to modern structures: government buildings, shopping galleries, urban mansions, and churches As noted above, the concern with the pre-Petrine past was part of a general cultural pattern in Russia during the mid-nineteenth century, and this national reawakening (descending from European Romanticism) led to impressive developments in literature, music, and intellectual history. But in architecture, the espousal of an *echt* Russian style in a rapidly changing social environment produced only a shallow synthesis. In churches some attempt was made to reproduce the structure as well as the decorative elements of seventeenth-century Muscovite architecture, but in most cases Moscow Revival consisted merely of facades, in brick and stone or plaster, heavily decorated with what were assumed to be seventeenth-century motifs—motifs whose origins were themselves quite eclectic. Two of the most prominent proponents of this revival were Ivan Ropet (Petrov) and Viktor Gartman, whose drawings inspired Mussorgsky's *Pictures at an Exhibition*.

295. *Krushchev mansion. Moscow. 1814. Architect: Afanasy Grigorev. Side facade, incorporating part of an eighteenth-century mansion that stood here before the 1812 fire. Stuccoed wood, on a stone foundation.*

296. *House on Little Molchanovka Street. Moscow. Circa 1820. As this photograph demonstrates, many of Moscow's nineteenth-century mansions, with their classical orders and rusticated facades, are simply large log houses with an overlay of wattle and stucco. The sign proclaims that the poet Mikhail Lermontov lived here between 1830 and 1832.*

297. *Lopukhin mansion. Moscow. 1817–22. Architect: Afanasy Grigorev. Stuccoed wood, on a stone foundation.* [LEFT]

298. *Zaikonospassky Trading Rows. Moscow. 1890s. Architect: M. T. Preobrazhensky.*

299. *Polytechnical Museum. Moscow. 1875–1907. Architects: Ippolit Moninghetti and Nikolay Shokhin.*

By the 1890s, the disjunction between a building's structural system and its facade had reached its height in such designs as Red Square's Upper Trading Rows (1889–94; now known as the Moscow State Department Store, or GUM). Built by Alexander Pomerantsev on the site of a neoclassical commercial arcade (Quarenghi's, rebuilt by Bove after 1812), the new Trading Rows were designed on the principles of Milan's Galleria, with shops opening on to a covered gallery, and they utilized advanced techniques in structural-steel and reinforced-concrete construction. Yet the Moscow Revival clichés that cover the building's facade could easily have been replaced by the clichés of any other style popular at the time. (In fairness to Pomerantsev, it must be noted that the ambience created by the Kremlin and Saint Basil's determined the use of Moscow Revival decoration.)

Muscovite eclecticism has its defenders, and in areas of the city that have remained largely untouched, such retrospective structures have acquired whatever virtues nostalgia and the sociology of taste can bestow. In comparison with earlier monuments, however, the results are insipid. Only a genius such as Bazhenov, with apparently unlimited resources at Tsaritsyno, could succeed in reviving the spirit of medieval Moscow (while calling it Gothic)—and even he ultimately failed, by reason of his empress's caprice. The significant developments in architecture of the late nineteenth century center on new building technologies and materials, not on the attempt to reproduce the texture of a style that had reached its culmination during the reign of Alexey Mikhailovich (father of Peter the Great).

In a chaotic and rapidly expanding Moscow, new solutions were called for, and revolutionary idealism—as short-lived in architecture

300. Upper Trading Rows (GUM).
Red Square, Moscow. 1889–94.
Architect: Alexander Pomerantsev.

as in politics—provided them in its radical proposals for the city's reconstruction and in its support of a new technological functionalism (see chapter six). Yet the transformation of Moscow in the twentieth century was not Russia's first experiment in comprehensive planning and sweeping architectural innovation: for this we must return to a period two centuries earlier, to the city founded by Peter the Great.

5. SAINT PETERSBURG:
The Imperial Design

An aerial ship and touch-me-not mast,
serving as a straightedge for the successors of Peter,
its lesson is that beauty is no demigod's caprice:
it is the simple carpenter's ferocious rule-of-eye.
  —OSIP MANDELSTAM, 'The Admiralty'

If we consider the matter thoroughly, then, in justice,
we must be called not Russians, *but* Petrovians.
  —YEGOR KANKRIN, Minister of Finance, 1823–1844

Historians have long debated the significance of Peter I's accomplishments. Although certain of his projects and reforms were ephemeral, it is beyond question that Peter the Great oversaw the transformation of the Muscovite state into a major European power. This transformation, occurring in the face of considerable opposition from many levels of society, was realized through massive forced-labor enterprises, as well as a series of wars demanding as much as ninety percent of the state budget and occupying twenty-eight of the thirty-one years of Peter's effective reign (from 1694, following his mother's regency, to his death, in 1725). From this sacrifice exacted from an unwilling populace Peter established an empire with acquisitions ranging from the Baltic to the Caspian seas; he introduced fundamental social, economic, religious, administrative, and educational reforms; he created a modern army and navy, which roundly defeated Sweden, one of Russia's oldest and most troublesome enemies; and he laid the foundations of a great city.

Peter was not, however, present at the founding of Saint Petersburg (May 16, O.S., 1703), nor did he at first intend to 'hack a window through to Europe.' His concerns at this time were intensely practical: simply to construct a fortified point as soon as possible, for he was in the third year of a conflict with Sweden that would last until 1721 and finally establish Russia's power in northern Europe. The Great Northern War had begun inauspiciously for Peter, but the eighteen-year-old Swedish king, Charles XII, lulled by his early success over the Russians, turned his attention to Peter's ally, Augustus II of Poland. During this respite Peter rebuilt the Russian army and went on to supervise its methodical conquest of Swedish garrisons along the northeastern Baltic.

Peter was particularly interested in the area around Lake Ladoga and the Neva River—a sparsely inhabited strategic territory disputed by the Swedes and Russians since the thirteenth century. By May 1703

301. *The Great Palace and Samson Fountain, Peterhof. 1714–52. Palace completed by Bartolomeo Rastrelli. Near Leningrad.*

Russian forces could sail unhindered from Ladoga down the Neva to the Gulf of Finland, but Peter now needed a fortress at the mouth of the Neva to control access to his newly won and still quite precarious position. In a reconnaissance of the estuary he chose a small, well-protected island (Hare's Island, as it was called by the local Finns) as the site of his fortification. On this marsh the imperial design began.[1]

Some twenty thousand men were conscripted to surround the island with earthen walls and bastions. Conditions were brutal: the workers dug with sticks, carried dirt in the tails of their long shirts or coats, lived with little or no shelter, drank contaminated water, and ate meager rations. The number of fatalities mounted rapidly, yet work proceeded at a brisk pace, and by November the fortress of Sankt Piter Burkh—'Saint Peter's Burg'—was essentially completed. The name was derived from the Russian Orthodox Festival of Saints Peter and Paul (June 29) but rendered in Dutch, the language of a culture much admired by Peter I.

After the completion of the fortress, the city's first structures were placed haphazardly on the islands surrounding Hare's Island, but as early as 1704 Peter intended to design the new settlement as a shipbuilding and commercial center—and, eventually, as a new capital. (He calls it that in a letter of September 1704 to his supporter Prince Alexander Menshikov.) That year the government instituted an annual conscription of 40,000 peasants for the construction of the city in shifts of two or three months (from April to October); and although only 30,000 to 34,000 peasants were actually summoned, and far fewer appeared (owing to administrative snarls), significant progress was made in draining marshes, driving piles, and building such basic institutions as the Admiralty and its shipyards. In addition to peasant conscripts, criminals, and prisoners of war employed in heavy construction, Peter brought in craftsmen, tradesmen, and members of the nobility to populate his new city. The lower classes settled in neighborhoods according to their crafts or trade, while the noblemen were expected to build houses of a certain type and size, determined by their wealth (as measured by the number of serfs they possessed).

Working conditions remained abysmal, even by Russian standards. Foreign visitors spoke of hundreds of thousands of deaths, and although such figures are undoubtedly inflated, historians have concluded that disease, overwork, and exposure killed thousands during the first two decades of the city's construction. The peasants, who quite rightly viewed work in Petersburg as little better than hard labor in Siberia, frequently deserted their convoys in large numbers; for not only were they being subjected to the rigors of building a city on a swamp, they were also being driven from their land at the height of the planting and harvesting seasons, to be sent—in some cases hundreds of miles—to an incomprehensible undertaking. Government measures for dealing with evasion or flight were predictably harsh. Workers were often marched to Petersburg in chains, families of escapees were liable to imprisonment, and many of those captured in flight were knouted or executed.

Gradually, however, some pragmatism was introduced into these

302. The Bronze Horseman: *'Petro primo Catherina secunda* MDCCLXXXII.' *Senate Square, Leningrad. Sculptor: Étienne Falconet.*

303. *The Neva estuary. Engraving by Grimel, 1737. The confluence of the Neva River and the Gulf of Finland provided Peter the Great with a strategic outlet to the Baltic Sea, a setting for future commercial and naval operations. The fortress island of Kronstadt (left) protected access to the new city of Saint Petersburg. On the southern shore of the Gulf of Finland, Peter and his most able assistant, Alexander Menshikov, built their country palaces—at Strelna (E), Peterhof (D), and Oranienbaum (C). By permission of the Houghton Library, Harvard University.*

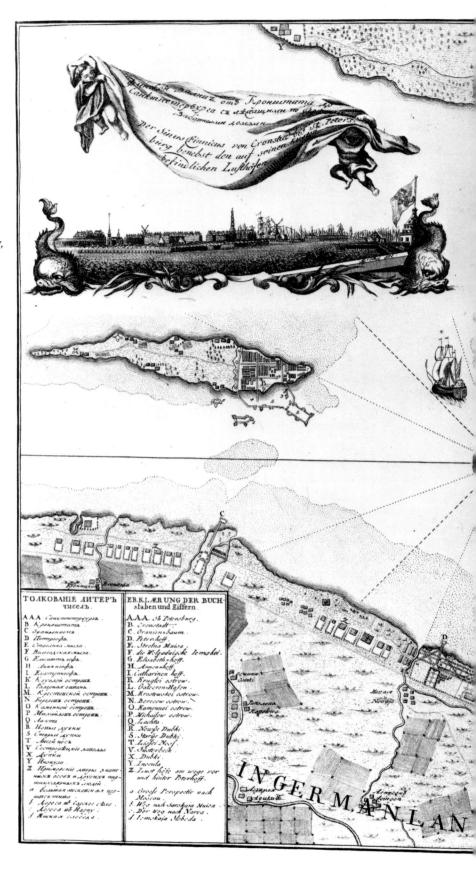

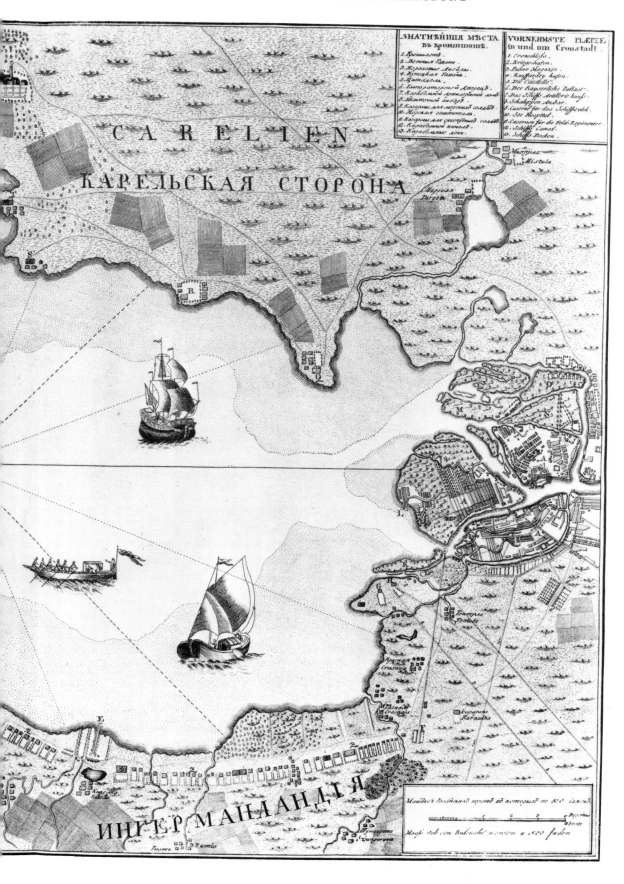

ЗНАТНѢЙШІЯ МѢСТА ВЪ КРОНШТАДѢ.

1. Кронштотъ.
2. Военная Гавань.
3. Пороховые Анбары.
4. Купецкая Гавань.
5. Цитаделла.
6. Императорской Дворецъ.
7. Карабельной Артиллерской домъ.
8. Шлюпочной анбаръ.
9. Казармы для морскихъ солдатъ.
10. Морской госпиталь.
11. Казармы для сухопутной солдатъ.
12. Карабельный каналъ.
13. Карабельные доки.

VORNEHMSTE PLÆTZE in und um Cronstadt.

1. Cronschloss.
2. Kriegeshafen.
3. Pulver Magazin.
4. Kauffardey hafen.
5. Die Citadelle.
6. Der Kayserliche Pallast.
7. Das Schiffs Artillerie hauß.
8. Schaluppen Anbar.
9. Casern für das Schiffsvolck.
10. See Hospital.
11. Casernen für die Feld-Regimenter.
12. Schiffs Canal.
13. Schiffs Docken.

C A R E L I E N

КАРЕЛЬСКАЯ СТОРОНА

ИНГЕРМАНЛАНДІЯ

304. *The Fortress of Sankt Piter Burkh.*
1703. An engraving from the first
history of the architecture of Saint
Petersburg, written by Andrey Bog-
danov in 1750. Bogdanov describes
this earliest version of the fortress
cathedral of Saints Peter and Paul as
'wooden, in the shape of a cross, with
three spires from which pennants
were flown on Sundays and holidays.'
As was frequently the case in Peters-
burg's first years, the facade was
painted to resemble masonry.
Widener Library, Harvard University.

draconian recruitment policies. By 1712 no more conscripts were brought in from distant Siberia, and by the end of the decade hired labor had largely replaced the conscription system, which was not only wasteful of manpower, but also inefficient. As the settlement acquired rudimentary services, peasants started to volunteer for work in large numbers—particularly during famine years.

Peter's Imperial Capital: The Pursuit of Order

In the first ten years of its existence, there was little to distinguish Saint Petersburg from a frontier outpost. Although its Department of Construction had been established in 1706, the town's buildings, almost entirely wooden or clay-walled, were distributed with little thought of a general plan. Peter was still preoccupied with his desperate struggle with Sweden, and even though the final assault on Petersburg was repulsed in 1708, the city was not secure until the decisive Russian victory over Charles at Poltava, in 1709. The capture of Vyborg in 1710 provided additional insurance, and in the same year the tsar—now 'Imperator'—commanded that a monastery be founded in honor of Saint Alexander Nevsky, who had been victorious over the Swedes in this area almost five centuries earlier. With the transfer of the saint's relics from Vladimir and the designation of the monastery as a *lavra* (the highest rank of monastery), Petersburg had acquired the trappings of a major religious center, however secular Peter's intentions.

In 1712 the imperial court was moved from Moscow to Saint Petersburg. Even though many important administrative departments continued to function in Moscow, there could now be little doubt as to Peter's commitment to the new capital, symbol of the transformation of the Muscovite state into the Russian Empire.

Construction of the city at this point began in earnest, under the supervision of Peter, or of his delegate Alexander Menshikov. No detail was too small for the ruler's attention, from the design of model houses to the decree ordering citizens to boil the moss used in insulating wooden structures (supposed to prevent cockroach infestation). Peter knew what he wanted: a well-ordered, solidly built city of the sort he had seen in Holland during his tour of Europe (1697–99), a city with Western spires (instead of the onion domes of Moscow) and a rationally planned network of streets (in contrast to Moscow's chaotic pattern)— a city, finally, of stone, with imposing secular monuments that would reflect the glory of an empire.

So eager was Peter to achieve monumentality that he ordered the wooden buildings painted to resemble stone and brick, and in 1714 he forbade masonry construction throughout the rest of his empire, in order to insure a supply of qualified workers and materials for Petersburg. Stone for foundations and streets was obtained by a 'stone duty,' levied from 1714 to 1776: three stones of not less than five pounds each were exacted from wagons entering the city, and ten to thirty stones were paid by ships entering the port. In fact, every form of building material—glass, lead, construction stone, bricks, roofing tile, cement, lumber (everything but dirt)—had to be imported, or else produced by workshops and mills hastily erected on site.

Despite this effort, spurred by a series of ukases from Peter and his assistant Menshikov, resources proved inadequate to the grand design, and Peter, a pragmatist when necessary, modified certain of his more ambitious plans. After 1714 large areas of the city were reserved for masonry construction only, but for lack of materials the decree was honored in the breach, and by 1723 masonry construction was actually forbidden throughout most of the city: in all of Russia, in fact, the construction of brick and stone houses was permitted only along the Neva embankments and a few streets on Vasilevsky Island, the city's putative center and site of yet another of Peter's grand schemes. The island—virtually inaccessible from the mainland for long periods during the formation and melting of river ice in the fall and spring—was to become a new Amsterdam, intersected with a network of canals and boulevards and embellished with the grandest buildings in the city. Peter's wealthy subjects were ordered to build houses on this island, but the location proved so impractical that many left their houses unfinished and continued to live on the left (mainland) bank of the Neva, in defiance of decrees between 1719 and 1725 threatening the recalcitrant with severe punishment. Contemporary accounts of Vasilevsky Island convey the impression of an abandoned project, imposing from a distance but on close inspection rotting and uninhabited.[2]

A City Plan

Peter the Great's rage for order, regardless of cost or suitability, was carried to its full, irrational extreme in the early plans for Saint Petersburg's development. The first coherent city plan, designed by the Italian-Swiss architect Domenico Trezzini and approved by the emperor in 1716, maintained contact with topographical and social reality

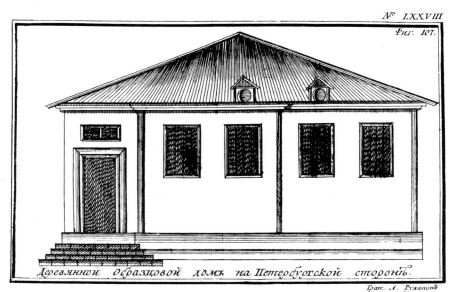

305. Although the Russian caption states 'wooden model home,' the structure is probably the mazanka, or clay, type. Peter enthusiastically designed such houses for his subjects and issued decrees concerning the most minute details, from siting and construction to the boiling of moss—used as insulation—to prevent cockroach infestation. Engraving from Andrey Bogdanov's history, 1750. Widener Library, Harvard University.

306. *Plan of Saint Petersburg, circa 1720, by Jean Covens. The jumble of buildings on the Admiralty and Petersburg sides of the Neva (south and north, respectively) stands in sharp contrast to the well-ordered grid of streets and canals designed (1715–16) by Domenico Trezzini for Vasilevsky Island. Peter's dream of a re-created Amsterdam never materialized, although Trezzini's grid was retained as the pattern for the island's streets. Widener Library, Harvard University.*

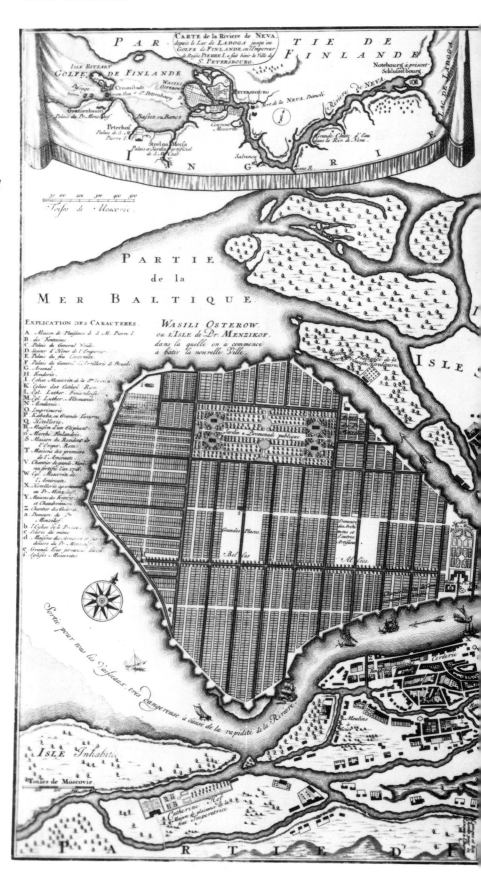

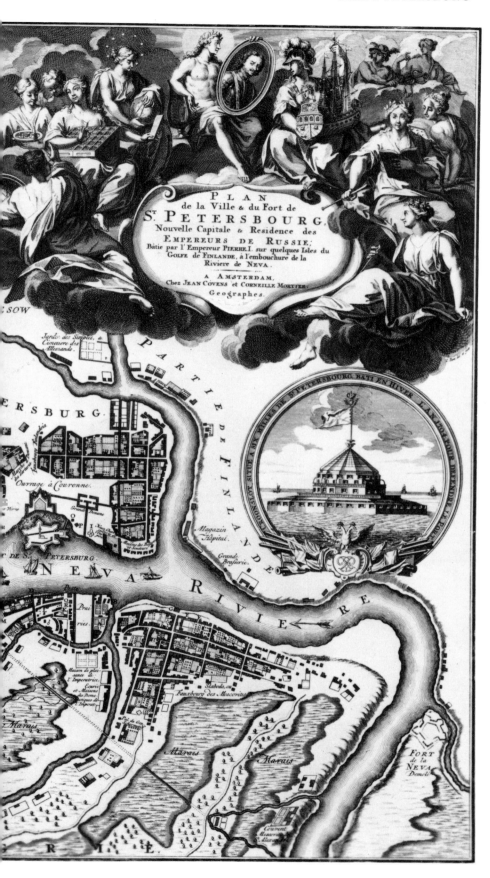

PLAN
de la Ville & du Fort de
St. PETERSBOURG,
Nouvelle Capitale & Residence des
EMPEREURS DE RUSSIE;
Bâtie par l'Empereur PIERRE I. sur quelques Isles du
GOLFE de FINLANDE, à l'embouchure de la
Riviere de NEVA.
A AMSTERDAM.
Chez JEAN COVENS et CORNEILLE MORTIER
Geographes.

307. *Project for Saint Petersburg. 1717.
Jean-Baptiste Alexandre Le Blond.
Order ignores topography in this ver-
sion of the imperial design. Le Blond's
fortified ellipse—one of the most im-
probable fantasies in the history of
city planning—centers on Vasilevsky
Island, with its network of parks and
intersecting boulevards. From I. N.
Bozheryanov,* Nevsky Prospekt, *Saint
Petersburg, 1908. Widener Library,
Harvard University.*

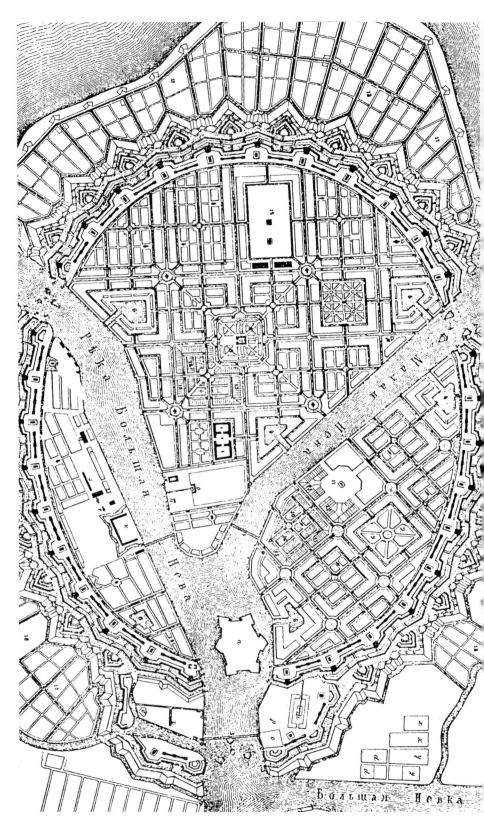

even as it incorporated Peter's intention to re-create Amsterdam on Vasilevsky Island. The following year, however, it seems that Trezzini's plan was supplanted by a wildly impracticable scheme submitted by the French Jean-Baptiste Alexandre Le Blond, a student of the great landscape architect André LeNôtre and, as of 1716, Peter's chief architect. Le Blond proposed a massive fortified wall in the shape of an ellipse, encompassing four islands (including Vasilevsky) in the Neva delta and containing a system of parks and squares arranged in various rectangular and diagonal configurations. No serious attempt was made to implement the plan, which is of interest only as an indication of the irrational extent to which architects were prepared to go in their pursuit of a 'rational' design.

Despite the absurdity of such projects, much of contemporary Leningrad owes its design to the Petrine era. Although Peter's hopes for a thriving city on Vasilevsky Island were not realized until decades after his death, the island's streets—or 'lines,' laid out with a straightedge, creating vistas—conform to the pattern first conceived in Trezzini's plan of 1716. And on the left bank of the Neva the magnificent arrangement of three major 'prospects' radiating from the Admiralty also originated with Peter's concept of a grand avenue leading into the city. But apart from these specific elements, reaffirmed with the adoption of a master plan in the late 1730s, Peter's greatest legacy to the form of his city consisted in the very notion of a comprehensive urban design, within which Petersburg's architects created the palaces, churches, parks, and squares that compose perhaps the most remarkable eighteenth-century ensemble in Europe.

308. *Peter's Summer Palace. The Summer Garden, Leningrad. 1711–14. Designed by Domenico Trezzini and Andreas Schlüter, this palace displays the modest Dutch style Peter found so attractive. The building was largely forgotten by his successors and is therefore preserved in its original form, on the banks of the Neva River and the Fontanka Canal.*

309. *The Menshikov Palace. Vasilevsky Island, Leningrad. 1711–16. Architects: Giovanni Mario Fontana and Gottfried Schädel. At the time of its construction, the palace of Peter's statesman Alexander* Menshikov *was the grandest structure in Saint Petersburg, overshadowing the tsar's own palaces. In 1732 the residence was transformed into a military institute, and its steeply pitched roof with flanking towers* was removed, *as were allegorical statues over the entrance. A current reconstruction attempts to regain what is assumed to have been its original appearance.*

310. The Great Palace at Oranien-baum. 1711–25. Architects: Giovanni Mario Fontana and Gottfried Schädel. Situated on the Gulf of Finland, Alexander Menshikov's 'pleasure palace' typifies the simple style of the Petrine baroque. Engraving by F. Vnukov and N. Chelnakov from a drawing by Mikhail Makhaev, 1761. Shchusev Museum, Moscow.

311. The Cathedral of Saints Peter and Paul (left). Peter-Paul Fortress, Leningrad. 1712–32. Architect: Domenico Trezzini. On the right is Bartolomeo Rastrelli's Third Winter Palace, begun in 1732. Designed to replace the earlier wooden church, Trezzini's cathedral is the first important example in Saint Petersburg of the elongated Latin-cross plan. Peter ordered that the bell tower be completed as quickly as possible so that he might have a vantage point for viewing his new city. Engraving by E. Vinogradov from a drawing by Mikhail Makhaev, 1753. Shchusev Museum, Moscow.

The Early Baroque: Trezzini et al.

Very little remains from the first decade of construction in Saint Petersburg, but surviving sketches and plans provide a sense of the early architectural forms, shaped by a variety of European styles. Fascinated by details, Peter had a propensity for changing his mind about the proposed appearance of a building as soon as its foundation was laid. 'Quite often one architect would begin a certain building, another would continue it, a third finish it, and at the very end a fourth would again redo it.'[3] The result was a hybrid different from anything Russia had seen, but not easily attributed to any particular European school. The city's first architects were themselves of widely differing origins—Italian, Dutch, German, French—whose talents, real or

imagined, had come to the attention of Peter's recruiting network.
However favorable the terms of their contracts, the primitive conditions
under which they worked strained their endurance to the limit, and
the rate of attrition from death or early departure was extremely high.
Nevertheless, these architects created a coherent baroque style, which
characterizes the Petrine monuments of Saint Petersburg.[4]

Domenico Trezzini, one of the most gifted, influential, and long-
lived of these architects, was present at the earliest stages of the
city's construction. Born in about 1670 near Lugano (the region that
had produced Carlo Maderna and Francesco Borromini), Trezzini received his education locally, and by 1699 was employed in Denmark
as a fortification engineer. In this capacity he arrived in Petersburg
with a group of craftsmen in 1703 (with the understanding that he

312. *Cathedral of Saints Peter and Paul. Leningrad. 1712–32. Architect: Domenico Trezzini.* [OPPOSITE]

313. *The Cathedral of Saints Peter and Paul. The cathedral tower and spire dominate the body of the building and to this day form Leningrad's tallest structure (almost 400 feet). Destroyed by lightning in 1756, the spire was reconstructed in something like its original shape by Giuseppe Trezzini, son of the building's architect. Although little of Domenico Trezzini's decoration has been preserved, the large volutes are characteristic of the city's early-baroque style.* [LEFT]

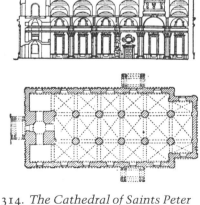

314. *The Cathedral of Saints Peter and Paul. Plan, elevation.*

might leave should the air prove 'very harsh and injurious to his health'), and remained there until his death, in 1734.[5]

The first years of Trezzini's service were occupied primarily with work on the city's wooden fortresses, which were being rebuilt in brick and stone, but he rapidly assumed the duties of a general architect, designing churches, palaces, and the boxlike model houses whose standardized form reflected Peter's desire for uniformity in his ordered, 'European' city.

Trezzini's first major architectural project—the reconstruction of the cathedral within the Peter-Paul Fortress—represented a radical

315. Alexander Nevsky Monastery. Leningrad. 1715. Plan according to Domenico Trezzini's design, with Ivan Starov's Trinity Cathedral (1776–90).

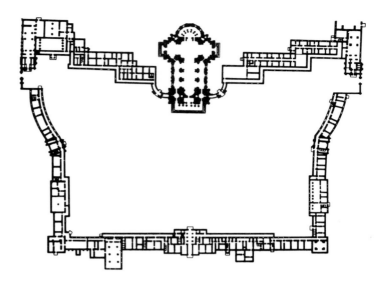

316. Cathedral of Saints Peter and Paul. Iconostasis by Ivan Zarudny. 1722–26. [OPPOSITE]

departure from traditional Russian church architecture, based on the cross-domed plan. Trezzini created instead a greatly elongated rectangular structure, whose modest baroque dome, on the eastern end, is clearly subordinate to the tower and spire placed over the west entrance. The austere appearance of the cathedral (modified by Bartolomeo Rastrelli and Savva Chevakinsky after a lightning strike and fire in 1756) reflects the influence of the northern-European baroque; but the spire's height—almost four hundred feet from the ground to cross— and its sheathing of gold leaf make the church one of the city's most dramatic landmarks.

Concurrently with the reconstruction of the Peter-Paul Cathedral, Trezzini was commissioned to design another of the city's religious monuments, the Alexander Nevsky Monastery. Although the monastery's construction continued until the end of the eighteenth century—with substantial modifications in the architect's conception— Trezzini's plan of 1715 established fundamental principles that would characterize much of Petersburg's religious architecture during a period of reaction against the traditional Russian forms. In contrast to Russia's earlier monasteries, with their seemingly haphazard distribution of structures accrued over a long period of time, Trezzini envisioned a highly organized, symmetrical complex, whose schools, chapels, and administrative buildings were joined in a single structure, dominated by the monastery cathedral. The plan exemplifies Peter's notion of a comprehensive architectural design, and, appropriately enough (if not ironically), its appearance is for the most part resolutely secular: the stuccoed walls, brightly painted in red and white and decorated with pilasters and panels, resemble nothing so much as Petersburg's early palaces and administrative buildings.

The last of Trezzini's major projects extant in Leningrad, the Building of the Twelve Colleges, contained the offices of the ten state ministries ('colleges'), as well as the Senate (the highest judicial body) and the Holy Synod, all administrative units devised by Peter (with the advice

317. *The Building of the Twelve
Colleges. Vasilevsky Island, Leningrad. 1722–41. Architects: Domenico
Trezzini, Theodor Schwertfeger, Giuseppe Trezzini. The center of Peter the
Great's bureaucracy, the Twelve Colleges was begun by Trezzini and
Schwertfeger and completed by Trezzini's son, Giuseppe, who added a
gallery connecting all twelve segments. Few buildings better illustrate
the horizontal principle so prevalent
in Saint Petersburg's architecture:
rows of windows, separated by pilasters, appear to converge at some
indefinably distant point. Engraving
by Ekim Vnukov, from a drawing by
Mikhail Makhaev, 1753. Library of
Congress.* [ABOVE]

of Leibnitz) in an attempt to organize the Russian bureaucracy on
Western principles. Emblematic of Peter's reforms, the building also
provides an example of the era's experimentation with construction
methods—organized in this instance to the point of chaos. According
to Peter's instructions of 1723, the various departments were to be
joined in a single row (more than four hundred yards long), but each
kollegiya was to have its own roof and was to be responsible for the
construction of its own unit. The aim of this peculiar system was to
accelerate what Peter considered intolerably slow work. But his pro-
cedure only compounded the confusion, particularly in the delivery of
building materials, and on Trezzini's advice he modified the order.
Although little more than the foundation was completed by the time
of the emperor's death, in 1725, the structure epitomizes Peter's concept of architectural and administrative order.

Trezzini's work, and that of the architects who collaborated with
him during the reign of Peter (Le Blond, Gottfried Schädel, Georg Johann Mattarnovy, Mikhail Zemtsov), established an architectural style
that represented a desire to create and impose a modern, Western form
on the native institutions of church and state. In this respect the
Alexander Nevsky Monastery and the Building of the Twelve Colleges
are complemented by a third major structure from the Petrine era,
built to house Petersburg's first academic institution: the Chamber of
Curiosities, or, as it was called in German, the Kunstkammer. (Peter

318. *The Twelve Colleges. Plan.*

319. *The Twelve Colleges. The faces of each segment display the usual devices of the Trezzini style: white pilasters on a red stucco facade, a rusticated ground floor, white trim, and simply articulated windows. In 1835 the building was converted to house the Imperial (now Leningrad) University.*

often adopted German as well as Dutch terms. Russians also call it the Kunstkamera.)

Peter was well aware of the role of modern scientific thought in the development of a secular state, and in February 1718 he issued a decree concerning the collection of various 'rarities' and 'monsters' to be displayed in the Kunstkammer for the edification of the populace and the promotion of what he considered scientific research. He was willing to pay well for these 'curiosities'—live and dead human freaks and deformed animals—and the results of his search were all that he might have wished.

The rapidly expanding collection outgrew its quarters, and in 1718 it was transferred from the modest Petersburg Summer Palace to the palace

321. *The Academy of Sciences (left).*
1783–89. Architect: Giacomo
Quarenghi. The Kunstkammer (right).
1718–34. Architect: Georg Johann
Mattarnovy. Vasilevsky Island.
Leningrad.

320. *Church of the Annunciation,*
Alexander Nevsky Monastery.
Leningrad. 1717–22. Architects:
Domenico Trezzini and Theodor
Schwertfeger. [OPPOSITE]

322. *Plan of Saint Petersburg, 1737.*
Engraving by G. I. Unvertzagt. By the
middle of Anne's reign, which was
from 1730 to 1740, building in Peters-
burg had shifted to the south, the
mainland side of the city. Rastrelli's
Third Winter Palace is just to the
right of the Admiralty, and the tree-
lined Nevsky Prospekt has begun to
acquire the look of a boulevard.
Trezzini's general plan for Vasilevsky
Island has been preserved in the form
of a street grid, but the actual devel-
opment is decidedly more modest
than that intended by Peter. (See
Trezzini's plan, Figure 306). By per-
mission of the Houghton Library,
Harvard University.

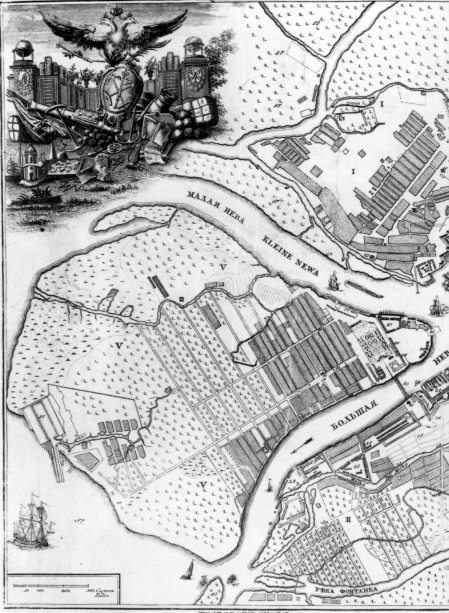

Tab. I

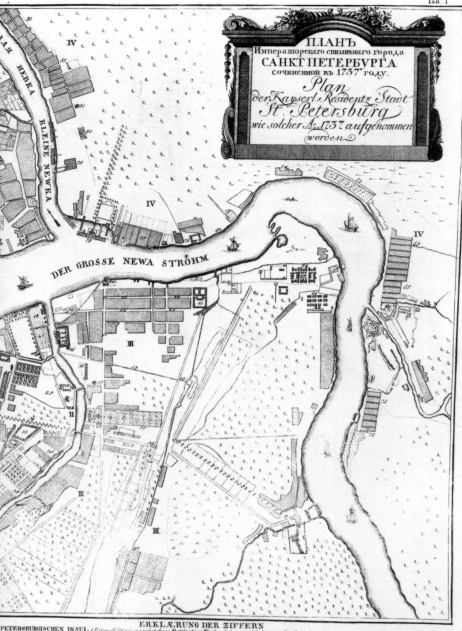

ПЛАНЪ
Императорскаго столичнаго города
САНКТ ПЕТЕРБУРГА
сочиненной въ 1737 году.
Plan
der Kayserl. Residentz Stadt
St. Petersburg
wie solcher A: 1737 aufgenommen
worden

ERKLÆRUNG DER ZIFFERN

323. *The Kikin Palace. Leningrad.*
1714. Architect unknown. One of
several residences built by Admiral
Alexander Kikin, the Palace was
briefly used to house the Kunst-
kammer Collection after Kikin's
execution for treason, in 1718. Its
plan corresponds in miniature to that
of Le Blond's Great Palace at Peterhof
(also begun in 1714).

formerly belonging to Admiral Alexander Kikin. In 1718 Kikin was condemned to death for his implicit participation in the abortive flight from Petersburg of Peter's son Alexey. This disturbed and malleable youth was looked on by opponents of Westernization as their one hope for returning to an earlier epoch; but Peter's capture, torture, and execution of the tsarevich, along with those associated with him, destroyed whatever feeble conspiracy might have existed. Whether or not Peter specifically chose to place his collection in the home of one who had wished for the destruction of the tsar and his innovations, the symbolism of this move could not have escaped notice.

The Kikin Palace, a whimsical example of the early baroque in Petersburg, soon proved inadequate to contain the collection, and in 1718 the German architect Georg Johann Mattarnovy submitted plans for a new Kunstkammer and library, to be built as part of the cultural center Peter intended for Vasilevsky Island. After Mattarnovy's premature death in 1719, construction was carried forward by a series of

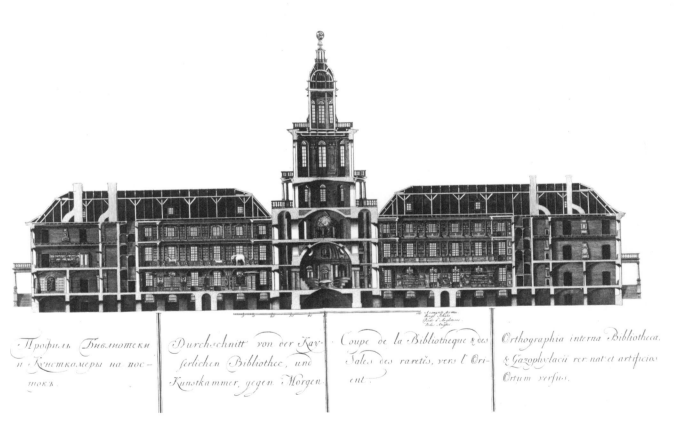

324. *The Kunstkammer (interior).*
Vasilevsky Island, Leningrad.
1718–34. Architect: Georg Johann
Mattarnovy. The Academy of Sciences
library (right) and the Kunstkammer
Collection (left) flank the central
tower, *which houses an anatomy*
theater and an observatory—the first
in Russia. The collection, with its
stuffed animals, skeletons, preserved
fetuses, and artifacts, served as a
museum of both anthropology and
natural history; its purpose as en-
visioned by Peter was to spread
scientific enlightenment in Russia.
Engraving by Grigory Kachalov,
1741. By permission of the Houghton
Library, Harvard University.

architects who introduced modifications and simplifications of the original plan; but despite these changes, the building—not completed until 1734—displays the features of the Petrine baroque in both form and detail. Its painted-stucco facade, in light blue marked with white trim for the simple but liberally applied decorative elements, perfectly reflects the blue and sparkle of the river on which it faces. The center of the building, with projecting rusticated angles, supports a polygonal tower, at whose summit is a globe, symbol of Peter's interest in science and its application in an era of exploration and expansion.

By the end of Peter's reign, in 1725, Saint Petersburg had acquired an economic and administrative base for further development. Its position as imperial capital, however, remained a source of discontent among those who resented the Westernization symbolized by the new city. The brief reign (1725–27) of Peter's second wife, Catherine I, saw a continuation of his projects, as buildings rose and others, completed only a few years earlier, were demolished to make way for yet grander structures. But Catherine had little of Peter's energy. On the succession in 1727 of the eleven-year-old Peter II (Peter's grandson by his first marriage), power was assumed by a Supreme Council dominated by the Dolgoruky family, which promptly exiled the corrupt though energetic Alexander Menshikov—Peter the Great's closest associate and one of the most vigorous participants in the building of Petersburg.

By 1728 reaction against Peter the Great's reforms had gained momentum. The court returned to Moscow, Petersburg was threatened with the exodus of a large part of its population, the army and fleet were neglected (Peter II is reported to have said that he had no wish to 'roam about the sea like his grandfather'), and the country's strained financial position was exacerbated by the widespread refusal of an impoverished peasantry to pay taxes. When in 1730 Peter II died of smallpox, the Romanov male line was temporarily exhausted. The eventual choice as empress of Anne, Peter I's niece (daughter of Ivan V) and widow of the duke of Courland, seemed to promise further limitation of imperial power by the Supreme Council.

The High Baroque: Bartolomeo Rastrelli

EMPRESS ANNE

Hopes for containment of imperial power were disappointed, however, when Anne, after first accepting restrictions on her authority, only nullified them upon her accession to the throne. With the support of the guards regiments and large segments of the gentry in service to the state (both the creations of Peter's reign), Anne restored absolutism to Russia and in 1732 transferred the capital back to Saint Petersburg, an act symbolizing the return to Peter's concept of imperial autocracy. Although Anne's reign has been characterized as one of Russia's most despotic, dominated by a clique of Baltic Germans with little sympathy for the empress's Russian subjects, the construction of Petersburg flourished with the revival of imperial patronage.

Indeed, the 1730s were the first period of the capital's achievement

325. *View of the Admiralty. Engraving attributed to Ottomar Elliger, circa 1730. In this festive scene a warship is launched from the Admiralty docks as crowds cheer and skiffs ply the water. To the right is Mattarnovy's Church of Saint Isaac of Dalmatia (1717), the second church to be built on that site. By the middle of the century it was demolished and a new church constructed, set back from the embankment; the old site is now occupied by Étienne Falconet's* The Bronze Horseman. *By permission of the Houghton Library, Harvard University.*

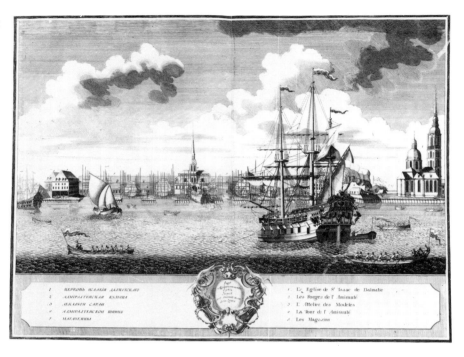

326. *View of the left bank of the Neva, circa 1730. Engraving by Ottomar Elliger. This view was engraved before Rastrelli had begun construction of a new (third) Winter Palace (1732) on the site of Admiral Fyodor Apraksin's mansion (number one, far right). To the left (number seven) is the second Winter Palace, built in 1716–18 by Mattarnovy and expanded by Domenico Trezzini in 1726. The final Winter Palace complex would eventually occupy the entire length of the embankment shown here. By permission of the Houghton Library, Harvard University.*

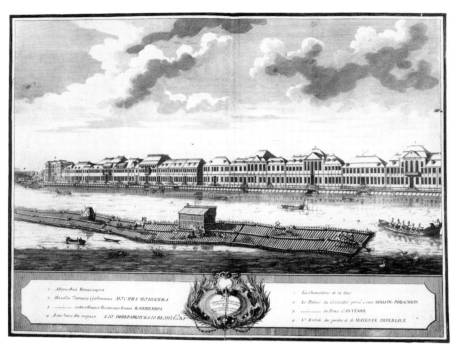

327. *The left bank of the Neva, circa 1730. Ottomar Elliger's use of the foreground to enliven his engravings of the grand quay is evident in this view of a raft carrying one of the city's most valuable commodities— lumber. Seen from the Neva, Saint Petersburg presented an imposing row of palaces (concluding with Peter's Summer Garden and Summer Palace at the far left), behind which very little was yet built. By permission of the Houghton Library, Harvard University.*

of magnificence, the first decade in what was to become a century of monumental expenditure and spectacle. The empress, an avid hunter who enjoyed shooting birds from the windows of her palaces, devoted unprecedented sums to imperial hunts, stupefying displays of fireworks, grand balls, and other forms of court entertainment. In order to indulge her taste for the lavish (and bizarre) in an appropriately luxurious setting, Anne commissioned a series of palaces in both Petersburg and Moscow. These large wooden edifices, none of which survives, represent an important episode in the history of Russian art, for the young Italian architect who designed them, Bartolomeo Rastrelli, was to become the greatest practitioner of the baroque in Russia.

In 1715, upon the death of France's Louis XIV, Peter the Great's foreign agents had been instructed to recruit French architects and artisans—newly without court appointments—for service in Russia. Among this group was Count Carlo Bartolomeo Rastrelli, a Florentine sculptor and architect, whose title derived from his service at the French court. In 1715 he left Paris with his fifteen-year-old son, Bartolomeo Francesco, and two years later he entered Peter's service as an architect, sculptor, decorator, and theatrical-set designer for the burgeoning imperial theater. (The combination of theater and architecture seems auspicious in light of the stagy quality of Petersburg's baroque buildings, many of whose facades in their colorful two-dimensionality resemble outsize stage sets.) The elder Rastrelli's reputation now rests on his sculpture, which includes a fine bust of Peter and an equestrian statue of the emperor. But he also competed for architectural projects, and although he was singularly unsuccessful in this respect (in part because of a feud with Le Blond), his work on project designs provided his son with an introduction to the principles of architecture and draftsmanship.

The younger Rastrelli's first works, two small palaces in Petersburg, date from the early 1720s, but with Peter's death and the consequent decrease in building activity, the architect left Russia for further study in Europe, apparently to remain there until the beginning of Anne's reign. (We know nothing about his itinerary or the details of his study.)[6]

By February 1730 both Rastrellis had moved to Moscow, site then of the imperial court. That same month the younger Rastrelli received the imperial commission that initiated his prolific career: the construction of Winter Annenhof ('Anne's Palace' in German, the predominant language at the court of this Germanophile), a wooden structure of some 130 rooms within the Kremlin. This was followed by a commission for the much larger Summer Annenhof, a palace of 220 rooms that included an extensive park with pools, fountains, flower gardens, and large trees transplanted to the site in Moscow. The rapidity with which these wooden palaces were completed (fifty-eight days in the case of Winter Annenhof!) is testimony not only to the skill of Russian craftsmen—above all, carpenters—but also to the substantial resources Rastrelli commanded, and would continue to command for the next thirty years. (According to the architect's account, during the construction of the Summer Annenhof he had at his disposal 6,000 carpenters, in addition to stonemasons, sculptors, and painters.)

Rastrelli's rise to prominence continued with yet another imperial commission in 1730 (for a wooden summer palace and park on the banks of the Neva), and in November he was designated Court Archi-

328. Empress Elizabeth's Summer Palace. Saint Petersburg. 1741–43. Architect: Bartolomeo Rastrelli. Destroyed by the Emperor Paul. Engraving from a drawing by Mikhail Makhaev. Library of Congress.

tect, the highest architectural post in the country. He was now at work in Petersburg, on the eve of its resurgence as imperial capital, and in order to provide ample accommodation for the court's rapidly increasing size, Anne commanded Rastrelli to build a large three-story palace facing the Neva. When completed, in 1735, this Winter Palace—the third to be constructed on the site—was the most imposing structure the city had seen, and the most richly appointed. Contemporary prints by Mikhail Makhaev convey a rather ungainly external appearance, with large hipped roofs bulging upward at the corners and a rambling horizontal line (due in part to the empress's stipulation that the architect incorporate two previously existing palaces in his design). The interior, however, according to sketches, reveals the rococo ambience that Rastrelli was to create to such striking effect in his later palaces.

329. *The Great Palace, Peterhof. North facade.*

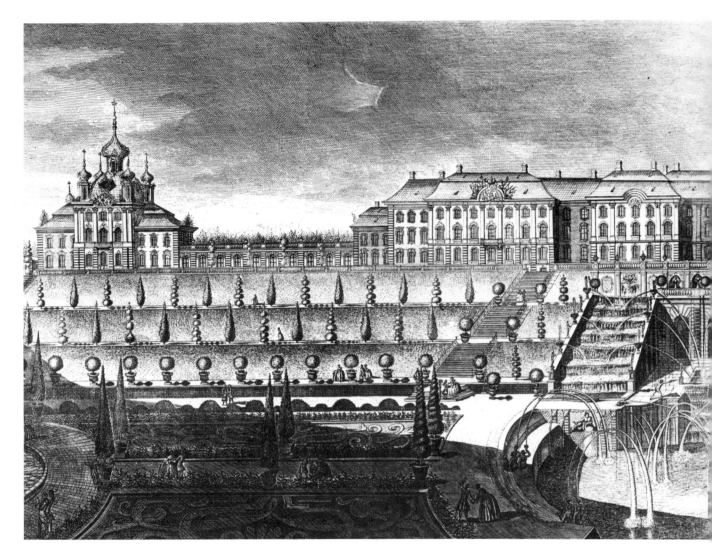

330. The Great Palace, Peterhof. 1714–52. Architects: Jean-Baptiste Alexandre Le Blond, Johann Friedrich Braunstein, Nicolo Michetti, Bartolomeo Rastrelli. Engraving from a drawing by Mikhail Makhaev, 1761. The central portion of Peter's largest palace is primarily the work of Le Blond and Braunstein, with galleries added by Michetti in 1721. Between 1746 and 1752 Rastrelli enlarged the structure for the Empress Elizabeth, without, however, substantially modifying the early baroque of Le Blond. In ruins after World War II, Peterhof has since been restored to Rastrelli's design. Shchusev Museum, Moscow.

EMPRESS ELIZABETH PETROVNA

Following the death of Anne, in 1740, and the subsequent arrest of her hated adviser Ernst Johann Biron, duke of Courland, Russia passed through the obligatory struggle for the throne. Succession was eventually resolved in favor of Elizabeth Petrovna, second daughter of Peter the Great and Catherine, who ruled from 1741 to 1761. The new empress, whose candidacy had been supported by the guards regiments, appeared to be everything that Anne was not: attractive, generous, and independent of the German clique that had dominated Anne's court. Fortunately, Rastrelli not only survived the downfall of Biron, who had been his patron, but rapidly assumed still greater authority as architect to the court of the new empress. Elizabeth intended to build on a scale unheard of in Russia, and she found Rastrelli's style thoroughly congenial to her tastes.

Rastrelli's first project for Elizabeth, the construction of a wooden summer palace (160 rooms) commissioned shortly before her accession

to the throne, proved a harbinger of his Baroque period, with its elaborate decoration and landscaping, enhanced by its location at the meeting of two canals. The walls were light pink, trimmed in white, and rose from a gray-green rusticated ground floor. The palace was razed in 1797 to make way for Emperor Paul I's forbidding Mikhailovsky Castle (in each case architectural taste providing an insight into the ruler's character), but we do have eighteenth-century colored prints that give some idea of the extravagance of Rastrelli's pastel flourish.

Inundated with commissions, Rastrelli was engaged throughout the western part of the empire in the design of Elizabeth's palaces and churches. In 1744 he began plans for one of his greatest monuments, the cathedral of Smolny Convent; in 1745 he completed sketches for the delicate and superbly proportioned Cathedral of Saint Andrew, in Kiev; and in the same year he initiated the expansion and rebuilding of the Great Palace at Peterhof. Several years were required for construction of these projects: the interior of Saint Andrew's was not completed until 1757, and the Smolny cathedral—still unfinished

331. *The Great Palace, Peterhof.*
East wing (court chapel).

at Rastrelli's death, in 1771—underwent so many modifications that
it more properly belongs to his last period. But by the mid-1740s
Rastrelli's late-baroque style had jelled, and his work during the
following two decades is part of a consistent architectural vision.

The much enlarged Great Palace at Peterhof, on the Gulf of Finland,
is the first of Rastrelli's three grand imperial residences, the first in
which he applied the experience of Courland (where he had built two
palaces for Biron) and Petersburg on such a vast scale. Peterhof had
been established by Peter the Great as a summer retreat, and its original
palace and park were designed first by Le Blond, in 1716–17, then,
after Le Blond's death, by Johann Friedrich Braunstein and Nicolò
Michetti. The complex consisted of a large structure situated on
a bluff overlooking the water, as well as a number of pavilions and
small palaces, or retreats. The descent from the central building was

332. *The Stroganov Palace. Nevsky Prospekt and the Moika Canal, Leningrad. 1752–54. Architect: Bartolomeo Rastrelli.*

marked by a cascade that emptied into a canal leading to the Gulf of Finland. When Rastrelli reconstructed the palace, he wisely decided to retain not only this dramatic conjunction of land and water but also the spirit of Le Blond's early baroque: the use of pilasters and rusticated corners—virtually the only ornamental features of the facade—is restrained, even austere, compared with the exuberant baroque decoration of Rastrelli's later works (which had already begun to appear in his cathedral designs).[7] The building's color, however, belies all notions of austerity: the brilliant ocher facade, highlighted by white trim, glows, pulsates in the sun. As is so often the case with the architecture of imperial Petersburg, the colors are enhanced by the continual variations in light, the tone of the northern sky, and the cloud patterns floating off the Gulf of Finland that match the most extravagant baroque fancy.

If in the simplicity of its form the Great Palace at Peterhof represents Rastrelli's homage to an earlier manifestation of the Russian baroque, his succeeding palaces express the spirit of Elizabeth's reign: extravagant, capricious in detail, yet ordered by the rhythmic insistence of massed columns, caryatids, and baroque statuary. The elements of this style appear in the palace Rastrelli built between 1752 and 1754 for Baron Sergey Stroganov, a relative of the empress's and one of the wealthiest men in Russia, possessor of tens of thousands of serfs and extensive salt mines and foundries in the Urals. Although small (fifty

333. *The Stroganov Palace. Detail, Moika facade. Rastrelli was a master of the use of wrought iron for architectural emphasis—seen here under the central windows of the piano nobile.* [RIGHT]

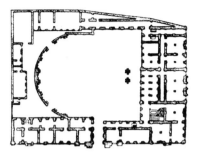

334. *The Stroganov Palace. Plan.*

335. *The Stroganov Palace. Courtyard window. An example of the decoration Rastrelli was to apply so extensively in his later imperial palaces. The caryatids originally were gilded, as was much of the plaster detailing. The ascent from rusticated ground floor (with lions over the portals) to the pattern of verticals and curves above epitomizes Saint Petersburg rococo.*

rooms) compared with the imperial palaces, the Stroganov residence displays a similar application of window decoration, as well as clusters of attached columns, which support the central pediments of each facade. The emphatic white trim on green stucco culminates in a cornice whose line is broken to accommodate the projection of column and pediment. A rise in the street level over the years has altered the building's ground design and proportions, yet the palace today retains the dynamic quality admirably suited to the Stroganov motto: 'Life in Energy.'

Energy, alas, runs amok at the Catherine Palace, commissioned by Catherine I and rebuilt by Rastrelli during Elizabeth's reign. In his report of 1764 to Catherine II ('the Great'), Rastrelli gave the following account of his work on the palace:

At Sarskoe selo I built a large palace of stone in three floors. . . . This extensive structure contains, in addition to the main apartments, a large gallery with several large reception rooms, a large main staircase, decorated with colonnades and statues, with rich

336. *The Catherine Palace. Tsarskoe
Selo (Pushkin). 1748–56. Architect:
Bartolomeo Rastrelli. Park facade.*

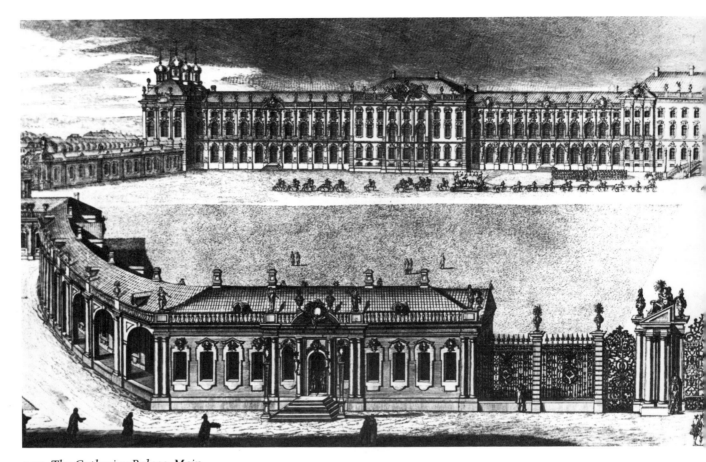

337. *The Catherine Palace, Main Court. Tsarskoe Selo (now called Pushkin, in honor of the poet, who attended the Tsarskoe Selo Lycée). 1748–56. Architect: Bartolomeo Rastrelli. Engraving from a drawing by Mikhail Makhaev, 1761. Named for Catherine I, Peter the Great's second wife, and first built by Johann Friedrich Braunstein (1718–24), the palace was completely reconstructed by Rastrelli for the Empress Elizabeth. With a facade almost a thousand feet in length, the Catherine Palace was the grandest of Russia's imperial country residences (the enormous sums for its construction came from the state salt monopoly). An eighteenth-century English visitor called it 'the Completest triumph of a barbarous taste I have seen in these northern kingdoms' (*A Tour through Some of the Northern Parts of Europe, Particularly Copenhagen, Stockholm, and Petersbourgh, *by Sir Nathaniel Wraxall, London, 1775). Engraving from the Shchusev Museum, Moscow.*

plaster and painted decorations . . . all richly gilded. In addition there is a large room, faced with magnificent work in amber, executed in the city of Berlin and given by the King of Prussia to Peter the Great during his passage on the way to France. . . . The facade of this large palace is decorated with magnificent architecture, all in capitals, columns, pilasters, window pediments, statues, vases, and in general everything gilded up to the balustrade. . . .[8]

'Large,' 'magnificent,' 'rich,' 'gilded'—Rastrelli's apparent hyperbole is in fact a sober, almost understated portrayal of the opulence that is the palace at Tsarskoe Selo.

The site of the palace, chosen by Catherine I as another summer residence for Peter the Great, incorporated a small Finnish farmstead called Saari Mojs ('high place'; the Russian variant, Sarskoe Selo, became Tsarskoe Selo, 'tsar's village'). During Catherine's reign, Braunstein constructed a small two-story palace, which at the beginning of Elizabeth's reign was being modified and enlarged. By 1748, however, the project of rebuilding the palace had reached such vast proportions that Rastrelli was summoned to design a new general plan for the main edifice, the park, and its pavilions. In 1750 work began in earnest with an army of 400 masons from Yaroslavl and 4,000 soldiers; six years later, after numerous changes introduced by Elizabeth ('Penelope's

labor,' according to Catherine the Great),⁹ the palace was essentially completed.

Since the removal during Catherine's reign of the gilt from much of the exterior, it has been difficult to imagine the effect this enormous mass must have produced in Elizabeth's time: gilded atlantes supporting white columns against a turquoise background, surmounted by a golden balustrade—decorated with golden vases and statuary—and culminating in the silver hue of a sheet-iron roof. With the passing of Elizabeth's reign, in the second half of the eighteenth century, such ostentation was condemned as the epitome of bad taste, by both Russians and European visitors. An English traveler, William Coxe, noted: 'This palace, which was built by Elizabeth, is a brick edifice stuccoed white; is of disproportionate length, and in a most heavy style of architecture. The capitals of the outside pillars, many other exterior ornaments, and the series of wooden statues which support the cornice and adorn the roof are all guilded and exhibit a most tawdry appearance.'¹⁰

The palace is indeed of disproportionate length (almost a thousand feet), and the facade is perhaps best appreciated in fragments, as seen through clearings in the park or from the palace gates. But when thus viewed in limited doses, the palace—with or without gilt—reveals Rastrelli's genius for color and form. (Like the other imperial residences to the south of Leningrad, the Catherine Palace was occupied by enemy

338. *The Catherine Palace. Detail, park facade.*

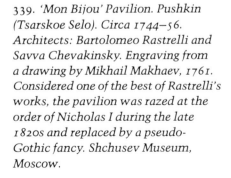

339. *'Mon Bijou' Pavilion. Pushkin (Tsarskoe Selo). Circa 1744–56. Architects: Bartolomeo Rastrelli and Savva Chevakinsky. Engraving from a drawing by Mikhail Makhaev, 1761. Considered one of the best of Rastrelli's works, the pavilion was razed at the order of Nicholas I during the late 1820s and replaced by a pseudo-Gothic fancy. Shchusev Museum, Moscow.*

forces during the Second World War, and by war's end it had been reduced to a blackened shell. The Soviets have since spent millions of rubles restoring not only the exterior of Rastrelli's monument, but also the rococo interior, room by room.)

Whereas the Catherine Palace suggests the fantasy of a baroque theatrical-set designer, Petersburg's Winter Palace is, in the words of art historian Igor Grabar, 'incontestably a genuine palace, stern and serious architecture.'[11] Many of the same devices are applied in both designs—clustered columns at points of emphasis, broken pediments, a balustrade surmounted with statuary, elaborate window pediments— but the effect of the Winter Palace is altogether more solemn. The atlantes are absent, and the massive rectangular form, open on three sides, conveys a three-dimensional solidity lacking in the Catherine and other great suburban palaces.

In the Winter Palace, his last imperial residence, Rastrelli operated under the same constraints imposed at Peterhof and Tsarskoe Selo: to incorporate an existing structure (in this case Rastrelli's own, 'Third,' Winter Palace) into the design of a much larger work, staggering in both its size and its cost. (It is a telling comment on the state of Elizabeth's finances that the 859,555 rubles originally allotted for construction were to be drawn from the revenues of state-licensed pothouses—no doubt frequented by Rastrelli's army of laborers, most of whom earned a monthly wage of one ruble.) Despite the huge sums designated for this palace built on vodka, cost overruns were chronic, and work was occasionally halted for lack of materials and money at a time when Russia's resources were strained to the limit by her involvement in the Seven Years' War (1756–63).

Elizabeth had hoped to see the work on the palace, begun in 1754, completed within the impossibly short period of two years. To that end Rastrelli exerted his considerable experience and talent in directing such a vast project, organized to a degree unprecedented even in Petersburg. But though construction continued year round, despite severe

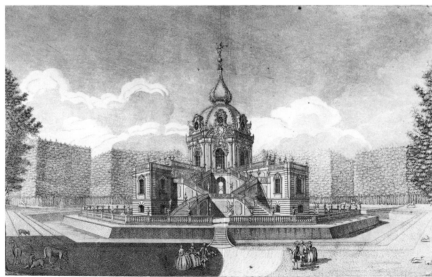

340. *The Winter Palace. Leningrad.*
1754–64. Architect: Bartolomeo
Rastrelli.

climatic conditions, the empress did not live to see the accomplishment of her greatest commission—she died December 25, 1761 (in yet another wooden palace constructed by Rastrelli). The interior of the new Winter Palace, with its more than seven hundred rooms, was habitable by 1763, but work on so elaborate a space was to continue for several decades, as rooms were refitted to suit the tastes of successive autocrats. Unfortunately, very little of Rastrelli's rococo decoration has been preserved: in 1837 the palace was gutted by a fire that burned unchecked for several days, and during the reconstruction most of the interior was designed in the style of the mid-nineteenth century. Only the Jordan Staircase (Iordanskaya lestnitsa) survives from Rastrelli's design.[12]

The exterior, however, has been preserved largely as the architect conceived it: 700 windows (not including those of the interior court), decorated in 20 different patterns; 250 columns, whose distribution provides an insistent rhythm to the facades; and a balustrade supporting 176 large ornamental vases and allegorical statues. Changes have, of course, been made: the stone statuary, corroded by Petersburg's harsh weather, was replaced in the 1890s by copper figures, and the sandy color Rastrelli intended for the stucco facade has vanished over the

341. *The 'New' (fourth) Winter Palace. Leningrad. 1754–64. Architect: Bartolomeo Rastrelli. Now the State Hermitage Museum, the palace incorporates Rastrelli's earlier Winter Palace in a quadrangle containing 700 rooms, some of vast proportions (the Marquis de Custine described one hall as accommodating a thousand guests for dinner). This photograph, taken from the Neva, includes the entire complex. From the right: Rastrelli's palace, the Small Hermitage (Vallin de la Mothe), the Old Hermitage (Veldten), and the Hermitage Theater (Quarenghi).*

years under a series of paints ranging from dull red (applied in the late
nineteenth century) to subsequent green and azure, as used at Rastrelli's
Catherine Palace. It is regrettable that the architect's intention has
been ignored, for the lighter color would provide not only an elegance
appropriate to Rastrelli's late baroque, but also an antidote to the
building's heavy horizontal proportions.

Despite these modifications Rastrelli's Winter Palace remains the
great expression of imperial Russian architecture. Yet not all critics
have been favorably impressed: Igor Grabar wrote that the building
does not inspire, that its weakness is inherent in the very conception,
in the 'incredible extension of this gigantic rectangle, whose lines are
interrupted only by feeble projections in the facade.'[13] There is much
to justify this opinion, for Rastrelli's valiant use of column and statuary
never quite succeeds in its struggle with the horizontal, the degree of
which makes even the varied combinations of Rastrelli's decorative
inventions seem repetitive. Yet the Winter Palace is admirably situated to display at greatest advantage qualities that might otherwise
seem ponderous. The entrance facade, on the south, opens on to a vast
square, contained and completed by the genius of another imperial
architect, Carlo Rossi; and on the north the palace fronts the Neva

River, whose sweep provides a setting commensurate with architecture of the grand design. Whatever faults may be found in the conception of the Winter Palace, it represents the quintessence of Saint Petersburg's monumental style, an assimilation of Western principles applied in a manner and on a scale uniquely Russian.

The achievement of the Winter Palace notwithstanding, the spirit of the late baroque in Petersburg is best revealed in Rastrelli's partially realized plan for the cathedral at Smolny Convent. This work's sculpted, compact form, reminiscent of the pavilions at Tsarskoe Selo, provides a focus lacking in Rastrelli's larger structures. Originally designated the Resurrection New-Maiden Convent, the complex acquired the name Smolny (from the Russian for tar) because of its location on the site where tar had been stored for Peter's navy. This unhappy association did not deter Elizabeth, who wished to found an institute suitably removed from the city for the education of young noblewomen; indeed, there may have been a more personal motive for the empress, who combined pleasure with piety and wished to retire to a convent that provided both. Rastrelli's design, redolent of imperial luxury, would certainly have met her needs.

Work on the design began as early as 1744, and by 1748 the foundations for the cells and the cathedral were begun, under the usual conditions: soldiers worked in shifts of 2,000, digging pits and driving some 50,000 four- and twelve-meter piles into the marshy soil along the Neva. During this preliminary phase Rastrelli submitted variants of a plan resembling Trezzini's design for the Alexander Nevsky Monastery: a large square enclosure containing living and administrative quarters, with churches placed at the corners and a cathedral dominating the center of the compound. Elizabeth further stipulated that the cathedral be built along the lines of the Cathedral of the Dormition in Moscow's Kremlin: a cross-domed plan with five cupolas. (During the reign of Peter the Great, the elongated Latin-cross plan had been adopted for such major Russian churches as the Peter-Paul Cathedral, and the Latin influence continued to appear in Petersburg's churches in the eighteenth and nineteenth centuries. The Elizabethan period marks the resurgence of the traditional Orthodox plan, however modified by Western influence.)[14] In addition, the entrance to the convent was to support a large bell tower, some 450 feet high, constructed in a style derived from the bell tower of Ivan the Great, also in the Kremlin.

Work proceeded very slowly: six years (1750–56) were required just for the construction of a detailed model—in itself an example of the Russian genius for woodworking—and only in the early 1760s did the exterior of the cathedral begin to assume its final state. Because of technical difficulties, construction delays, and the enormous cost, the Smolny Convent was never completed as Rastrelli, or Elizabeth, had intended; in particular, the bell tower, which might have proved the culmination of Rastrelli's engineering achievements, was eliminated from the plan after the empress's death, in 1761, and various other modifications were introduced into the design. The complex was not finished until 1764 (under the direction of Georg Friedrich Veldten, not Rastrelli), and by the time the interior was finally decorated, in the

342. *The Winter Palace. Main archway, south facade (from Palace Square).* [OPPOSITE]

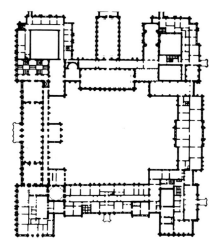

343. *The Winter Palace. Plan.*

344. *Cathedral, Smolny Convent.*
Leningrad. 1748–64. Architect:
Bartolomeo Rastrelli. Detail. [RIGHT]

345. *Corner chapel, Smolny Convent.*
One of four chapels at the corners of
the interior court. [OPPOSITE]

1830s, Rastrelli's rococo had long since become unfashionable; the interior created by Vasily Stasov bears little relation to Rastrelli's intention.

Rastrelli's design of the cathedral's exterior, however, is relatively intact and reveals the ingenuity with which he fused Eastern and Western elements. The four subsidiary cupolas, placed on double-tiered towers, are grouped around a central dome supporting the fifth cupola, in a pattern derived from the Russian Orthodox five-domed church; their placement and design, however, as well as the form of the ribbed dome, are reminiscent rather of Borromini and the seventeenth-century Roman baroque. When viewed from the front, the corners of the cruciform structure—marked by pilasters and clusters of columns—advance toward the entrance portal and the central dome, rising to a height of some 300 feet and clearly visible from the surrounding area. In the usual Petersburg manner, the rhythm of the building's structural and decorative elements is underscored by the use of color—in this case, white on a pastel-blue stucco facade. As a final touch, the crosses that soar above the five cupolas are mounted on golden orbs, whose surface, in the proper light, glows with a celestial radiance.

It is said that each time the Italian architect Giacomo Quarenghi passed the Smolny cathedral he doffed his hat and exclaimed, 'Ecco

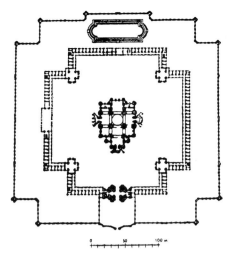

346. *Smolny Convent. Plan, with cathedral in center and four corner chapels in bold outline.*

una chiesa!' Quarenghi was one of the leading proponents of neoclassicism during Catherine the Great's reign, and his severe monuments display the taste of an era quite antipathetic to the exuberance of Russia's Elizabethan baroque. His remark, however, indicates that the perfection of Rastrelli's greatest work transcended the conflict of architectural schools in its inspired union of two disparate cultures. *Ecco una chiesa!*

EXIT RASTRELLI

Following the death in 1761 of Rastrelli's patron Elizabeth, the architect's career suffered an abrupt and irreversible decline. Catherine the Great, who attained the throne in 1762 (after the usual murderous intrigue), possessed an abiding interest in architecture, but her tastes

347. *Cathedral, Smolny Convent. This drawing by Rastrelli shows his original rococo decoration for the interior, as well as the piles on which the building rests. From* Zodchy Rastrelli, *by Yu. M. Denisov and A. N. Petrov.*

348. *Cathedral, Smolny Convent.*
Leningrad. 1748–64. Architect:
Bartolomeo Rastrelli.

ran counter to the rococo fancies of the reign of her predecessor. Having received the Order of Saint Anne in 1762 for his services in the creation of the new Winter Palace, Rastrelli was now given notice that he was no longer Master of Imperial Construction, subordinate only to the empress. On learning that he would have to report to Ivan Betskoy, supervisor of the Department of Construction, Rastrelli tendered his resignation—accepted with great alacrity—and by 1763 he had been relieved of all further duties, ostensibly on the grounds of ill health. Upon leaving Russia, probably in 1765, he interrupted his journey to Italy with a stay of several weeks at Ruenthal, in Courland. Here the duke, Biron, returned from exile, was at work on the interior of the palace designed by Rastrelli in his youth, a monument to the beginnings of a brilliant career, now ended.

During his final years, in Lugano, Rastrelli organized and provided a commentary for his architectural sketches, in the hope that they might be published in Russia. (This plan, unfortunately, was never realized. The sketches and Rastrelli's description passed in the eighteenth century from Russia to Poland, where they were finally sold, in 1932, to the National Library in Warsaw.) In 1770 Rastrelli petitioned for membership in the Russian Academy of Sciences—this, at least, was granted him—and in the following year he died in Lugano. No one in Russia seems to have taken note of his death.

Rastrelli had survived the reigns of two empresses, and, in a transplantation of Western forms to a Russian setting, had created a style whose scale and ingenuity are among the great achievements of the late baroque in Europe. His fall from favor is attributable not to any decline in ability but rather to a complex series of events related to politics and changing architectural tastes—most notably, the replacement of the baroque (and its rococo elaboration) by the principles of classicism, which were being assimilated in Russia well before Rastrelli had completed his last work. To this transition must be added the new empress's disapproval of the frivolity she had witnessed as a young woman at Elizabeth's court. Catherine the Great was no ascetic, but her personal manner and her notion of imperial power—its obligations and privileges—created a much altered concept of style, in architecture as well as in imperial comportment. With her accession begins a new era in the imperial design.

Catherine the Great: The Classical Form

In 1779, the seventeenth year of her reign (1762–95), Catherine described her passion for architecture in a letter to the philosophe Friedrich Grimm:

> Our storm of construction now rages more than ever before, and it is unlikely that an earthquake could destroy as many buildings as we are erecting. Construction is a sort of devilry, devouring a pile of money; and the more you build, the more you want to build. It's simply a disease, something like a drinking fit—or, perhaps, just a habit.[15]

349. *The Cathedral of Saint Nicholas. Leningrad. 1753–62. Architect: Savva Chevakinsky. Designed by one of the most talented architects of the Rastrelli period, this cathedral bears comparison with its contemporary at Smolny: although less emphatic in the vertical development of its towers, Chevakinsky's church displays a melding of baroque and Orthodox elements as extravagant as anything by Rastrelli.* [OPPOSITE]

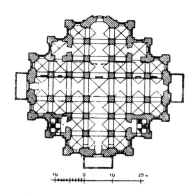

350. *The Cathedral of Saint Nicholas. Plan.*

351. *The Cathedral of Saint Nicholas. Detail.*

352. *Bell tower, the Cathedral of Saint Nicholas. The finest baroque interpretation of this traditional Russian structure.* [RIGHT]

353. *Cathedral of Saint Nicholas. Leningrad. 1753–62. Architect: Savva Chevakinsky.* [OPPOSITE]

It would indeed seem that no other Russian ruler, with the exception of Peter the Great, was more addicted to the pursuit of architecture as a manifestation of progress and of imperial glory. Not only did Catherine the Great initiate a multitude of projects in both Petersburg and Moscow—projects that led to the reconstruction of large areas within those cities—but she also founded a planning commission whose mandate was to impose the imperial design on scores of provincial cities; the architecture and planning of these administrative centers were to reflect the rationalism of the Enlightenment, which Catherine associated with the classical style. Although her accomplishments fell short of the ambitious goal, many provincial cities in Russia still bear the imprint of her desire for architectural order: architecture as a statement of rationality.

It was Petersburg, however, that bore the brunt of the 'storm,' as Catherine presided over the extraordinary enterprise that defines the first phase of neoclassicism in Russia. The architects of this period are

354. *The Academy of Arts.*
Vasilevsky Island, Leningrad.
1764–88. Architects: Jean-Baptiste
Michel Vallin de la Mothe and Alex-
ander Kokorinov. The Academy is
one of the earliest examples of neo-
classicism in Petersburg—the detached
Tuscan columns, simple window de-
tail, and unbroken cornice line signal
a new sensibility in imperial taste.
[ABOVE]

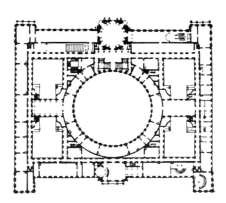

355. The Academy of the Arts. Plan.

as thoroughly cosmopolitan as those of previous reigns: Jean-Baptiste Michel Vallin de la Mothe, from France; Antonio Rinaldi and Giacomo Quarenghi, from Italy; Georg Friedrich Veldten, from Germany; Charles Cameron, a Scot; and, for the first time, an impressive array of native Russians, educated in Europe, or in the European manner. The designs of Vasily Bazhenov (in Moscow as well as Petersburg) and Ivan Starov are of particular interest as examples of the complete assimilation of the Western idiom by Russian architects.

The origins of neoclassicism in the eighteenth century cannot easily be traced because of the variety of tendencies that contributed to the movement: the Italian Renaissance and classical French architecture of the seventeenth century as well as Palladianism in England all provide interpretations of what was seen as the essence of classical architecture—particularly as expressed in the writings and work of Palladio. (Russian interest in Palladio and Vitruvius dates from the beginning of the eighteenth century, but no sustained interpretation of their work occurred during the country's relatively brief apprentice-ship in Western architecture.) Above all other nations, however, France provided for Russia the model for the application of classical architec-tural principles, as defined by the 'Roman' imperial style of Louis XIV and by later, 'purer' variants, derived from the more severe statement of Hellenism.

The rapidity with which Russia accepted neoclassicism reflects the influence of the intellectual and artistic movement that occurred in France during the middle of the eighteenth century. Russia did not make any original theoretical contribution to this development, merely

356. *The Church of Saint Catherine (Roman Catholic). Nevsky Prospekt. Leningrad. 1762–83. Architect: Jean-Baptiste Michel Vallin de la Mothe.*

appropriating it, but the reason for its success in both countries is the same: neoclassicism was welcomed as a rejection of the 'disorder' of the late baroque, and a reaffirmation of the principles of reason expressed in the philosophy and the architecture of antiquity. As one critic has described the movement in France, 'This revulsion against the Rococo and all the values it was felt to express, or at any rate to imply and condone, amounted in certain cases to an instinctive nausea; but in general the new moralizing fervour which began to penetrate the arts around the mid century was rational and stoic in tone.'[16] Much the same could be said of Russia, or, more precisely, of Catherine, who experienced 'instinctive nausea' for the baroque extravagance of Elizabeth's style, and who took pride in the role of enlightened autocrat—a role assiduously cultivated by her correspondence with such French philosophes as Diderot, Voltaire, and d'Alembert.

The style of Catherine's neoclassicism varies considerably, depending on the function of the structure and the individual architect's interpretation of classical principles. But the general intent is always clear: a new restraint—especially in the decoration of the exterior—and an adherence to elements of the classical order.

VALLIN DE LA MOTHE AND RINALDI

The departure from the style of Rastrelli is evident as early as 1759 in Vallin de la Mothe's design for the facade of the Imperial Academy of Arts. This French architect's other monuments in Petersburg—such as the Small Hermitage, designed to house Catherine the Great's art collection (the basis of the later vast repository of Western art)—demonstrate a similar vision: greater simplicity in the use of columns, which are frequently detached but not clustered; modest window decoration, devoid of rococo detail; and a severe cornice line, articulated with the traditional classical elements (triglyph, dentils, guttae, and so forth). The Doric and Ionic were the most commonly used orders. In addition to a greater simplicity in design, the new austerity is particularly noticeable in the muting of the vivid colors that had characterized the Petersburg baroque from its beginnings; stucco remained the primary building surface, but it was now painted in subdued tones. Nonetheless, baroque forms, especially in the window detail, continued to appear in the work of Vallin de la Mothe and other architects during this transitional period of mixed styles. The rejection of earlier tastes was by no means total.

Vallin de la Mothe's contemporaries—Rinaldi, Bazhenov, Veldten, Starov—extended the interpretation of imperial classicism, loosely defined, in what might be called the era of the column. Not that the uses of the column were unknown to Rastrelli, but the decoration of his palaces submerged the column within an array of statuary and plaster ornament. Both Vallin de la Mothe and Rinaldi, like Rastrelli, exploited the column and pilaster as means of segmenting an extensive facade, yet the articulation is restrained in comparison with Rastrelli's

357. *Gostinny Dvor (Merchants' Yard). Nevsky Prospekt, Leningrad. 1757–85. Architects: Bartolomeo Rastrelli and Jean-Baptiste Michel Vallin de la Mothe. Rastrelli provided the design—a large, two-storied quadrilateral, with arcades connecting the shops. After 1761 Vallin de la Mothe assumed control of the project and greatly simplified its appearance, in accordance with neoclassical tastes.* [LEFT]

358. *Gostinny Dvor. Corner entrance.*

359. *The Small Hermitage. Palace Quay, Leningrad. 1764–75. Architect: Jean-Baptiste Michel Vallin de la Mothe.*

360. *Cathedral of Saint Nicholas. Bell tower. 1756–58.* [OPPOSITE]

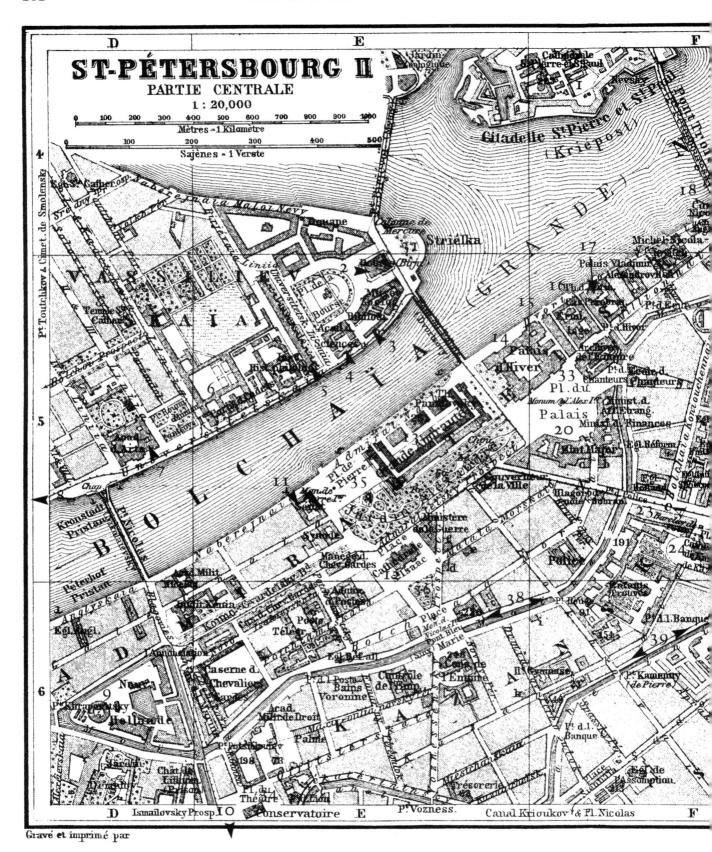

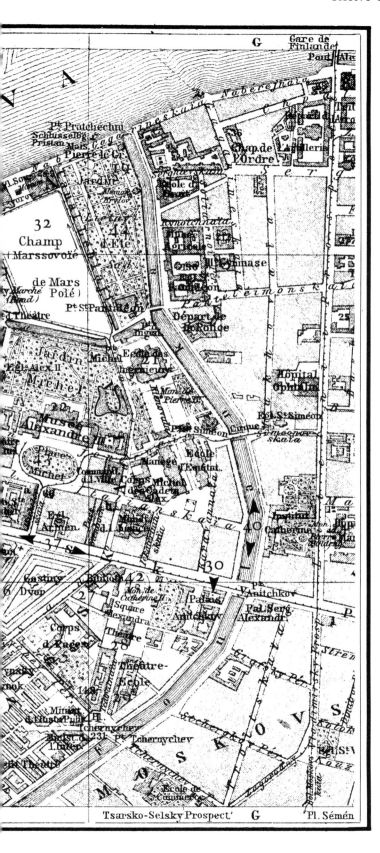

Central Saint Petersburg, 1897

Buildings

1. *Cathedral of Saints Peter and Paul*
2. *Bourse*
3. *Kunstkammer*
4. *Academy of Sciences*
5. *Building of the Twelve Colleges*
6. *Menshikov Palace*
7. *Academy of Arts*
8. *Mining Institute*
9. *New Holland*
10. *Cathedral of Saint Nicholas*
11. *Senate and Holy Synod*
12. *Cathedral of Saint Isaac*
13. *Admiralty*
14. *Winter Palace*
15. *Small Hermitage*
16. *Old Hermitage*
17. *Hermitage Theater*
18. *Marble Palace*
19. *Summer Palace of Peter I*
20. *General Staff*
21. *Mikhailovsky Castle*
22. *Mikhailovsky Palace*
23. *Stroganov Palace*
24. *Kazan Cathedral*
25. *Church of Saint Catherine*
26. *Gostinny dvor*
27. *Public Library*
28. *Alexandrine Theater*
29. *Directorate of Theaters, Ministry*
    of Education
30. *Anichkov Palace*

Streets, Squares, and Parks

31. *The Point, Vasilevsky Island*
32. *Mars Field*
33. *Palace Square*
34. *Theater Square*
35. *Senate Square*
36. *Saint Isaac's Square*
37. *Nevsky Prospekt*
38. *Moika Canal*
39. *Catherine Canal*
40. *Fontanka River*
41. *Chernyshev Square*
42. *Alexandrine Square*
43. *Mikhailovsky Square*
44. *Summer Garden*

361. *New Holland Arch. Leningrad.
1765–80s. Architect: Jean-Baptiste
Michel Vallin de la Mothe. The architect's genius in combining the monumental and the utilitarian is evident
in his entrance to New Holland, a
complex of canals and lumber warehouses built by Ivan Korobov in
the 1730s and redesigned by Savva
Chevakinsky in the 1760s. As at
Gostinny Dvor, Vallin de la Mothe
here used paired Tuscan columns and
a sharply defined cornice to grand
effect. Granite on brick.*

exuberance. For Vallin de la Mothe, this restraint derives from a variety
of the late baroque exemplified in the French *hôtel* of the first part of
the eighteenth century. For Rinaldi, who arrived in Petersburg in 1754,
the model is a similar style applied to the Italian palazzo—notably by
his teacher, Luigi Vanvitelli.

If we assume that Rinaldi assisted Vanvitelli in the construction of
the Royal Palace at Caserta, begun in 1751, the results of his apprentice-
ship are clearly evident in two of his mature works: the Marble Palace,
in Petersburg, and the palace at Gatchina (both built for Prince Grigory
Orlov, one of Catherine's favorites).[17] In contrast to the brick-and-
stucco construction applied in almost all of Petersburg's monuments,
each of Rinaldi's palaces is faced in stone; and in the case of the Marble
Palace—built of granite with details in various colors of marble—no
expense was spared in obtaining materials of the highest quality. In
this most imposing of Petersburg's palaces from the late eighteenth
century (1768–85), the facade is defined by two-story Corinthian
pilasters—doubled on the corners of the structure—and surmounted,
above the cornice, with a balustrade and ornamental vases. Although

362. *The Marble Palace. Palace Quay, Leningrad. 1768–85. Architect: Antonio Rinaldi. One of the few buildings in Saint Petersburg to be faced with stone, this palace is the most imposing residence constructed in the city during the reign of Catherine the Great. The development of quarries in Russia during the eighteenth century provided Rinaldi with marble and granite of delicate colors, ranging here from the rose gray of the ground floor to the light pink of the pilasters. The walls are of light-gray granite.*

the main, court entrance is somewhat obscured by a service building to the east, the river and street facades (north and south) epitomize the stern luxuriance that characterizes Petersburg's transition from the baroque to the neoclassic.

363. *The Summer Garden Gates. Palace Quay. Leningrad. Georg Friedrich Veldten(?). 1760s.*

IVAN STAROV

The most influential architect of this transition, Ivan Starov (1744–1808), graduated with distinction from the Petersburg Academy of Arts in 1762, and subsequently spent six years studying in Paris and traveling throughout Europe. After his return to Petersburg, he accepted a teaching position at the Academy and designed a number of country mansions in the environs of Moscow and Petersburg. In Petersburg itself, his first major project was the Cathedral of the Trinity at the Alexander Nevsky Monastery (1776–90), the earliest church clearly to show the influence of Roman baroque on Russian ecclesiastical architecture. (Although the central cupola of Rastrelli's Smolny Cathedral derives from the Italian baroque, the plan of that church is based on the Greek cross.) Starov adopted the elongated cross, surmounted by a drum with attached Corinthian columns, above which rises a ribbed dome supporting a lantern with volutes. Corinthian pilasters decorate the two square bell towers of the west facade, and a hexastyle Tuscan Doric portico frames the main entrance.

The complexity of articulation on the west facade of Trinity Cathedral is absent from Starov's next exercise in the Tuscan order, the Tauride

364. *The Summer Garden Gates. Design. Shchusev Museum, Moscow.*

365. *The Neva embankments. Leningrad. 1762–80s. Chief architect: Georg
Friedrich Veldten. The son of Peter the
Great's chef, Veldten served as an
apprentice to Bartolomeo Rastrelli
after a period of study in Tübingen,
and is the architect of the Old
Hermitage, one of the additions to
Rastrelli's Winter Palace (see Figure
341). His greatest achievement is the
design and construction of the granite
embankments along the Neva—an
engineering project transformed into
a work of art invaluable to the sense
of architectural ensemble. Pictured
here is the Upper Swan Bridge over
the Lebyazhy Canal.* [ABOVE]

366. *Ornamental ironwork along the
Palace Quay. Designer: Georg Friedrich Veldten.*

367. South Pavilion, the Small Hermitage, Million (now Khalturin) Street, Leningrad. 1760s. Architect: Georg Friedrich Veldten. During the construction of Vallin de la Mothe's Small Hermitage on Palace Quay (Figure 341), Veldten added this structure to the south. A hanging garden connected the two buildings, which were used to house Catherine the Great's rapidly expanding collection of Western art. In 1840 Vasily Stasov added a fourth floor to the pavilion. [LEFT]

368. *The Chesme Church. Leningrad (outskirts). 1777–80. Architect: Georg Friedrich Veldten. This pseudo-Gothic caprice commemorates the victory in 1770 of the Russian fleet over the Turks at Chesme. Such Gothic Revival was fashionable in the latter part of Catherine the Great's reign.*

Palace (1783–89), commissioned by Catherine the Great for yet another of her favorites, Grigory Potëmkin, Prince of the Tauris. The palace is a model of neoclassical simplicity, and was widely imitated, though on a more modest scale. The center of the front of the building is defined by a hexastyle Tuscan Doric portico and a rotunda with a low dome; the lack of ornamentation is most striking in the facade, whose only decoration is a frieze of metopes and triglyphs. The main courtyard is flanked by wings, each of which has a Doric portico of four columns. The back, or park, facade of the wings displays the Ionic order, the effect of which is equally severe. Starov's minimal use of architectural decoration on the exterior is in contrast to the richness of the interior, but in each case an elegant neoclassical restraint dominates.

The palace has not survived in its original form. The Emperor Paul, in one of his rages against his mother and her supporters, converted the building into a stable for the Horse Guards, thus destroying much of the interior. And despite a reconstruction by Luigi Rusca at the beginning of the nineteenth century, Starov's design for the interior was substantially altered. Later in the nineteenth century much of

369. *The Tauride Palace. Leningrad. 1783–89. Architect: Ivan Starov. Catherine the Great presented the palace to her favorite, Grigory Potëmkin, Prince of the Tauris, whose title and the name of the building derive from his services in the conquest of the Crimea. The palace's severe neoclassical exterior—subsequently a model for Russian country mansions—belies a lavishly appointed interior. A large park behind the palace was designed by the Englishman William Gould.*

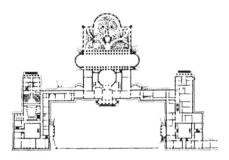

370. *The Tauride Palace. Plan.*

the grand park surrounding the palace was sold for speculative development, and in 1906–07 the palace was adapted for use by Russia's short-lived *duma*, or parliament. But in spite of its vicissitudes, the Tauride Palace remains the best example of the austere style of neoclassical domestic architecture favored by the wealthy nobility of Catherine's reign.

CHARLES CAMERON

Among the varieties of neoclassicism during the reign of Catherine the Great, the most productive was Palladianism, introduced to Russia by Charles Cameron and Giacomo Quarenghi. Cameron (1743–1812), an enigmatic Scotsman highly recommended to the Empress, arrived in Petersburg about 1779, and worked there over the next two decades. But before going to Russia, he had made a prolonged stay in Rome, where he studied classical monuments, as well as the work of Palladio. His book, *The Baths of the Romans Explained and Illustrated, with the Restorations of Palladio Corrected and Improved* (published in England in 1772), serves as an introduction to the style he pursued in Russia.

Cameron's first task for Catherine consisted of redecorating a number of rooms in the palace at Tsarskoe Selo, where she liked to spend her summers. The empress was justifiably pleased with the results—now restored after severe damage during the Second World War. In a letter to Grimm (June 22, 1781) she wrote: 'I have an architect here named Kameron, born a Jacobite, brought up in Rome. He is known for his book on the ancient Roman baths; the man has a fertile brain, and a great admiration for [Charles-Louis] Clérisseau; so the latter's drawings will help Kameron to decorate my new apartments here, and these

371. *Alexander Park. Tsarskoe Selo
(Pushkin). Chinese Bridge designed
by Charles Cameron, 1782–88.*

372. *Trinity Cathedral, Alexander Nevsky Monastery. Leningrad. 1776–90. Architect: Ivan Starov. The most resolutely Latinate of Petersburg's cathedrals, Trinity is set within the early-baroque ensemble created by Trezzini and Schwertfeger.* [RIGHT]

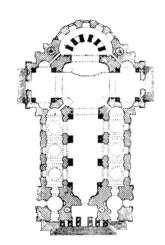

373. *Trinity Cathedral, Alexander Nevsky Monastery. Plan, elevation.*

apartments will be superlatively good. So far only two rooms have been finished, and people rush to see them. . . .' (Cameron apparently played on the empress's sympathy for a deposed royal line by claiming affiliation with the Jacobites, but there is no evidence that he was associated with the cause, either in London—where he grew up—or in Rome.)[18]

In 1780, soon after his completion of Catherine's apartments at Tsarkoe Selo, Cameron began work on the Agate Pavilion and the Colonnade (subsequently renamed the Cameron Gallery), both of which are located next to Rastrelli's palace. Each is an eminently successful example of Cameron's interpretation of antiquity: the Agate Pavilion, with its Cold Baths, reflects his study of the Roman Baths, while the Gallery is one of the happiest conceits in eighteenth-century Russian architecture—a massive rusticated ground floor, surmounted by delicate Ionic columns.

Cameron's Palladianism is fully evident in the palace he built at

374. *The Cameron Gallery, adjoining the Catherine Palace. Pushkin (Tsarskoe Selo). 1783–86. Architect: Charles Cameron. Although Catherine the Great had no fondness for* Rastrelli's baroque extravagance, his Great Palace at Tsarskoe Selo became one of her favorite residences, with a redesigned interior and various galleries provided by her notable *Palladian architect, Charles Cameron. His design for this gallery reconciles opposites with its heavily rusticated foundation and delicate Ionic peristyle.*

375. *The Imperial Palace. Pavlovsk.*
1780–96. Architect: Charles Cameron.
Park facade.

376. The Agate Rooms and Cold Baths. Pushkin (Tsarskoe Selo). 1780–85. Architect: Charles Cameron. Part of the Cameron complex at the Catherine Palace. His gallery adjoins at left.

Pavlovsk for Catherine's son, Paul. Although the palace, interior as well as exterior, was not completed according to the architect's specifications, and although he was frequently at odds with Paul and his wife, Maria Fyodorovna—who entrusted much of the work to the less gifted Vincenzo Brenna—the central structure provides fair measure of Cameron's practice of the Palladian ideal. A two-storied portico composed of paired Corinthian columns dominates the courtyard facade, but the more impressive view is from the opposite side— again, a Corinthian portico, of paired and single columns supporting a pediment. From this side, ornamental trees obscure Brenna's additions and allow a clearer perception of Cameron's building, surmounted with rotunda and colonnade. By virtue of its detail as well as its site, a knoll descending to the Slavyanka River, the palace has been compared to Palladio's design for the Villa Trissino at Meledo.[19] The park, incidentally, is the most beautiful in Russia, and may have been designed according to plans furnished by 'Capability' Brown, although it is frequently credited to Cameron.[20] Cameron's pavilions in it—particularly the Doric Temple of Friendship—and their setting within the park are among the best examples of the eighteenth-century ideal of noble simplicity in architecture and in nature.

GIACOMO QUARENGHI

The last of Catherine's pleiad of architects, Giacomo Quarenghi (1744– 1817), like Cameron an admirer of Palladio, created the most austere

377. *The Imperial Palace. Pavlovsk. 1780–96. Architect: Charles Cameron, with galleries constructed by Vincenzo Brenna. The courtyard facade.* [RIGHT]

378. *Temple of Friendship. Pavlovsk. 1782. Architect: Charles Cameron.*

379. *Pavilion of the Three Graces. Pavlovsk. 1780s. Architect: Charles Cameron. Ceiling detail.*

form of Petersburg's Roman classicism, as exemplified by the English Palace at Peterhof, the Academy of Sciences, and the Alexander Palace at Tsarskoe Selo.[21] Although the last is graced with a balustrade, Quarenghi's buildings represent a rigorous statement of column and mass almost devoid of ornamentation. The Hermitage Theater, with its decorative niches and window pediments, offers a partial exception to this austerity, but here too the effect derives largely from the finely calculated spacing of the columns and windows.

The most distinctive feature of Quarenghi's style, however, is his Palladian-inspired portico. Throughout Quarenghi's career in Russia, beginning with his design of 1780 for the English Palace at Peterhof and concluding with the construction of the Smolny Institute (1806–08), he used the portico as a means of organizing a large, simply detailed structural mass. Typically, his portico consisted of eight columns, in the Ionic order, culminating in a pediment marked with dentils. In a flawless understanding not only of the spatial relation between the columns and the angle of the pediment incline, but also of the relation of the portico to the proportions of the rest of the structure, Quarenghi achieved a clarity of statement that epitomizes the classical in architecture.

Quarenghi continued to work as imperial architect during the reign (1801–25) of Catherine's grandson Alexander I, providing a transition from the Roman classicism of the eighteenth century to the rise of Hellenism in the first part of the nineteenth. There was, however, a major disappointment at the end of Quarenghi's career: at Alexander's command, construction of his project for the Bourse (Stock Exchange), on Vasilevsky Island, was halted, the building razed, and its reconstruction entrusted to the young French architect Thomas de Thomon, whose

380. *The Imperial Palace. Pavlovsk.*
View across the Slavyanka River.

new design—with peristyle—is Petersburg's most radical exercise in column and mass.

Catherine's reign had witnessed the creation of an imperial style based on an order that can be broadly characterized as classical, however eclectic and varied the interpretations of it. The architectural monuments of the late eighteenth century in Saint Petersburg display a grandeur founded on an autocratic utilization of human and material resources and tempered by the enlightened autocrat's understanding of classical dignity. Like Elizabeth, Catherine spent enormous sums on the construction and renovation of palaces, those symbols of imperial rule, but her plans for the provincial administrative centers and such monuments as Petersburg's Academies of Arts and of Sciences attest to a concept of civic order that underlies the modern secular state—a concept that originated, in architecture as much as in politics,

381. *Temple of Friendship. Pavlovsk.*
1782. Architect: Charles Cameron.

382. *The Academy of Sciences. Vasilevsky Island, Leningrad. 1783–89. Architect: Giacomo Quarenghi.* [ABOVE]

383. *The Hermitage Theater. Palace Quay. Leningrad. 1783–87. Architect: Giacomo Quarenghi. In the foreground, the Hermitage Bridge.*

during the Petrine era. Both Peter and Catherine, concerned with the rational organization of the state according to principles articulated by Leibnitz and Montesquieu, were equally concerned with the rational design of the center of that state, the imperial capital.

Alexander I: The Rational Plan Achieved

The architectural mission pursued by Peter and Catherine culminated in the reign of Catherine's grandson Alexander I, from 1801 to 1825. In his own interpretation of the grand design, Alexander either completed

384. *The Smolny Institute for Noble-women. Leningrad. 1806–08. Architect: Giacomo Quarenghi.* [RIGHT]

385. *The Alexander Palace. Pushkin (Tsarskoe Selo). 1792–96. Architect: Giacomo Quarenghi.*

386. *Monument of Peter the Great. Mikhailovsky Castle, Leningrad. Sculptor: Carlo Bartolomeo Rastrelli. Cast in 1745–47; placed at its present site in 1800.*

or initiated the majority of the neoclassical architectural ensembles that exist today. In the words of an observer of the time,

> He wanted to make Petersburg more beautiful than any of the European capitals he had visited. For this purpose he decided to set up a special architectural committee under the chairmanship of [General Augustin de] Béthencourt. Neither the legality of private ownership, nor the structural durability of public or private buildings was the business of this committee: it was to be concerned only with examining designs for new facades, to accept, reject, or alter them, and also to engage in the planning of streets and squares, projects for canals, bridges, and the better construction of the outlying parts of the city—devoted, in a word, solely to the city's external beauty.[22]

No building, private or public, was to escape the scrutiny of this most thorough of Saint Petersburg's planning commissions.

In the implementation of his design, Alexander was fortunate to have at his command a group of architects whose vision equaled his own: Andrey Voronikhin, Thomas de Thomon, Adrian Zakharov, Vasily Stasov, and Carlo Rossi—the most prolific creator of monumental architectural space in Petersburg.[23] The harmony that pervades their neoclassical style can be traced in part to earlier works by Starov and Quarenghi, but the boldness with which the classical revival was expressed in Petersburg unquestionably owes a debt to French neoclassicism, represented in theory, if not in practice, by such architects as Claude-Nicolas Ledoux and Étienne-Louis Boullée. For three decades during the nineteenth century they provided Alexander and his successor, Nicholas I (reigning from 1825 to 1855), with a coherent Russian neoclassicism, expressive of a new confidence in Russia's destiny among European nations.

387. *Mikhailovsky Castle, Leningrad. 1797–80. Architects: Vasily Bazhenov and Luigi Brenna. Idiosyncratic in design, the Mikhailovsky Castle was intended by the Emperor Paul to serve as an impregnable fortress, surrounded by a moat; his private guard assassinated him there in 1805. The building's design was first entrusted to Bazhenov, but Paul replaced him with Brenna, who is responsible for the final form. In 1823 the castle was adapted for use as a military-engineering academy: among its students in the 1840s was the young Dostoevsky.*

ANDREY VORONIKHIN

This new phase in city planning originated during the brief reign of Alexander's predecessor, Paul I (1796–1801). This is not the place to examine Paul's megalomania, or the contradictory, tragic, and frequently ludicrous events of the five years preceding his assassination by the palace guard. The reign did, however, have its moments of triumph, particularly in Italy, with the victorious campaign of Generalissimo Alexander Suvorov over the revolutionary armies of France. Indeed, Russia's renewed role in European affairs demanded yet another monument to the glory of the Romanovs, and in 1800, the year before his assassination, Paul commissioned one of Petersburg's most imposing cathedrals, dedicated to the icon of the Kazan Mother of God.

Its architect, Andrey Voronikhin, was not well known in the capital, having built no structure remotely comparable in size or complexity to the Kazan Cathedral.

Voronikhin was born a serf in 1759, on one of the Stroganov estates in the Urals. The circumstances of his birth were fortunate. The Stroganovs were not only one of the richest families in Russia, but also generous and knowledgeable patrons of the arts, and Voronikhin was drawn into the family circle by virtue of his artistic talents; he frequently accompanied Count Alexander Stroganov's son Paul on his travels in Russia and, between 1786 and 1790, in Europe (primarily Switzerland and France). When in 1786 the count granted Voronikhin his freedom, he by no means intended to release the young artist from his service.

Little is known of Voronikhin's training, either in Russia or during the period he spent in Paris with Paul Stroganov. But what remains of his first major project—the remodeling in 1793 of Rastrelli's Stroganov

388. *Mikhailovsky Castle. Detail.*
[RIGHT]

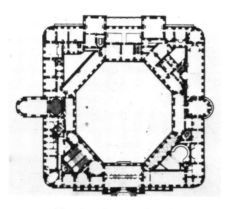

389. *Mikhailovsky Castle. Plan.*

Palace—shows a thorough understanding of decoration and architectural form. Although Voronikhin's other work for the Stroganovs is not extant, it is clear that by the end of the eighteenth century he had made his mark with his noble patrons, as well as at the Academy of Arts, which elected him an academician in 1799. (The Academy's president was Alexander Stroganov.)

Voronikhin's debut as a major architect was nonetheless sudden and unexpected. As early as the 1780s, there had been plans to rebuild Mikhail Zemtsov's modest Church of the Nativity of the Virgin on Nevsky Prospekt, the repository of the miraculous icon the Kazan Mother of God, which had been brought to the city by Peter the Great and was considered the palladium of the Romanovs. Quarenghi is known to have submitted a proposal for the church's reconstruction, though it has not survived. In 1799 Paul reopened the competition for the new cathedral, which was to symbolize his desire to effect a reconciliation with Roman Catholicism—his desire, indeed, to establish his capital as the *new* Rome, bastion of militant united Christianity. He intended the cathedral to emulate Saint Peter's in Rome.

Cameron and de Thomon were among those competing for the project, and though Paul had approved Cameron's design in October 1800, he reversed himself a month later and appointed a commission, headed

390. Cathedral of the Kazan Mother of God. Nevsky Prospekt. Leningrad. 1801–11. Architect: Andrey Voronikhin. The grand Corinthian portico and colonnade (96 columns) are part of an architectural illusion designed to emphasize the side of the church facing Nevsky Prospekt. Despite its appearance, the north-facing Nevsky side does not contain the main entrance, which, in accordance with Russian Orthodox architectural tradition, is at the western end of the church, opposite the altar.

391. *Cathedral of the Kazan Mother of God. West facade.* [RIGHT]

392. *Cathedral of the Kazan Mother of God. Apse.*

393. *Cathedral of the Kazan Mother of God. Plan, elevation.* [ABOVE AND RIGHT]

by Stroganov, to direct the construction. The commission promptly chose Voronikhin as the architect.

The wisdom of this decision and Stroganov's faith in 'his' architect have been amply substantiated. Voronikhin's cathedral is redolent of monumental classicism as interpreted in Saint Peter's and, more to the point, Jacques Germain Soufflot's Sainte Geneviève in Paris (the Panthéon, 1755–92). The body of the Kazan Cathedral is in the form of a Latin cross, with Corinthian porticoes on the north, south, and west, and a semicircular apse, with attic frieze, on the east. The structure is surmounted by a large attic. Over the crossing is an elongated dome, above a drum whose pilasters echo the rows of columns below. In an earlier variant of the plan, the dome and drum were considerably larger, and the drum was surrounded by a colonnade—a detail reminiscent of the Panthéon. In its present form, slender over so massive a structure, the dome produces a curiously light effect, quite unlike either Saint Peter's or the Panthéon.

Voronikhin's ingenuity was most taxed by the problem of adapting the cathedral to its setting. Although Nevsky Prospekt was marked by a number of palaces, the street was not particularly imposing at the beginning of the nineteenth century; the new cathedral was to be the first of its great monuments. Because the cathedral's main axis, east-

394. *The Mining Institute. Vasilevsky Island, Leningrad. 1806–11. Architect: Andrey Voronikhin. Pluto abducts Persephone in front of Voronikhin's magnificent Doric portico.*

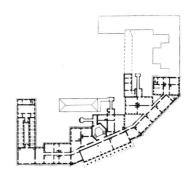

395. *The Mining Institute. Plan.*

396. *The Bourse. Vasilevsky Island,
Leningrad. 1805–10. Architect:
Thomas de Thomon. From Voronikhin to de Thomon, the severe style of
the Hellenistic revival was applied in
Saint Petersburg on a scale and with
a determination unrivaled in Europe.
In commissioning the Bourse (Birzha),
Alexander I provided de Thomon
with the opportunity to realize what
his teacher Claude-Nicholas Ledoux
had only proposed—monumental
civic structures in an austere classical manner. Although devoid of
channeling, the pronounced entasis
and large echinus of the Tuscan Doric
columns forming the peristyle show a
familiarity with the ancient temples
at Paestum. Above the peristyle is the
allegorical sculpture* Navigation with
Mercury and Two Rivers. [RIGHT]

397. *The Bourse. Detail.*

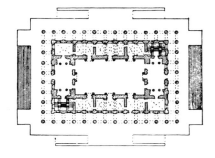

398. *The Bourse. Plan.*

west as dictated by Church tradition, parallels the Prospekt, the architect had to create a more striking resolution for the cathedral's north
facade, facing the street, than for its official main entrance, on the
west. His 'deception' is wholly satisfying—a vast curving colonnade,
anchored at the east and west ends by a portico of square pylons,
culminating in an attic frieze. With its sharply defined entablature
and balustrade, the colonnade sweeps from both ends toward the north
portico and dome, which are barely strong enough to focus the energy
released along this grand arc. In the original plan there was to be a
second colonnade on the south side, which, fortunately, was not built:
the combined strength of two colonnades would have overpowered
the cathedral.

   Although the impression the cathedral gives is of grand austerity,
Voronikhin did decorate his creation. He used the frieze and other
ornamental sculpture to embellish the building's stone facing (the
walls underneath are of brick); the Pudost stone, a limestone tufa
quarried near Petersburg, is tractable when quarried but hardens on
exposure to air and provides an ideal substance for detailed sculpting.
The exterior columns are of the same material, and various details are
rendered in granite (three different types), limestone, and marble—
heretofore only Rinaldi's Marble Palace had made such lavish use
of stone. Conceptually, Voronikhin's sole predecessor in a Roman
classical exercise of this magnitude was Bazhenov, whose designs for
the Great Kremlin Palace and, possibly, the Pashkov Mansion may
well have influenced Voronikhin.[23]

   The Kazan complex of colonnade and cathedral is one of the earliest
examples of coherent spatial planning in Petersburg (with the exception of self-contained monasteries). During the eighteenth century,
large palace ensembles had been erected along the Neva River and the
canals, but the design of the areas surrounding such monuments as
the Winter Palace had been deferred. And by the time of the cathedral's
completion, in 1811, the development of the capital's parks and squares

399. *The Bourse, Vasilevsky Island.*
Leningrad. 1805–10. Architect:
Thomas de Thomon.

400. The Admiralty. Leningrad. 1806–23. Architect: Adrian Zakharov. The greatest work of Alexandrine classicism, Zakharov's version of the Admiralty resolved the problem of horizontal repetition by applying classical orders to simple geometric forms. The simplicity of the surfaces of the Admiralty provides the ideal setting for Zakharov's large rusticated arches and high-relief sculpture. But the focus of the quarter-mile facade is, appropriately, his inspired re-creation of the 'needle' (igla) of Peter the Great's original Admiralty.

was in progress, under the direction of architects such as Zakharov (although to be interrupted by the events of 1812–14). But in its integration of architectural form and public space, Voronikhin's work remains unique in Petersburg.

Voronikhin's other large structure in Petersburg, the Mining Institute, was completed the same year as the cathedral, but the style is radically different. In 1806 he had been commissioned to unify and expand the five buildings of the Mining Institute, located on the right bank of the Neva (Vasilevsky Island). To provide a focal point for the Institute, Voronikhin devised for the main entrance a portico of twelve Greek Doric columns (channeled and without base) and the proper entablature with pediment; the columns are echoed by channeled pilasters on the interior of the portico. The effect of this grand simplicity is worthy of Quarenghi, but Voronikhin worked on a larger scale. Whereas Quarenghi used Tuscan Doric porticoes, usually of eight columns, to mark the center of long, simple facades, Voronikhin extended the dodecastyle portico almost the length of the Institute's

401. *The Admiralty. East wing pediment.*

central building. As the last of the baroque and neoclassical monuments that flank the Neva on its course to the gulf, the Mining Institute and its portico provide a splendid terminus to the city's main thoroughfare.

THOMAS DE THOMON AND ADRIAN ZAKHAROV

At the opposite end of Vasilevsky Island, its eastern point (*strelka*), stands another monument illustrative of early Alexandrine neoclassicism in its Greek form—the Bourse, or Stock Exchange (1805–10). Its architect, the French émigré Thomas de Thomon, received his education in Paris (where he studied with Claude-Nicolas Ledoux), settled in Petersburg in 1790, and remained there until his death, in 1813. The Bourse, the most important of his works to have survived, had been begun in 1783 according to plans by Quarenghi; but at the beginning of Alexander's reign, Quarenghi's uncompleted building was razed and de Thomon received the commission to design a new structure. (The reason for this drastic change may have been Adrian Zakharov's comprehensive plan for the tip of Vasilevsky Island, a plan that envisioned a more severely classical structure than Quarenghi's.)

De Thomon's Bourse displays his familiarity with the temples at Paestum: its Doric peristyle rises above a granite base and encloses a simply articulated building, at each end of which, above the entablature, stands allegorical statuary representing maritime commerce. In its archaic plainness, the Bourse embodies one of the most rigorous exercises in Hellenistic neoclassicism; it is admirably conceived to dominate the tip of Petersburg's largest island. To emphasize this strategic point, de Thomon erected two rostral columns in front of the Bourse, with allegorical figures personifying Russia's major rivers. In addition to their decorative function, the columns were to serve as

402. *The Admiralty. Main entrance.*

403. *The Admiralty. Leningrad.*
1806–23. Architect: Adrian Zakharov.
[OPPOSITE]

404. *The Admiralty. Pediment detail.*
[ABOVE]

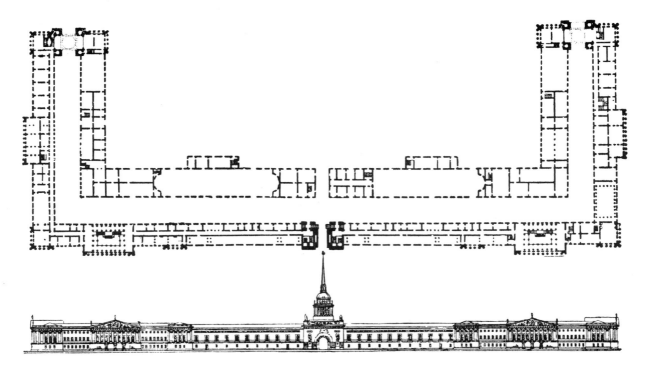

405. *The Admiralty. Plan.*

beacons, and on national holidays they are still lit, casting a theatrical light on de Thomon's temple of commerce.

By the time de Thomon had completed the Bourse, in 1810, Adrian Zakharov, on the opposite bank of the Neva, was well into a much larger project: the third version of the Admiralty. First built by Peter the Great and then rebuilt, in the 1730s, by Ivan Korobov, the Admiralty was addressed a third time only after the emperor's advisers had debated the wisdom of leaving this utilitarian structure (which included a shipworks) in the center of the capital. Indeed, following a fire in 1783 there had been plans to move the Admiralty to the fleet base at Kronstadt on the Gulf of Finland, but nothing was done. By 1806 Zakharov's plans for rebuilding the Admiralty had been approved, and although he died (in 1811) before the completion of construction— 1823—no significant changes were made in his design. (Later, however, a third row of windows replaced the plaster frieze that had originally run along the upper part of the facade.)

Born in 1761 to the family of a minor Admiralty official, Zakharov attended the Petersburg Academy of Arts, and after graduation, in 1782, he studied in Paris for four years under the direction of Jean François Thérèse Chalgrin, creator of the Arc de Triomphe. During this period Zakharov traveled extensively in Italy, where he gained a thorough understanding of Roman classicism. Although appointed in 1787 to the faculty of the Petersburg Academy—where he became a senior professor of architecture—Zakharov soon devoted more of his attention to the practice of architecture. His plan for the tip of Vasilevsky Island provided a setting for the work of de Thomon and subsequent architects, and although few of his projects were actually built, his reputation in European architecture was secured by his design for the Admiralty.

In rebuilding Korobov's partially destroyed structure, Zakharov had to contend with a facade a quarter of a mile in length and two wings, each of which was almost half that long. Located on the Neva River, the complex consists of two pi-shaped buildings, one within the other, which were originally separated by a narrow canal; the inner building served the Admiralty dockyard, which it enclosed on three sides, while the outer contained administrative offices. The center of the main facade is anchored by a tower and spire, which envelop Korobov's original tower (see front end leaf), and contains an arch, flanked by statues of nymphs supporting the globe (sculptor: Feodosy Shchedrin). The attic frieze portrays Neptune handing Peter the Great the trident, symbol of power over the seas; above the attic are statues of Alexander the Great, Ajax, Achilles, and Pyrrhus. The base of the spire rests on an Ionic peristyle, whose cornice supports twenty-eight allegorical and mythological statues representing the seasons, the elements, the winds, and so forth. Not since the twelfth-century Cathedral of Saint Dmitry in Vladimir had architecture and sculpture combined so richly to proclaim temporal power and divine protection.

Zakharov understood the virtues of simplicity: on either side of the tower a rusticated ground floor defines the base of the main facade, above which are two rows of simply articulated windows. At each end

406. *The Admiralty. West end block. Zakharov's neoclassicism is at its most heroic here: a large pavilion with arch and rotunda, flanked by Doric columns and proper entablature.*

407. *The Yelagin Palace. Yelagin Island, Leningrad. 1818–22. Architect: Carlo Rossi. Portico, park facade. The first of Rossi's major works in Petersburg, the palace is more successful in its decorative detail than in its architectural form.*

of the facade is an 'autonomous' unit, marked in the center by a Doric portico (dodecastyle, with pediment) and flanked by projections with six Doric columns. Each of the wings has a similar Doric portico, with flanking hexastyle projections; and each culminates at the Neva in a pavilion, or end block, with a large rusticated arch flanked by Doric columns. The use of portico, pavilion, and spire, the restrained window detail, the placing of heroic sculpture on pediments and at the base of the spire produce both visual stimulation and a sense of absolute control—a sense, miraculously, of richness and simplicity.

CARLO ROSSI

With the completion of the Bourse, the Admiralty, and the Kazan Cathedral, Petersburg had acquired foci around which its landscape could be organized. The Bourse defined the tip of Vasilevsky Island, while the Admiralty dominated not only the left bank of the Neva but also the three major arteries radiating from its tower and spire into the interior of the city. The final development of a coherent design linking and complementing the city's monuments occurred under the direction of Carlo Rossi (1777–1849), the last of Alexander's 'immortals,' an architect and urban planner of genius. He created or redesigned no fewer than thirteen squares and twelve streets in the central part of Petersburg, and as an architect he is responsible for four major ensembles, each of which forms an essential link in his grand design.[24]

Rossi was born to an Italian ballerina who had settled in Pavlovsk— a fortunate choice for Rossi's architectural education. His youth was spent in apprenticeship to Vincenzo Brenna, who was employed for the last decades of the eighteenth century in the decoration of the imperial palace at Pavlovsk. By 1796 Rossi was named Brenna's assistant, and he presumably participated in Brenna's work on Cameron's palace at

408. *The General Staff Building and Arch. Palace Square, Leningrad. 1819–29. Architect: Carlo Rossi. The Roman design of the arch owes more than a passing debt to the main entrance of Zakharov's Admiralty.*

409. *Palace Square, with the General Staff Building and the Alexander Column. Designed by the French architect Auguste Ricard Montferrand, in 1830–34, the Alexander Column (commemorating the victory over Napoleon) was another of Petersburg's impressive engineering achievements. But like Montferrand's Saint Isaac Cathedral, it is irremediably graceless.*

Pavlovsk, on Rinaldi's palace at Gatchina, and at the Mikhailovsky Castle in Petersburg. In 1802 Brenna and Rossi left for a three-year sojourn in Europe (Florence, Rome, Paris). It is clear from Rossi's writings and, more important, from his designs that the architecture of Rome produced a deep effect on him. In a note attached to his early, gargantuan plan for an Admiralty quay, he wrote: 'Why should we fear to be compared with them [the Romans] in magnificence? By this work one should mean not a surfeit of decoration, but grandeur of form, nobility of proportions, and indestructibility.'[25]

From 1806 to 1814 Rossi worked primarily in Moscow and in the provincial city of Tver, but on returning to Petersburg after the war of 1812–14, he rapidly assumed a position of authority in the design and implementation of Alexander's general plan for the city. A thorough examination of Rossi's projects would be too extensive for this survey, for he worked not only as an architect but also as the interior designer of numerous palaces, including the Gallery of 1812 in the Winter Palace (1826). In Petersburg his first major project as an architect and designer of parks was a palace ensemble (1818) on Yelagin Island for the mother of Alexander I. The order of the palace is Corinthian, and its main portico bears some resemblance to that of Cameron's palace at Pavlovsk.

Rossi's work on the plan of the city begins with the Mikhailovsky Palace (1819–25), built for Alexander's brother Mikhail and not to be confused with Bazhenov and Brenna's Mikhailovsky Castle. The facade is in Rossi's opulent Roman style: a rusticated ground floor, supporting a portico and attached columns—all in the Corinthian order. The upper part of the facade displays a frieze, and the entire structure is capped with a balustrade. Two wings flank the main courtyard. To provide a proper setting for the palace, Rossi designed a square (now Pushkin Square) for the area in front of the palace, and either built or specified the style for the buildings on the square, as well as those along the street leading from the palace to Nevsky Prospekt.

Concurrently with the construction of the Mikhailovsky Palace, Rossi undertook a far greater project, in terms of both size and conceptual daring. The area between the south facade of the Winter Palace and the Moika Canal had been partially developed, but no comprehensive plan for the space had yet been implemented. Rossi's task consisted of two parts: to construct an administrative complex for the General Staff and the Ministry of Finance and, in so doing, to create an appropriately imposing square for the Winter Palace. His ingenious solution called for the General Staff Building to take the form of a large arc facing the palace and dominated at its center by a triumphal arch, surmounted by a chariot of victory. The plain facade—devoid of decoration except for a cornice frieze, a balustrade, and columns on either side of the arch—forms the perfect complement to the baroque panoply of Rastrelli's Winter Palace. The color scheme for this and Rossi's other monuments was to be light gray with white trim, but

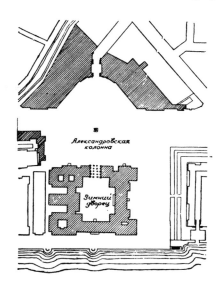

410. *General Staff Building (top), with Palace Square and Winter Palace. Plan.*

411. *The Senate and Holy Synod. Square of the Decembrists (formerly Senate Square), Leningrad. 1829–34. Architect: Carlo Rossi. Rossi's last monumental ensemble, facing Zakharov's Admiralty and Falconet's* The Bronze Horseman. [LEFT]

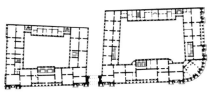

412. *The Senate and Holy Synod. Plan.*

413. *The Mikhailovsky Palace. Leningrad. 1819–23. Architect: Carlo Rossi.*
[ABOVE]

414. *Alexandrine Theater. Leningrad. 1828–32. Architect: Carlo Rossi.*
[OPPOSITE]

later generations have preferred more assertive tones: yellow with white trim, and the metallic sculpture painted black.

In his design for the General Staff Building and the Palace Square, Rossi not only created a magnificent ensemble, but also linked it to the surrounding area, most notably by the triumphal-arch passageway leading from the square to the Nevsky Prospekt. The passageway consists of a series of three arches, the first two of which are located on an axis with the main entrance to the Winter Palace, while the last follows the turn of the passage toward the Prospekt. The light that enters the spaces between the arches enhances the perception of depth and illuminates the decorative detail of this grand procession toward the city's main square.

The concepts of spatial and architectural planning illustrated at the General Staff Building were applied with similar éclat to Rossi's theater and administrative complex extending from Nevsky Prospekt to the Fontanka Canal. The Alexandrine Theater, center of the project, is connected to Nevsky Prospekt by a square, flanked by Rossi's Public Library and his pavilions for the garden of the Anichkov Palace. The rear facade of the theater is no less monumental than the front, and it is more effectively framed—the narrow corridor-street, formed by two long facades with paired Doric columns (the Ministry of Education and the Theater Directorate), leads from the theater to another square on the Fontanka. Dramatic perspective, so frequently a part of the Petersburg cityscape, here achieves a hypnotic effect, drawing the viewer toward the theater.

Rossi did not supervise the construction of his last monuments, the Senate and the Holy Synod (1829–34), and a certain clumsiness in detail, particularly in the statuary, shows the lack of the master's hand. His general plan, however, was realized in the creation of yet another large square, between the west facade of the Admiralty and his own Senate and Synod. Étienne Falconet's statue of Peter the Great is admirably displayed in this setting.

By 1832 Rossi had been relieved of his role as director of the city's construction; having done so much to create the architectural symbols of imperial pomp, he had little patience with imperial pomposity, and on at least two occasions in 1831 was sternly reprimanded (once by Nicholas I) for his 'crude and offensive expressions.' One of the most highly paid architects in Petersburg, he was generous to a fault—and scrupulous about the 60,000,000 rubles entrusted to his projects—and died, in 1849, in poverty. The minors among his ten children (by two marriages) were eventually granted state pensions.

The Imperial Legacy: Transition and Preservation

Petersburg neoclassicism did not end with Rossi's departure, in 1832, from an active role in the city's planning. Architects such as Rossi's contemporary Vasily Stasov (1769–1848) complemented the great ensembles with neoclassical monuments, for both elevated and prosaic purposes. Stasov built not only two large cathedrals that combined

415. *The Cathedral of the Transfiguration of the Savior. Leningrad. 1827–29. Architect: Vasily Stasov. The Transfiguration (Preobrazhensky) served as the church of Russia's oldest Guards Regiment. After a fire had gutted the original, baroque church on this site (architects: Mikhail Zemtsov and Pietro Trezzini, 1743–54), Stasov incorporated the walls into his neoclassical cathedral. In both versions the plan was derived from the traditional Russian cross-domed model.*

the cross-inscribed form with neoclassical articulation—the Cathedral of the Transfiguration of the Savior (1827–29) and Trinity Cathedral (1828–35)—but also various warehouses, whose simple detail possesses more nobility than many of the pretentious structures of the period. Unfortunately, Stasov did not always maintain this high level: it was he who rebuilt the Church of the Tithe in a graceless pseudo-Byzantine style, and in so doing destroyed the remnants of Kiev's first major church.

The turn toward eclecticism was already discernible in the last of Petersburg's great monuments, Auguste Ricard Montferrand's Cathedral of Saint Isaac of Dalmatia (1818–58). Originally constructed on the left bank of the Neva, in 1710, the church was rebuilt by Mattarnovy in 1717, and then again by Rinaldi, who moved its location inland, behind the newly created Peter Square (later Senate Square). Rinaldi's project, begun in 1768, was never completed to his specifications; Brenna hastily finished the church at the beginning of the nineteenth century. Alexander I decided to rebuild the entire structure on a grander scale—this was to be his cathedral, as the Kazan Cathedral had been Paul's—and in 1818 the project was entrusted to Montferrand, a young Parisian draftsman who had arrived in the capital in 1816. Montferrand's plan bore some resemblance to the large-domed Roman design of the

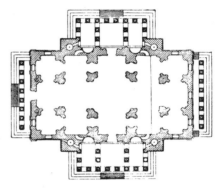

416. *The Cathedral of Saint Isaac of Dalmatia. Leningrad. 1818–58. Architect: Auguste Ricard Montferrand. This ponderous mass, constructed at enormous cost, signaled the end of the creativity that had imbued imperial architecture. No expense was spared in obtaining materials (the forty-eight monolithic columns of red Finnish granite each weigh 110 tons), but the architect, hindered by Nicholas I's interference, proved incapable of anything beyond pallid eclecticism. Nevertheless, the dome has become an indispensable part of the Petersburg landscape.* [LEFT]

417. *Cathedral of Saint Isaac. Plan.*

Kazan Cathedral, but over the forty years of construction, numerous modifications subverted whatever stylistic unity had once existed.

Montferrand's lack of experience soon showed in a number of structural defects, which led in the early 1820s to a revision of the project by an architectural commission that included Rossi and Stasov. In 1825 construction resumed; by 1830 the forty-eight monolithic granite columns (each weighing 100 tons) were in place on the porticoes; and in 1838 the iron cupola—seventy-one feet in diameter—was placed over the drum. Although the building was completed in 1842, work continued until 1858 on the interior, which is one of the most grandiose in the history of Russian architecture. No expense was spared: the walls, faced in gray marble on the exterior, on the interior were decorated with lapis lazuli, porphyry, malachite, and various sorts of marble; bronze and gilt work, mosaics, paintings, and sculpture supplemented the expensive stone. The effect is oppressive and tasteless, and the detail (such as the corner statuary on the exterior) seems inconsequential against the mass of columns and dome. Unlike Voronikhin, Montferrand was incapable of a coherent plan for so large a structure. No amount of technological ingenuity or assistance by other architects could overcome this deficiency.

The larger problem, however, lay not with any one architect, but with the loss of the eighteenth-century principles of clarity and reason, based on the forms of classical architecture. By the latter part of the 1830s, institutions such as Moscow's Court Architectural School were offering courses in Byzantine, Gothic, Renaissance, and other styles, although the Petersburg Academy of Arts attempted, with little effect,

418. *Church of the Resurrection. Griboedov (formerly Catherine) Canal, Leningrad. Architects: Ivan Makarov and Alfred Parland. 1886–1907. Moscow revival style, built on the site of Alexander II's assassination.* [OPPOSITE]

419. *The Hermitage Arch and Winter Canal. Leningrad. The arch is attached to Quarenghi's Hermitage Theater.*

to perpetuate neoclassicism. Tellingly, with the rise of eclecticism, Moscow—not Petersburg—became Russia's dominant architectural center, with its plethora of styles from five centuries.

In both cities the pressures of economic expansion and speculative building, caused by laws encouraging the formation of private capital, led to architectural chaos, but Petersburg, with its carefully planned ensembles, was particularly vulnerable. (The despoiling of the Admiralty courtyard with two large commercial buildings is a prime, but by no means unique, example of the expansionist menace.) As Dostoevsky noted in 1873: '. . . In truth, one does not know how to define our present architecture: here we have something nondescript which, however, is in full accord with all the nondescript things of the present moment.'[26] Although no architectural historian, the great writer and chronicler of Petersburg understood that beneath changes in architectural taste lay social changes, linked to the decline of the nobility and Russia's fitful progress toward capitalism. Preoccupied with social reforms, Alexander II, along with his less reform-minded successors, had little concept of comprehensive architectural planning, and was content to let nobleman and speculator alike build according to the latest fad, unhampered by zoning and other controls.[27]

The record of this urban transformation is clear, for few cities have been more exhaustively portrayed than Saint Petersburg. In surveying these depictions, one contrasts the elegant eighteenth-century drawings of Mikhail Makhaev and watercolors of Vasily Sadovnikov—views that display the ordered intent—with photographs of Nevsky Prospekt from about 1900, which show facades defaced by a jumble of advertising in both Latin and Cyrillic letters.[28] Present-day Nevsky Prospekt, with its neo-Romanesque, neo-Egyptian structures (banks and other buildings from just before the First World War), provides further evi-

420. The Moika Canal. Leningrad.

dence of the modern disfigurement of the city. The Singer Sewing Machine Building even managed to exceed the classical height restrictions with an advertising dome, although the building itself is a tolerable mixture of Louis Sullivan and art nouveau.

There was, to be sure, a preservationist movement from about 1900 to 1915, a movement stimulated in part by the city's bicentennial, but more significantly by a general revival in the arts and architecture. Nevertheless, the attractive guidebooks published at that time did little to stop the decay they described and illustrated. Only in the 1920s did the efforts of preservationists result in planning policy that recognized the city's architecture as part of a precious national heritage. Although there have been violations of that policy, no city has been more rigorously safeguarded on so extensive a scale: within the large industrial metropolis, the entire historic core is protected. Deprived of the imperial power that conceived and sustained the design—and then presided over its deformation—Leningrad has become in a very real sense an architectural museum. It is appropriate that this city, so purposefully created, at such great cost, should be jealously maintained; at its best the architecture of Saint Petersburg speaks of ideals whose order, clarity, and beauty transcend the boundaries of nations.

421. *Apartment house for the People's Commissariat of Finance. Moscow. 1928–30. Architects: Moisey Ginzburg and I. F. Milinis. Front facade.*

6. TWENTIETH CENTURY RUSSIAN ARCHITECTURE

REVOLUTION AND REGRESSION

Our new architecture does not just attempt to complete something that has been temporarily interrupted. . . . Its task is to comprehend the new conditions of life, so that by the creation of responsive building design it can actively participate in the full realization of the new world.

—EL LISSITZKY, *Russia: Architecture for a World Revolution* (1930)[1]

One of the most persistent themes in the frequent, and frequently strident, cultural pronouncements in Russia at the end of the nineteenth century concerned the sterility of old forms and the need to create a new artistic sensibility. In whatever area of the arts, the message was essentially the same, and architecture provided no exception. Indeed, by its drift into various forms of eclecticism or historicism, architecture was particularly vulnerable to the charge of aimlessness and confusion so pointedly noted by Dostoevsky as early as the 1870s. Echoing Dostoevsky, critics in the 1890s saw in the chaos of architectural styles the reflection of a greater social and cultural malaise, the product, as one architect put it, of 'the very fabric of contemporary life, in which we sense the lack of a unifying idea.'[2]

Russian intellectuals of the nineteenth century seemed to have a predilection for sweeping syntheses of social, moral, and æsthetic issues, and the preceding statement by the chairman of the Moscow Architectural Society (K. M. Bykovsky) might appear broad in its explanation of the vagaries of architectural fashion. This is, however, only one of many statements of a similar nature, issued by architects at the conferences that had become an integral part of their profession in the 1890s. (The professional organization of architects in Russia occurred in the latter part of the nineteenth century: the Moscow Society of Architects was founded in 1867, and the Petersburg society in 1871. The first general architectural conferences were held in 1892 and 1895.)

The opinions expressed at these meetings were not new. In the 1860s, historicism had been scathingly attacked as 'architecture from the shelf' by the art critic Vladimir Stasov. But despite his admiration of Joseph Paxton's Crystal Palace, as a harbinger of a new architectural era, Stasov foundered on his own attempt to resurrect a Russian national architecture, which contained many of the elements he decried in historicism.

STYLE MODERNE

The first cogent response to the pretentiousness of historicism, to the division between the facade as the architect's prerogative and the structure as the engineer's, emanated from the work of William Morris in England. In the 1870s his theories of integral design—not only in the structure of the building but also in its furnishings—transcended the concerns of architecture in a narrow sense and embraced social issues such as the democratization of art and the revival of craftsmanship in an age of machines. During the last decades of the century Richard Norman Shaw, Charles Voysey, and Charles Mackintosh created a style that freely interpreted Gothic motifs without the clutter of historicist decoration. In both architecture and design, the work of these architects served as a stimulus to the development of art nouveau in Russia, where a revival of interest in folk crafts and their reinterpretation by contemporary artists not only paralleled but also was influenced by the Arts and Crafts movement in Britain. In the late 1870s and '80s, Savva Mamontov, a railroad magnate, converted his Moscow country estate at Abramtsevo into a center for the study of folk art and a retreat for a group of artists who wished to incorporate folk motifs into their work. Other such enclaves existed—in Finland as well as in Russia—but the Abramtsevo colony sponsored the widest range of activities. Commissioned by Mamontov, the artist Viktor Vasnetsov designed and supervised the construction of the Abramtsevo estate church (1880–82), modeled on the architectural forms of medieval Pskov. The calculated simplicity of the church and its lapidary structure—so different from the historicist architecture of the period—signaled the development of a Russian equivalent of art nouveau.

In Russia, as in Europe, the new style (known in Russia as *style moderne*) drew on a mixture of medieval and folk motifs, for architectural decoration as well as for the design of accessories such as furniture. But the ambience was as much international as Russian. By the turn of the century, the lavishly illustrated journal *The World of Art* (Mir iskusstva, 1898–1904) informed its readers of the latest developments in the various branches of art nouveau, and included photographs of the interior and exterior of works by architects such as Mackintosh and the Austrian Joseph Maria Olbrich, both of whom had visited Moscow in 1903 for a major art-nouveau exhibit. It must be admitted that the numerous Russian examples of *style moderne* demonstrated little of the rigor characteristic of Mackintosh's work (such as the Glasgow School of Art) or that of Otto Wagner in Vienna. Many Russian practitioners of the style were content to transplant the curvilinear, botanical motifs from continental art nouveau to the facades of office buildings and apartment blocks in Moscow and Petersburg.[3]

Despite the occasional exercise in triviality, *style moderne* introduced to Russia a form of rationalism resembling, and to a large extent
derived from, the Vienna Sezession. Otto Wagner's equation of practicality and beauty established an æsthetic usually associated with the
Jugendstil in Germany and Austria, but equally applicable to the
architecture of Petersburg and Moscow at the turn of the century.
An emphasis on the functional and æsthetic properties of modern
building materials such as reinforced concrete, plate glass, and steel
complemented a concept of design employing the latest advances in
lighting, sanitation, and the arrangement of apartment and office space
to meet new standards of comfort. An increase in window size admitted
more light, and permitted a greater unobstructed view, while corridor
space within apartments decreased in an attempt to achieve a more
convenient, rational grouping of rooms. The concern for design from
within and the lessening importance of the exterior wall as the domi-

422. *The Levenson Press. Moscow.
1900. Architect: Fyodor Shekhtel.*
[LEFT]

423. *The Levenson Press. Corner
detail.*

nant architectonic feature anticipated developments in constructivist architecture of the 1920s. The molded contours and exaggerated gables of so many *style moderne* buildings seem more than slightly affected, but the exotic decoration notwithstanding, the *moderne* represented a significant advance toward the creation of a rational, and attractive, urban environment.

FYODOR SHEKHTEL

Style moderne produced one major architect, Fyodor Shekhtel (1859–1926), who developed a remarkably laconic style based on the ferroconcrete structural skeleton. Shekhtel received his art education in Moscow, where he explored a number of media: commercial illustration, graphic arts, icon painting, theater-set decoration, furniture designing—and architecture. The wide range of his interests prepared Shekhtel for the new style's ideal of comprehensive design; but his earliest architectural projects and sketches, from the late seventies and eighties, were unabashedly historicist, with a heavy imprint of the Muscovite revival.

While continuing to work in a retrospective mode in the 1890s, Shekhtel made an interesting foray into the English Gothic revival with a mansion for Z. G. Morozova (1893). In contrast to earlier examples of the neo-Gothic in nineteenth-century Russia, Shekhtel's mansion avoided the heavily decorated facade in favor of a clear architectonic statement, with large, sharply etched lancet windows on a simple facade.

Shekhtel's first major exercise in *style moderne* consisted of an ensemble of pavilions for the Russian exhibit at the 1901 International Exposition in Glasgow. Built to imitate Russia's wooden churches, the pavilions demonstrated an effective combination of the national

424. *'Boyars' Court' office building. Moscow. 1901. Architect: Fyodor Shekhtel. Despite the obtrusive details of the facade, the Boyars' Court marks an important stage in the development of an open, skeletal structure in Moscow's commercial buildings. Southeast corner.*

425. *Sytin Typography on Tver (now Gorky) Street. Moscow. 1905. Architect: A. E. Erikhson. Erikhson's application of* moderne *ornament to a grid facade represents a typical combination of the decorative and the functional in early twentieth-century commercial architecture.*

style (as interpreted by such artists as Vasnetsov in his Abramtsevo church) and the contoured forms of art nouveau. It is an appropriate tribute to the international character of art nouveau that Shekhtel built in the city of Charles Mackintosh, and was honored for his work with membership in the Royal Society of Architects.[4]

In the following year he repeated the combination of nationalism and *moderne*, in more durable materials, for his Yaroslavl Railway Station in Moscow. Its curves and bulges border on the grotesque, but Shekhtel's panache sees the design through. (The interior, unfortunately, has not been preserved.) Equally flamboyant are the interiors of his mansions for S. P. Ryabushinsky (1900–02) and A. I. Derozhinskaya (1901)—both firmly in the international style of art nouveau, and both designed with careful attention to detail, from door handles to ornamental ironwork. (The Ryabushinsky house, now under repair, is open to the public as a museum dedicated to Maxim Gorky.)

These mansions reflect Shekhtel's mastery of the Vienna Sezession (cf. Olbrich), but his boldest and most innovative work occurred in the realms of commerce that underlay the fortunes of families such as the Ryabushinskys and Morozovs. Here—in department stores, office buildings, banks, and printing houses—the demands of efficiency effected a synthesis between new construction techniques and Shekhtel's sense of form and rhythm. Although his earliest commercial buildings, dating from the turn of the twentieth century, were not devoid of art-nouveau ornament, Shekhtel was among the first Russian architects to realize that a structural skeleton need not be masked by a decorated facade.

The evolution of Shekhtel's commercial design begins with his building for the A. A. Levenson printing works (1900), in which he used a Gothic variant of early *moderne*, with the large windows and grid design characteristic of a new rationalism. In fact, the Gothic part of the Levenson building is an office front for the printing works, whose considerable length is designed in the best severely functional manner.

The integration of structure and facade was exploited on a larger scale in the 'Boyars' Court' office complex (1901), whose long expanse on Old Square bears comparison with Louis Sullivan's design for the Carson Pirie Scott department store in Chicago (1899–1904). Although less streamlined than Sullivan's building (note the heavy balconies and decoration on the fifth floor), the Boyars' Court follows a similar principle of exterior segmentation, with large window space reducing the walls to little more than an outline of the reinforced-concrete skeleton. The technology employed at Boyars' Court differs little from that in Pomerantsev's Upper Trading Rows, completed a few years earlier; and yet the contrast between the two buildings is that of two eras, of two very different ways of perceiving the relation between structure and appearance.

By 1903 Shekhtel had eliminated the last vestiges of *moderne* decoration from the facades of his buildings. His bank for the Ryabushinsky brothers (1903) and a printing house for the same clients (*Utro Rossii*, 1907) display the simplest of grid patterns. The only concessions to *style moderne* are the rounded corners, glazed bricks, and, at the printing house, the curves above the window shafts and the entrance.

426. Utro Rossii *Typography. Moscow. 1907. Architect: Fyodor Shekhtel. The Ryabushinsky brothers, prominent Moscow industrialists, commissioned a number of buildings by Shekhtel, including this printing works for their newspaper. The structure is illustrative of Shekhtel's development of an austere* moderne *style. The attic windows are a later addition.*

427. *Office building of the Moscow*
Merchants' Society. Moscow. 1909.
Architect: Fyodor Shekhtel.

At the final stage of Shekhtel's functionalism—the Moscow Merchants' Society Building (1909)—the skeleton dominates completely. As in the Ryabushinsky buildings, there are subtle traces of late *moderne*: the slightly convex piers, the glazed brickwork, and the varied articulation of the top floor. But its clean lines and balanced proportions anticipate some of the best work in Moscow architecture of the 1920s.[5]

Shekhtel did not, however, choose to pursue this development. His work about 1910 became increasingly influenced by the neoclassical and medieval revivals (see the following section), and he continued to maintain his interest in theater design, leading in 1902 to his project for the interior and facade of the Moscow Art Theater (the design for the facade was not realized in its entirety). A friend of Anton Chekhov, Shekhtel built a library and museum (1910) as a memorial to the great writer in Taganrog, Chekhov's birthplace.

Although few of Shekhtel's projects were constructed after 1910, he continued to work until 1926, the year of his death. In addition to his practice as an architect, he served as president of the Moscow Architectural Society from 1908 to 1922, and between 1896 and 1926 he taught at the Stroganov Art Institute, merged after the revolution into the Higher Artistic-Technical Workshops (Vkhutemas). Appropriately for one who had done so much to create a functionalist æsthetic, Shekhtel's final project was a design (unrealized) for the great power station and dam on the Dnieper River. The project was awarded to his students, the Vesnin brothers.

428. *The Meltser House. Stone Island, Leningrad. Circa 1905. Architect: Roman Meltser. A leading proponent of the* moderne *in Petersburg, Meltser applied 'folk' motifs—more Scandinavian than Russian—in the construction of his house on one of the fashionable islands to the north of the city.*

The Twilight of Imperial Architecture: Neoclassical Revival

In the history of late-imperial architecture, Moscow unquestionably takes precedence over Petersburg: it was in Moscow that *style moderne* originated and developed in its diverse ways; and it was in Moscow that the *moderne* evolved from a decorative, eclectic style to the functionalism of Shekhtel. Nonetheless, Petersburg was not untouched by these developments. Its apartment buildings from the beginning of the twentieth century display the decorative motifs as well as the contours of *moderne*; and at least one commercial structure on Nevsky Prospekt—Pavel Syuzer's Singer Sewing Machine Building (1904)—combines the flamboyant molding of the *moderne* with an innovative skeletal construction. Examples of the folk revival style can also be found in certain mansions on the outskirts of Petersburg.

But the dominant tendency in Petersburg architecture lies in another movement, which was at once an outgrowth of and a reaction to the *moderne*. Designated the neoclassical revival, one of the many retrospective styles of the time, the movement flourished in Moscow as well as in Petersburg, and can be compared with various classicist reactions to art nouveau in Europe before the First World War. Yet in Russia the movement's origins derive in no small part from an attempt to rehabilitate the classical heritage of Petersburg, with particular emphasis on the late phase of neoclassicism (called by the revivalists 'empire').[6]

It has been noted in the preceding chapter that this heritage was in considerable danger during the latter part of the nineteenth century, both from the lack of proper zoning regulations and from a general indifference to the imperial monuments of the eighteenth and early nineteenth centuries. The public, as well as many architects, frequently dismissed neoclassicism as an uninspired, alien style. This opinion was reinforced by the poor condition of many neoclassical monuments and by the government's disregard for the architects' original color schemes (always a complex issue in Petersburg-Leningrad, but never more ineptly resolved than with the late-imperial repainting of the Winter Palace in dull red).

The reversal of these attitudes first appeared prominently in the

429. Singer Sewing Machine Building (now House of Books). Nevsky Prospekt, Leningrad. 1902–04. Architect: Pavel Syuzer. The first building in Petersburg to use the steel skeleton, with floors of reinforced concrete.

pages of *The World of Art*, the same journal that had played so important a role in the introduction of art nouveau to Russia. There, in the early 1900s, artists such as Alexander Benois and the architect Ivan Fomin not only lovingly described the neoclassical monuments of Petersburg and Moscow, but also conveyed their vision more directly in nostalgic sketches and drawings. During this period, elements of the classical order appear on the facades of commercial and apartment buildings in both cities.

Although competent architects such as Shekhtel and Ilarion Ivanov-Schitz worked in this style, most such designs involved little more than the application of classical details to structural types that had evolved under the banner of *style moderne*. Ivan Rerberg's Northern Insurance Company building, in Moscow (1910–11), is a good example of this uneasy synthesis—a *moderne* business tower capped with neoclassical urns and a rotunda. G.K. Lukomsky, one of the most vocal defenders of classical Petersburg, scathingly denounced such efforts as 'false-front architecture,' designed by mediocre builders.[7] About 1910, however, the revival passed from the stage of appreciation

430. *Yeliseev Building (now the Comedy Theater). Nevsky Prospekt, Leningrad. 1903–07. Architect: Gavriil Baranovsky. Functionalism yields to decorative display in this* moderne *structure for the Yeliseev firm—purveyors of fine foods.*

431. *Azov-Don Bank. Leningrad. 1907–09. Architect: Fyodor Lidval. One of the most prominent examples of the blending of* style moderne *and neoclassical revival in Petersburg's late-imperial commercial structures.*

and pastiche to the development of a classical theory—but without solving certain inherent problems in its modern architectural usage.

The arrival of this new phase was signaled by neoclassicist exhibits in 1910 and 1911 and by Igor Grabar's *History of Russian Art*, the third volume of which presented a lucid survey of the various late-neoclassical styles and their relation to French neoclassicism at the turn of the nineteenth century. One of the collaborators in this scholarly reappraisal, Ivan Fomin, provided a convenient case study of the achievements of the late phase of neoclassical revival. As an art critic he was thoroughly familiar with the subtleties of neoclassical design, and as an architect he was prepared to reinterpret them. In 1904 he had published an article on Moscow neoclassicism in *The World of Art*, and had recorded neoclassical monuments in Moscow in a series of sketches for postcards. He valued both the Moscow and the Petersburg variants of neoclassicism (the former being somewhat bolder and more exaggerated in its use of classical details); and his most notable work—the Polovtsov mansion, in Petersburg (1912)—derives primarily from the Moscow 'empire' style of Gilardi, Grigorev, et al.

In comparison with other examples of the neoclassical revival, Fomin's Polovtsov mansion is a model of scrupulosity in its reinterpretation of a style prevalent a century earlier. From the main portico to the furnishings and detail of the interior, the house renders homage to 'empire'; but the effect of this enumeration of neoclassical elements is of excessive condensation, a distorted echo of a lost culture.[8] Ironically, the professionalism of the best revival architects, with their art-historical knowledge, mitigated against the vigorous yet measured spirit characteristic of early nineteenth-century neoclassicism.

Other practitioners of the style, in particular Vladimir Shchuko and Ivan Zholtovsky, made a strenuous attempt to apply the classical order to large structures, such as multistoried apartment buildings. In their commercial buildings, Zholtovsky, Andrey Belogrud, and Marian

432. *Northern Insurance Company.
Moscow. 1910–11. Architect: Ivan
Rerberg. A classical rotunda graces
one of the earliest skyscrapers in
what was once Moscow's commercial
district. After the Revolution, Rerberg
continued to flourish, building the
ungainly Central Telegraph Office on
what is now Gorky Street.*

433. *Polovtsov Mansion. Stone Island, Leningrad. 1912–16. Architect: Ivan Fomin. Central portico and front court.*

Peretyatkovich also revived a neo-Renaissance style—fortress-like in appearance and heavily rusticated.

The desire to utilize neoclassical forms on the scale demanded by modern urban construction is epitomized by one of the revival's last major projects, designed by Fomin, with the assistance of Fyodor Lidval. As its name, New Petersburg, implies, this gargantuan development for Goloday Island was intended as a return to the days of large-scale monumental planning in the city. Fomin himself mentioned the inspiration of French neoclassicism in his design, and there are echoes of Rossi as well, particularly in the appearance of the project's main square. Very little of New Petersburg was completed before the First World War began, and investor interest then waned. Indeed, had Fomin been less enamored of the formal qualities of neoclassicism, he might have noticed—as did certain of his contemporaries—the oddity of applying the trappings of imperial grandeur to a middle-class housing development.[9] But he was not the last architect in this century not to do so.

While the New Petersburg project exemplified the attenuation of classical ideals in the neoclassical revival, with its application of hypertrophied forms, the influence of the revival on Russian architecture should not be underestimated. On the most immediate level, it led to a concerted effort to preserve the neoclassical heritage in Petersburg and Moscow, through such foundations as the Commission for the Study of Old Petersburg and the Society for the Defense and Preservation in Russia of Monuments of Art and Antiquity (founded in 1911). Although they accomplished little before the war, these societies provided the basis for preservation policies developed after 1917.

Concomitant with the concern for preservation was a renewal of interest in city planning as it had been practiced in the neoclassical era, and as it might once again be applied to control the rapid growth of Russia's cities. Urban-planning academic courses were established as early as 1911, and despite the war's curtailment of large projects such as New Petersburg, concepts of city planning developed during these years were to be pursued vigorously after the Revolution.[10] From 1908 to 1916, L. N. Benois fought for a comprehensive approach to the growth of Petersburg (his project for a position on the planning and construction of Petrograd, 1916), a cause taken up in 1919 by Fomin and others, who developed a 'project for the regulation of Petrograd.' In Moscow, general plans for urban growth were largely a post-Revolutionary phenomenon; but here too, their formulation was entrusted to a prominent late-imperial architect, Alexey Shchusev.

Finally, it must be noted that the architects of the neoclassical revival not only served as mentors to a number of the most talented architects of the post-Revolutionary period (the Vesnin brothers, Konstantin Melnikov, and others—all of whom had received a grounding in neoclassical architecture); they also were to find their ideas once again in favor during the 1930s. Rigid Party control of the arts, following Stalin's consolidation of power, would bring to an end the experiment in modern architecture that had flourished after the Revolution. The neoclassical revival suited Stalin's requirements for a style that was at once grandiose and conservative, and with the revival revived, architects such as Zholtovsky, Shchusev, and Fomin returned to the late-imperial styles.

Nor was the return limited to neoclassicism. Retrospectivism in the decade preceding the First World War had also included yet another phase of the Russian medieval revival, on a scale unknown to the Mamontov circle. Secular buildings as well as churches emulated various medieval models—often with astonishing precision—as part

434. *Rozenshteyn apartment building. Leningrad. 1913–17. Architect: Andrey Belogrud. Built in imitation of a medieval English castle, the Rozenshteyn house typifies the elaborate retrospective design of Petersburg's last luxurious apartment buildings.*

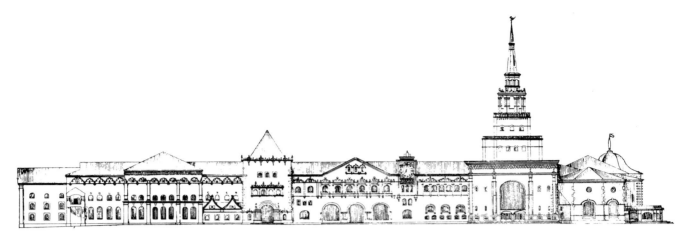

*435. Kazan Railway Station.
Moscow. 1914–40. Architect: Alexey
Shchusev. Elevation.*

of a movement associated with the Romanov tercentenary celebrations of 1913. When Stalin wished to rekindle the spirit of Russian nationalism, he had at his disposal Shchusev, whose Kazan Railway Station was designed in 1911 in a medieval Muscovite stylization, begun in 1914, and eventually completed in 1940—with no substantial change in appearance.

In summary, the most striking characteristic of late-imperial architecture is its diversity of styles and ideologies, from Shekhtel to Shchusev, from retrospectivist to rationalist. And while the retrospective might seem to have predominated, it by no means excluded innovative and progressive approaches to building and urban planning. At the last pre-Revolutionary Congress of Russian Architects (Moscow, 1913), the papers presented included 'Ferro-concrete Architecture,' 'The Construction of Skyscrapers in New York,' 'The Question of Urban Planning,' and 'Cooperative Building Ventures': a forward-looking agenda. While Petersburg built its New Petersburgs, Moscow flirted with the skyscraper, spoke of American tempos of construction in 'Moscow-City,' and pursued visions of Chicago.[11]

The Reconstruction of Russian Architecture

'October 1917 marked the beginning of the Russian Revolution and the opening of a new page in the history of human society. It is to this social revolution, rather than to the technological revolution, that the basic elements of Russian architecture are tied.'[12] In 1930, when this passage appeared in El Lissitzky's essay *Russland: Die Rekonstrucktion der Architecktur in der Sowjetunion* (the English title is *Russia: Architecture for a World Revolution*), little remained of the foment that had motivated the radical experiment in Russian architecture in the 1920s. With an irony no doubt unintended, Lissitzky had stated a truth that would acquire a new dimension in the Stalinist era, as the Communist Party erected its monuments with little concern for the technological revolution and still less for the innovative and pluralistic spirit of the preceding decade. But for the fifteen or so years of its existence, the great post-Revolutionary experiment in its many manifestations endeavored to alter conceptions of architectural space, to create an environment that would inculcate new social values, and at the same time to utilize the most advanced structural and technological principles.

The assumption that a revolution in architecture (along with the other arts) would inevitably accompany a political revolution was soon put to the test by social and economic realities. Russia's rapidly developing industrial base lay in a shambles after a war, a revolution, and a civil war; technological resources were extremely limited in what was still a predominantly rural nation; and Moscow's population—poorly housed before the war—increased dramatically as the city became the administrative center of a thoroughly administered state.

To be sure, the pre-Revolutionary building boom had established a viable foundation, in both architectural theory and practice, for urban development on a large scale. Russian architecture was little affected by the emigration that decimated certain other areas of Russian culture after the Revolution (what architect would leave what promised to be the greatest building site in history?). And the most prominent art and architectural schools in Moscow and Petrograd were capable of providing a base for the development of new cadres, despite sometimes sweeping changes in the composition of the faculty. Nonetheless, the task of resuscitating these institutions, of allocating resources for new construction, and of devising a plan for coordinating further development could only have been Herculean.

Paradoxically, the poverty and social chaos seemed to encourage the most radical architectural ideas, many of which were related to an already thriving modernist movement in the visual arts. For example, Lissitzky's ideas on space and form, along with those of Kazimir Malevich and Vladimir Tatlin, played a major part in the development of an architecture expressed in 'stereometric forms,' purified of the decorative elements of the eclectic past. The radical experiments of Lissitzky, Wassily Kandinsky, and Malevich in painting and of Tatlin and Alexander Rodchenko in sculpture had created the possibility of a new architectural movement, defined by Lissitzky as a synthesis with painting and sculpture.[13]

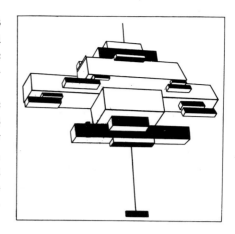

436. Future 'Planits' [habitats] for Earthlings. *Artist: Kazimir Malevich. Suprematist architecture of pure forms.*

A New Rationalism

Within the diversity of architectural schools and alliances in the immediate post-Revolutionary period, one Moscow institution was preeminent as a gathering ground for architects and artists dedicated to innovation. Called Vkhutemas (the Russian acronym for Higher Artistic and Technical Workshops), the organization was formed from the merger, in 1918, of two pre-Revolutionary art schools: the Stroganov School, founded in 1825 by Count Sergey Stroganov and including Shekhtel on its faculty, and the Moscow School of Painting, Sculpture, and Architecture. Originally known simply as the Free Workshops, the new entity was given its elevated name when it was reorganized in 1920. In 1925 it was reorganized yet again, this time to be called the Higher Artistic and Technical Institute (Vkhutein). Vkhutemas-Vkhutein was by no means the only Moscow institution concerned with the teaching and practice of architecture in the 1920s, but it was unique in the scope of its concerns (which included the visual and the applied arts) as well as in the variety of programs and viewpoints that existed there before its closing, in 1930.

Theoretical direction for Vkhutemas was provided by the Institute of Artistic Culture (Inkhuk, also founded in 1920), which attempted to establish a science 'examining analytically and synthetically the basic elements both for the separate arts and for art as a whole.'[14] Its first program-curriculum, developed by Kandinsky, was found too abstract by many at Inkhuk, and Kandinsky soon left for Germany and the Bauhaus. But the concern with abstract, theoretical principles was not abated by Kandinsky's departure. Indeed, the issue of theory versus construction became a major source of factional dispute in Russian modernism.

In the early 1920s a group of faculty members at the Higher Workshops established the Working Group at Inkhuk, and began to exhibit architectural sketches, both in Russia and in Germany (for example, in Berlin in 1922). In 1923 the nucleus of the group—which included Nikolay Ladovsky, V. Krinsky, N. Dokuchaev, and for a time Lissitzky—formed the Association of New Architects (Asnova), an organization devoted to the 'establishment of general principles in architecture and its liberation from atrophied forms.'[15] Its members called themselves rationalists, a term signifying the study of basic geometric principles, their development in space, and the psychological bases of perception of architectural forms. The pedagogical and theoretical programs developed by Ladovsky and his colleagues were closely related to the work of Lissitzky and Malevich, whose abstract architectonic models represented the ultimate refinement in 'pure' spatial forms—Suprematism, as Malevich called it.[16]

Both Malevich and Lissitzky were actively involved in another organization propagating the ideas of a new architecture. Known as the Affirmers of New Art (Unovis), the group originated in Vitebsk under the direction of Malevich; and three years after its founding, in 1919, most of the members moved with Malevich to the Petrograd Institute of Artistic Culture, where they combined forces with the artists Tatlin and Nikolay Punin. There were branches of the Affirmers in several Russian cities, Moscow included, and doubtless the staff at Inkhuk was familiar with the objectives of Unovis, which sought 'the optimal harmony of the simplest geometric forms.' The Unovis curriculum began with 'the study of color, and of the principles of contemporary movements in art, beginning with Cézanne and concluding with Suprematism; then a transition to the study of the properties of various materials; and only afterwards, concentrated work on specific projects.'[17]

The pedagogical program developed by Ladovsky, Dokuchaev, and others was not accepted without protest by many architects (including Alexander Vesnin), who considered the Asnova approach pseudo-

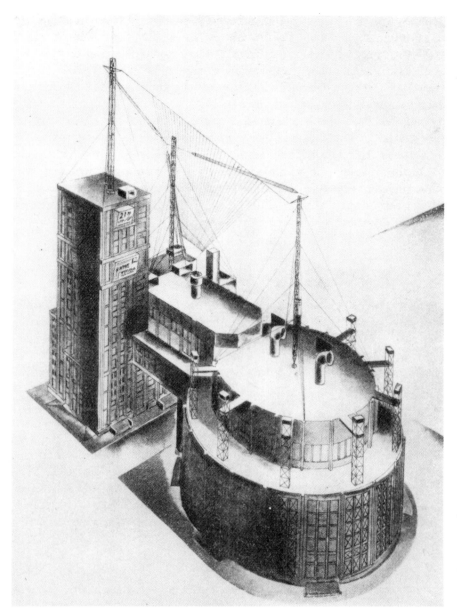

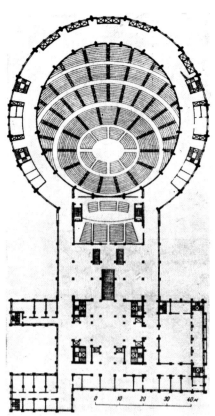

437. *Project for the Palace of Labor in Moscow. Circa 1922. Architects: Alexander, Viktor, and Leonid Vesnin. Although the project was awarded only third prize, it is a landmark in the development of a constructivist æsthetic, combining both monumentality and severe functionalism in its massing of simple geometric shapes. Plan, sketch from M. A. Ilin,* Vesniny.

scientific and excessively abstract. As early as 1922, Zholtovsky, commissioned to assess the Ladovsky group, found many of their views untenable, but suggested that they be allowed to function as a studio, 'in view of their sincerity and passion.'[18] Such was the tolerance of the twenties. For much of that decade, Ladovsky, Dokuchaev, and other members of Asnova focused largely on æsthetic principles of architectural shapes that were designed to produce the ideal physical and psychological environment.

In terms of actual construction, the Asnova group produced little: Dokuchaev, in his article 'Contemporary Russian Architecture and Western Parallels' (1926), complained of bias in the award of projects by juries hostile to Asnova, and spoke of a 'blockade'; but by the end of the twenties, Asnova architects participated actively in architectural competition. In 1928 Ladovsky and his closest followers seceded from the association to found the Association of Architects-Urbanists, with a concentration on urban planning; and in 1932 Asnova was absorbed, along with other architectural groups, into the Union of Soviet Architects.[19] It would be a mistake to consider the Association excessively concerned with abstruse theoretical problems at the expense of architectural practice, for many of the designs from its studies were far-sighted and might have been quite practical, had the Soviet Union possessed the necessary technology and materials. (Cf. the Ladovsky studio's design for a skyscraper, several years in advance of Howe and Lescaze's Philadelphia Saving Fund building [1932], one of the first International Modern skyscrapers.)

Constructivism

Most of the projects realized during this period belong to a group of architects known as the constructivists (or functionalists). For all of the heat generated by polemics between the rationalists and constructivists, their origins and their goals had much in common. Like the rationalists, the constructivists drew inspiration from modernism in painting and sculpture—particularly the latter. In 1920, the year of genesis for so much in Russian modernism, Naum Gabo and Anton Pevsner released their 'Realistic Manifesto,' with its praise of kinetic rhythms and negation of outmoded concepts of volume; and in 1921 Alexander Rodchenko stated that 'construction is the contemporary demand for organization and the utilitarian application of materials.'[20] The works of these artists, and of Malevich, Lissitzky, and Tatlin (in particular, Tatlin's project for a monument to the Third International, 1919–20), served notice of a new movement—one that glorified the dynamic and the material, and that intended to participate fully in the shaping of Soviet society.

In the early twenties, the evolution of constructivist ideas at Inkhuk passed through a number of polemical phases (the term *constructivism* was still broadly interpreted and had not yet acquired the 'functionalist' architectural emphasis of the mid-twenties). The pure-art faction, influenced by Kandinsky, was opposed by the 'productionists'—associated with Left Front of the Arts—who anticipated an age of engineers supervising the mass production of useful, nonartistic objects. A reaction to both sides, particularly the former, led in 1921 to the formation of a group of artists-constructivists: Alexander Vesnin, architect; Alexey Gan, art critic and propagandist; Rodchenko, sculptor and photographer; V. and G. Sternberg, poster designers; and Varvara Stepanova, set designer. Never in Russia had there been such a comprehensive bringing together of the arts.

And never had Russian artists gained such a receptive audience in Western Europe. Lissitzky, who spent much of the twenties in Germany but maintained contacts in the Soviet Union, served admirably as a propagandist for the movement. During that decade many Russian artists active at Vkhutemas and Inkhuk visited the West (Kandinsky, Malevich, Gabo, Pevsner), while a number of Western architects visited, and in some cases worked in, the Soviet Union (Bruno Taut, Ernst May, Erich Mendelsohn, Le Corbusier). Exhibitions of modernist Soviet art were held in various German cities, in Holland, in Paris, Venice, and New York; and Western architectural journals such as *L'esprit nouveau* and *De Stijl* wrote of constructivism and of the latest developments in Russian architecture. The Soviets reciprocated: ties between Inkhuk and the Bauhaus were particularly close, and at exhibits in Moscow during the middle and late twenties, Russian architects could see the work of their counterparts in Germany (Mendelsohn, Max Berg, Walter Gropius, Mies van der Rohe), Holland (Gerrit Rietveld, J. J. P. Oud), and France (Le Corbusier).[21]

Until 1925 the constructivists had little more to show in actual

438. Izvestiya *Building. Moscow. 1927. Architects: Grigory and Mikhail Barkhin.*

construction than their more theoretically minded colleagues, the rationalists. The exigencies of social and economic reconstruction drastically limited the resources available, particularly for structures requiring a relatively intensive use of modern technology. In fact, the most advanced of constructivist works in the early twenties are of wood: Konstantin Melnikov's Makhorka Pavilion at the All-Union Agricultural Exhibition (1923), and the constructivist set designs by Alexander Vesnin, Stepanova, and Lyudmila Popova. Yet by 1924, constructivist architects, whatever their tangible achievements, had acquired vigorous leadership in the persons of Alexander Vesnin and Moisey Ginzburg, the latter of whom proved to be an articulate and combative spokesman in polemics with Asnova. In 1924 Ginzburg's programmatic book *Style and the Epoch* appeared in print; the following year, constructivists founded the Union of Contemporary Architects (OSA); and in 1926 the Union began publishing the journal *Contemporary Architecture*, edited by Ginzburg and Vesnin.

The crux of the debate between the rationalists, or formalists, and the constructivists lay in the relative importance assigned to æsthetic theory as opposed to a functionalism derived from technology and materials. In 1923 the poet Vladimir Mayakovsky exhorted the constructivists: 'Beware of becoming just another æsthetic school!'; while this statement could be dismissed as another bit of the 'infantile leftist' sloganeering so characteristic of the early twenties (in 1920 the constructivists had declared 'uncompromising war on art'), constructivist ideologues maintained that the work of the architect must not be separated from the utilitarian demands of technology. Ginzburg accused the rationalists of ignoring this principle. Asnova countered by finding the constructivists guilty of 'technological fetishism.' Constructivists responded with the terms 'naive,' 'abstract,' and 'formalist.'[22] Yet both groups shared a concern for the relation between architecture and social planning; and both insisted on a clearly defined structural mass, based on simple, uncluttered geometric forms.

This geometric laconism is uncompromisingly applied in the constructivist buildings erected in Moscow in the late twenties and early thirties. If we compare Shekhtel's building for the Moscow Merchants' Society—one of the most advanced pre-Revolutionary designs—with Grigory Barkhin's *Izvestia* Building (1927), we see that both are defined by the grid of the structural skeleton, both make extensive use of glass within the grid, both create an unobstructed glass shaft off-center (a stairwell, on the left), and both have a large service entrance at the left corner. But the visual effects are quite different, and it is a difference that says much about the constructivist æsthetic. Shekhtel softens the effect. He applies glazed brick facing to the piers, and he modulates the grid by a judicious use of the curve: over the service entrance, in the niches of the top story, and in the brick facing that covers the piers. Barkhin, by contrast, is resolutely angular: there is no rounding of the points of intersection between vertical and horizontal; both the horizontal and vertical lines are further stressed by a series of simple balconies, placed asymmetrically on the facade; and when the curve is

439. *Zuev Club. Moscow. 1927–29.*
Architect: Ilya Golosov. [LEFT]

440. *Zuev Club. Detail.*

used, it is used fully, as a circle in the four windows of the top story. The circle and square dominate here as clearly as they do in constructivist set designs by Stepanova.

Barkhin's geometrical display is limited to the street facade, but the juxtaposition of square and circle is developed in depth by Ilya Golosov in his Zuev Workers' Club (1927–29). Many such clubs were built in the late twenties and thirties, and in the most pragmatic sense they were intended to provide a meeting and recreational space for both workers and professionals (whose alternative might have been the *traktir*, or tavern). On a more idealistic level, the workers' clubs provided an opportunity for the integration of architecture and social concern in the creation of communal structures, and it is not surprising that the club concept (or 'palace of labor') stimulated some of the most interesting designs of the period.[23]

As of this writing, the Zuev Club looks rather shabby—like many constructivist buildings, it is in a state of disrepair. But the vigor of Golosov's design has not diminished. The large corner cylinder, containing a stairwell enclosed in glass, is clenched within a rectangular extension of one of the upper floors. The resulting contrast of shapes epitomizes constructivist architecture, both in its display of steel, glass, and concrete, and in its massing of sharply defined volumes. A new industrial æsthetic created a building that resembles a machine, symbolizing the machine age, and yet the bold modeling of its forms recalls the work of architects such as Bazhenov, whose heroic neoclassicism displays a similar volumetric approach. (The best example of this similarity is Bazhenov's Yushkov mansion, which by happy and fitting coincidence served as the home of Vkhutemas.)

441. *Rusakov Club. Moscow. 1927–29. Architect: Konstantin Melnikov. Side facade.* [RIGHT]

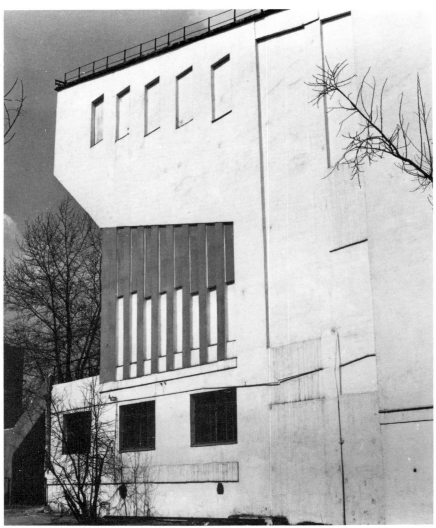

442. *Rusakov Club. Back facade.*

443. *Rusakov Club. Moscow.*
1927–29. Architect: Konstantin
Melnikov.

KONSTANTIN MELNIKOV

Although not a constructivist, Konstantin Melnikov (1890–1974) was acquainted with the movement, and his design for the Soviet Pavilion at the Paris Exhibition of Decorative Arts (1925) represented for the West one of the most advanced achievements of Russian modernism. A similar and equally splendid example of rhetoric in architecture appears in his Rusakov Club (1927–29), for the Union of Municipal Workers. It is the most dramatic of the workers' clubs, with its three cantilevered wedges plunging toward a point at the rear of the building. The effect of the three massive projections, separated by glass shafts in the front, is not only visually striking but functional as well, in providing a slope for the seats of the theater within. The building has been called 'expressionist,' and it does indeed proclaim of itself more loudly than most other structures of the period—Melnikov's included.[24] His Kauchuk Factory club, for example, bears a greater resemblance to the work of the constructivists, particularly in its use of the cylindrical form.

The cylinder dominates in the most private of Melnikov's buildings. Situated in a shaded nook on one of the side streets of Moscow's Arbat region, the Melnikov house (1927–29) consists of two interlocking vertical cylinders, whose entrance is defined by a rectangular glass facade between two pylons. The taller cylinder, to the rear, is perforated by numerous hexagonal windows that flood the artist's studio and bedroom with light, and in the spring and summer relieve the plain interior walls with swatches of green from the foliage outside.

Modern architecture has created many notable houses—from Frank Lloyd Wright's Robie House to Alvar Aalto's Villa Mairea—and the greatest can be seen as a distillation of the architect's thought, a credo. The Melnikov house does not resemble any of them; its contours are different from the angular slabs and planes of houses by Wright or Gerrit Rietveld or Le Corbusier.[25] Despite its open front, the house reminds one of a fortress—though not forbidding, but protected from the large blocks of flats that surround it. This rounded sufficiency suggests that the house's true affinity lies not with twentieth-century architecture, but with the late-eighteenth-century design for a spherical house by another visionary, Claude-Nicolas Ledoux, creator of secular temples.

There is a purified, altarlike quality about the interior of the Melnikov house, in its shape and in the way the light enters through a multitude of narrow windows—both reminiscent of the apsidal space of large fourteenth-century Novgorod churches. The individuality so uncompromisingly stated in the Melnikov house did little to protect its architect from the repression of the following decade, when he was in effect excluded from the practice of architecture for the rest of his life, left to draw sketches for projects whose grandiosity suggests comparison with Boullée or Ledoux. But the house has survived, in the care of his son and daughter, and its entrance still bears the signature *Konstantin Melnikov arkhitektor.*

444. *Experimental house. Moscow. 1927–29. Architect: Konstantin Melnikov.* [LEFT]

445. *Experimental house. Architect: Konstantin Melnikov. Rear cylinder.*

The Functional Æsthetic:
Moisey Ginzburg; Le Corbusier in Russia

Our survey has thus far focused on some of the more striking, dynamic examples of contemporary architecture in the 1920s. There were, however, other buildings of the period that avoided dramatic juxtapositions of form in favor of more severe lines. The main proponent of this functionalism, Moisey Ginzburg, noted that 'the method of functional thought by no means negates the extremely important task of architectural design. It merely establishes the laws for this design and forces the architect to locate [design] in functionally justified elements.'[26] In this and other statements of 1926–27, Ginzburg attempted to defend his constructivist, functional approach to architecture from those who considered it indifferent to the question of æsthetics, and at the same time to insist on the organic unity of form and function.

Despite technological and material limitations, there are Moscow structures that bear out his claim. One of the earliest, B. Velikovsky's building for the State Trade Agency (Gostorg, 1925–27), was never completed to the architect's specifications; its recessed central element was meant to rise another six floors above the flanking blocks that extend to the street line. As it exists, the six-floor structure is probably the period's most severely functional design, with its reinforced-concrete skeleton set within horizontal strips of glass, interrupted only by vertical slabs of concrete on the flanking projections. Despite the unkempt appearance of such buildings, the proportions of the window spaces and the variations in depth along Gostorg's street facade attest to an elegant sense of measure that is particularly noteworthy in comparison with recent 'functionalist' designs in Moscow.

Among Ginzburg's own creations, the apartment house for the People's Commissariat of Finance (Narkomfin, 1928–30) illustrates

446. *Melnikov House. Moscow. 1927–29. Architect: Konstantin Melnikov. Studio, rear cylinder.* [OPPOSITE]

447. *State Trade Agency. Moscow. 1925–27. Architect: B. Velikovsky. In the distance is the Soviet Ministry of Agriculture (1928–33), built in the constructivist style by the versatile Alexey Shchusev.*

448. *Apartment house for the People's Commissariat of Finance. Moscow. 1928–30. Architects: Moisey Ginzburg and I. F. Milinis. The finely balanced back facade of Ginzburg's apartment house will soon be obscured once again, as the new American Embassy complex rises in the foreground.*

admirably his statements on the necessary interdependence of æsthetics and functional design, 'from the interior to the exterior.' Built to contain apartments, as well as dormitory rooms arranged in a communal living system, the interior is meticulously designed, like that of many constructivist buildings. The main structure, adjoined at one end by a large block for communal services, rests on pilotis (now enclosed). The front of the building is dominated by the sweeping horizontal lines of window strips and, on the lower floors, of connecting balconies. The horizontal emphasis applies to the back facade as well, although its delineation is more complex: the floors are grouped in strips of two, and each end of the facade is marked by a stairwell shaft. The effect is austere, yet finely calculated in rhythm and balance.

The success with which Ginzburg implemented his concept of functionalism for Narkomfin not only created an outstanding example of modern Russian architecture, but also demonstrated how closely such works were related to contemporary architecture in the rest of Europe. Without losing its individuality, the building seems to echo Gropius and De Stijl; and within a few years of its completion, Alvar Aalto was to continue this enlightened experiment in communal living space with his Paimio Tuberculosis Sanatorium (1933), a building with many similarities to Ginzburg's. The closest affinity, however, is with Le Corbusier's notion of an Unité d'Habitation, which must have been discussed between the two. They were acquaintances, and in 1927 Le Corbusier was included on the board of *Contemporary Architecture*, edited by Ginzburg and Vesnin.

Le Corbusier's active collaboration in Russian architecture reached its culmination in his design for two large projects: the Palace of Soviets (not realized) and the headquarters for the Central Organization of Trade Unions (Tsentrosoyuz, 1929–36). Assisted by his brother, Pierre Jeanneret, and the Soviet architect Nikolay Kolli, Le Corbusier succeeded in completing the building on the intended scale, but without many of its planned technical refinements, such as a sophisticated system for circulating cooled or heated air through the double-paned

449. *Palace of Culture for the Likhachev Auto Factory. Moscow. 1932–37. Architects: Vesnin brothers. Sketch from M. A. Ilin,* Vesniny.

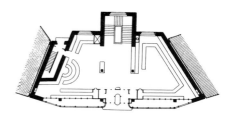

450. *Mostorg Department Store, on Krasnaya Presnya Square. Moscow. 1927–28. Architect: Leonid Vesnin. Elevation, plan from M. A. Ilin,* Vesniny.

glass facade. Although not very tall (eight stories), the building is impressive, with its three elongated blocks. The center block is set back from Kirov Street, while the other two flank it in a perpendicular arrangement extending to the street line. Two of the blocks are sheathed in a monolithic glass facade, framed by red tufa; and the central block rests on pilotis—now enclosed, although there are plans to restore the ground level to its original appearance.[27] The rear of the building contains subsidiary structures, including a meeting hall and club space. One unusual detail of the interior is the architect's use of spiral ramps, rather than staircases, to connect the various components.

Le Corbusier's building for the Tsentrosoyuz was one of the last modernist works to be completed in the capital. Other noteworthy examples of the constructivist-functionalist style from the 1930s include: Panteleimon Golosov's *Pravda* Building (1931–37); the large complex for the Likhachev Auto Factory club, by the brothers Vesnin (1932–37); and the same architects' club for the Society of Political Prisoners (pre-Revolutionary, of course; oddly enough, the society was disbanded in 1934, just as its building was nearing completion). Nor was Moscow the only site of constructivist activity: Leningrad, Gorky, and Kharkov commissioned projects that illustrate the extent to which ideas developed at Inkhuk had been assimilated into general architectural practice.[28] Even classicists such as Fomin and Shchusev built in the style (the latter designed the Lenin Mausoleum)—but not for long.

The Destruction of Russian Modernism

The Stalinist repression in architecture was conducted as skillfully and methodically as it was in the other arts. Various factions were allowed to continue their disputes, while the Party stepped in only reluctantly, as an honest broker, gradually extending its control. There was no organized resistance: *sauve qui peut*, and the odd man out—such as Melnikov—could be used as a convenient means of deflecting the increasingly self-righteous invective of hackdom. The

451. *Central Organization of Trade Unions. Moscow. 1929–36. Architects: Le Corbusier, assisted by Pierre Jeanneret and Nikolay Kolli.*

first phase of this process concluded in 1932, when the remaining architectural groups were abolished and the Union of Soviet Architects was established as the sole legitimate professional organization.

As the public campaign against 'formalism' intensified, a campaign within the profession proceeded to solidify ideological control over the union. One particular target was Ivan Leonidov (an associate of Ginzburg's), who built practically nothing but whose designs, ranging from the visionary to the functional, made his name a term of abuse for the Stalinists. At architectural conferences in 1934 and 1935, both formalism and retrospectivism were condemned, thus creating the curious situation in which architects as diverse as Ivan Fomin and Melnikov found themselves in open disfavor.

There were, however, indications that retrospectivism would carry the day: in 1934 Shchusev was allowed to resume work on his neo-Muscovite Kazan Railway Station, and in that same year Zholtovsky constructed a seven-story apartment building (at 16 Marx Prospekt) in a pompous neoclassical-revival style—its gargantuan attached columns reached five stories, and culminated in mammoth composite capitals. In 1935 the Vesnin brothers attempted a mild reply to the growing retrospectivist tendency by stating that 'the canonization of an old form, however excellent, is a brake on the development of content.'[29]

452. Apartment house (now head-quarters for Intourist). Moscow. 1934. Architect: Ivan Zholtovsky. Firmly in the style of the late-imperial neo-classical revival, Zholtovsky's edifice is an early example of the Stalinist reaction against modernism.

453. *Apartment building, Kotelniches-*
kaya Quay. Moscow. Architects:
D. Chechulin and A. Rostovsky.
Completed in 1952. View from the
Taganka region, with mid–nineteenth-
century buildings in the foreground.

But retrospectivism was not to be denied. The new concept of 'socialist realism' had to be given content, and by the Stalinist dialectic, that content was to be derived not from an innovative functionalism (now labeled formalism), but from reassuringly conservative neoclassical and neo-Muscovite styles (the epitome of formalism in a modern context).

The destruction of Russian modernism in architecture was complete by the First All-Union Congress of Architects in 1937—the beginning of the great Purges—as one architect after another recanted or remained silent. That they survived, unlike so many of their counterparts in literature, in no way signified that pluralism was still permitted. After the Second World War, the longed-for liberalization failed to occur,

454. *Children's Music Theater. Moscow. Completed in 1979. Architects: A. Velikanov and V. Krasilnikov. The use here of roughly textured prefabricated concrete panels is one of the better examples of creative adaptation to modern Soviet assembly methods.* [ABOVE]

455. *Universal Sports Pavilion. Moscow. 1979. Architects: Yu. Bolshakov, V. Tarasevich, and I. Rozhin.*

and the late forties and fifties witnessed the rise of 'Stalinist gothic.' Cities from Warsaw to Tashkent exhibited the style; but the center remained Moscow, where seven tower buildings arose, crowned with a pastiche of decorative motifs from the sixteenth and seventeenth centuries. Wasteful of interior space and bombastic, the towers do exactly what they were intended to do—dominate the city.

In the period following Stalin's death, in 1953, a sober reassessment of priorities—particularly the housing crisis in Moscow and other cities—led to a functionalism and rationalization of construction methods that had been among the goals of Soviet design and planning during the 1920s. Teams of engineers and architects now produce standardized plans that can be widely applied with relatively simple technology. And the pace of growth has been impressive: rows of office buildings, theaters, research institutes; hundreds of thousands of apartments.

456. *Troparevo Housing area. Moscow. 1970s. Architects: A. Samsonov, and A. Bergelson. In the foreground, a green zone with alternating strips of conifer and birch.*

The industrialization of building and the curbing of architectural pomposity have, however, produced a different set of problems. Apart from the general monotony of design, even the creative project must be adapted to the processes of standardized construction, based on prefabricated modules or precast concrete forms assembled on site. The seams and cracks that result from such a method of assembly give many contemporary buildings a shoddy appearance. There have been recent proposals for the greater use of poured concrete in the construction of multistoried buildings, but as of 1981 there is little evidence of it.[30]

If we ask whether Soviet Russian architecture has accomplished the goals set for it in the 1920s, the answer in many respects must be affirmative. Despite the havoc of the late thirties and the Second World War, living space has been greatly expanded in an intelligent way, with the preservation of open space and green zones. Yet the effects of the repression of the 1930s are still noticeable in Soviet architecture, even though modern functionalism has revived the names of those whose careers were cut short. Soviet architectural journals now place quotations from Melnikov, Ginzburg, and the Vesnin brothers, with illustrations of their work, among models of new structures in the latest modernistic style.[31] But the modernism is strained and in most cases pretentious. What is lacking is a sense of measure, a knowledge of modern art 'from Cézanne to Suprematism,' and the spirit of internationalism that informed the heroic period of the 1920s.

epilogue

In his article 'On the Architecture of the Present Time' (1834), the Russian writer Nikolay Gogol presented his readers with what he considered a 'strange idea': 'I thought it would not be bad to have in a city a street that would serve as an architectural chronicle. It ought to begin with ponderous, gloomy gates, from which the viewer would emerge to see on both sides the sublime, magnificent buildings of the primordial savage taste common to all peoples. Then a gradual change through a series of views: the high transformation to a colossal Egyptian [architecture], suffused with simplicity; then to that beauty, the Greek; then to the sensuous Alexandrine and Byzantine, with its squat domes; then to the Roman, with arches in several rows. . . .' And so on. The high point would be Gothic architecture, the 'crown of art,' and the promenade would end with some undefined new style. 'This street would become in a certain sense a history of the development of taste, and anyone too lazy to leaf through weighty tomes would only have to stroll along it in order to find out everything.'[1]

There is not in this fantasy one mention of medieval Russian architecture, in any of its manifestations; and the article's references to eighteenth-century architecture in Russia are not flattering. Gogol praises the cathedrals of Milan and Cologne as well as the Islamic architecture of India; yet the 'everything' that Gogol's cultured but indolent Russian might inspect includes nothing from eleventh-century Kiev or Novgorod, nothing from twelfth-century Vladimir or sixteenth-century Moscow. Nor can this omission be attributed to an unusual ignorance on the writer's part: he had an abiding interest in the history of architecture, and had at one time studied the architecture of the classical world.

Indeed, Russian architectural students of the period knew little more about their native building traditions than did Gogol, if we can judge by a public lecture delivered in 1837 by a student at the Moscow Court

School of Architecture. The speaker, Alexey Martynov, was to become a leading figure in the Russian medieval-revival movement in architecture during the 1840s and '50s, but his description of pre-Petrine architectural evolution displays an inventiveness worthy of Gogol: 'The first trace in Russia of architecture as a fine art is considered to begin with the time of Vladimir the Enlightener. From this time until the eighteenth century, the history of our architecture consists of three epochs in its ancient buildings: in the first we see the style of Syrian architecture; in the second, Asian or Mongolian; and in the third, Lombard-Venetian.' The periods overlap: Saint Basil's, according to Martynov, is a mixture of Mongol and Indian, although it belongs chronologically to the Lombard-Venetian epoch. This early attempt at periodization was to be accepted as valid well into the nineteenth century.[2]

From the above essays—one by an amateur critic, the other by a professional critic and architect—one might conclude that Russian architecture before the eighteenth century had virtually no history of its own, was a receptacle for alien influences: Mongol, Venetian, Syrio-Byzantine. The process, it seems, was not one of borrowing, but of imposition—of Russian 'culture' as a pliable undefined material on which any stronger or more highly developed culture placed its stamp. There were no 'Lives' of Russian artists and architects, no schools of painting (Russians had yet to discover the æsthetic value of icons), no Renaissance, no enlightened patrons, no sense of continuity. Gogol's boulevard of architectural history was a means of imagining that which Russia apparently did not have—a history, not simply an architectural chronicle, but a history of a people as revealed through its architecture.

Evident in these essays is the long eclipse of the medieval building tradition by the nonindigenous architecture of the Petrine and post-Petrine eras. In 1838 a Petersburg newspaper complained that Russian academicians were still preoccupied with the monuments of the ancient world, to the detriment of an understanding of Russian architecture and its relation to that of other cultures: 'It would also be desirable for our architects to turn their attention to the various monuments scattered throughout our provinces.'[3] In fact, by the beginning of the nineteenth century, architectural expeditions to the countryside were doing just that, and by the 1830s even so venerable an institution as the Imperial Academy of Arts had commissioned a survey of pre-Petrine monuments to be made by the artist F. G. Solntsev, whose work played an important role in publicizing the rediscovery of early Russian architecture.[4]

The rejection of neoclassicism—indeed, of architecture since the late Renaissance—can be further deduced from the interest taken by Russian architects and writers (such as Gogol) in exotic architectural styles from abroad. This meant above all the glorification of Gothic architecture, an attitude typical of the Romantic period everywhere, but especially adopted in Russia. There it not only inspired Gothic caprices, but also stimulated in the 1830s a desire to exalt Russian medieval architecture, however different it might be from that of Western Europe. Alexander Benois, writing of Russian architects on tours of Europe during the nineteenth century, noted: 'They believed in the theory that the medieval architecture of Italy had much in common with old Russian architecture, and therefore set for themselves the task of resurrecting this native architecture on their return to Russia.'[5]

Yet these two forms of medieval building differed so fundamentally as to make impossible any comparison between the European sense of architectural development and that of Russia. Even the term *medieval* is likely to be misleading when applied to Russian art and architecture, although it is widely used by Russian scholars to refer to a protean grouping of styles and periods before the eighteenth century. For Russians, 'medieval' could not mean the great cathedrals whose structural complexity symbolized not only the religious but also the intellectual thought of the time. There is no 'idea of scholasticism' in medieval Russian architecture; and there are no documents similar to those of Villard de Honnecourt, the thirteenth-century French architect whose notebooks provide an insight into the architectural mind of medieval Europe.[6]

Indeed, for the nineteenth-century Russian, 'Old Russian' architecture would most likely mean a rather modest, if highly decorated, church built only a century and a half earlier, during the reign of Peter the Great's father. Furthermore, the scholarly grounding of Russian architecture in the Byzantine tradition was tenuous, owing both to the lack of research and to the diversity of styles (hence the references to Syrian, Mongol, and Lombard influences). As Yelena Borisova has remarked in her study of Russian architecture in the second half of the nineteenth century, 'The hypnotic effect of the word "Byzantine" replaced all attempts to comprehend the relations between Byzantine and pre-Petrine architecture and cut off any possibility of such attempts.'[7] In the nineteenth century, the concept of the Byzantine was equated with the neo-Byzantine, a style appropriated for official ecclesiastical architecture during the reign of Nicholas I.

It is probable that had Peter the Great not reigned, Russian architecture would nonetheless have developed as it did, if less spectacularly. Recent scholarship has demonstrated the extensive Western influence on Russian culture during the latter half of the seventeenth century. The so-called Moscow baroque, an amalgam of traditional elements with borrowings filtered through Poland, the Ukraine, and White Russia, exemplifies Boris Vipper's concept of 'rusticalization'—the assimilation of a style taken from a more advanced culture.[8] But however significant, this indebtedness to other cultures was minor compared with the extent of the change that occurred with the founding of Saint Petersburg: to build his capital, Peter imported the necessary architects and artisans, who worked exclusively in a baroque idiom that might have been found in any number of northern-European countries.

The historical factors that underlie the cultural transformations of the seventeenth and eighteenth centuries reflect the larger question of Russian national identity. Suspended between East and West—and frequently invaded by both—Russia was the legatee of the Byzantine empire and church, whose collapse then propelled Muscovy, in the interests of survival, toward the suspect West: only the West could provide the requisite technical knowledge for Russian preservation— and expansion. Paradoxically, Peter the Great's modernization campaign assured Russia's place as a dominant European power, while revealing all the more clearly the cultural differences between Russia and the rest of Europe. In architecture, this revelation applied not simply to a change in the plan and appearance of ecclesiastical architecture, but, more important, to the introduction of secular building styles that had not previously existed in Russia.

It can be argued that this process of secularization appeared as early as the late seventeenth century, in the tiered churches on the estates of the Naryshkins, Sheremetevs, and Golitsyns near Moscow. Designed to accommodate only a small number of worshipers, these churches seem to have served primarily as ostentatious displays of the wealth and Western tastes of the upper stratum of an increasingly Westernized nobility, closely connected with the young tsar Peter. With the consolidation of the privileges of the nobility during the eighteenth century, the wealthiest representatives of that class discovered other ways of displaying their wealth and European culture—notably, by building or rebuilding their mansions and palaces on a scale approaching that of Western Europe. (Palace architecture in any refined sense is the creature of Peter the Great's reign; seventeenth-century Russian 'palaces' hardly qualify by any standard of style or convenience.) Hence, the pattern on estates in the Moscow area is of a seventeenth-century church flanked by an eighteenth-century mansion.

The creation within a few decades of an architectural type that in the West had evolved over centuries is one aspect of a cultural transformation that produced not only mansions for the wealthy nobility but also grandiose palaces for the imperial family and administrative buildings for the increasingly complex and pervasive tsarist bureaucracy. The rapidity and thoroughness of this imperial transformation left their mark not only on Petersburg, but also on Moscow and a score of provincial towns, each with its administrative center in the neoclassical style dictated by Catherine the Great.

The resultant sharply contrasting styles and all that this juxtaposition implied—pre-Petrine Russian culture, oriented toward the church and its Eastern, Byzantine heritage, and the post-Petrine secular, Westernized culture—could be observed in Vladimir, Novgorod, and Moscow. More to the point, however, was the contrast between Russia and the Russian imperial capital. Architecture thus became a material embodiment of the radical dislocation that accompanied Russia's acceptance of an imperial destiny. The acceptance was neither easy nor complete. In the nineteenth century, as Russia moved belatedly into the industrial age, the question of national identity became still more acute: the greater the dependence on Western technology and trade, the more obsessive the concern with the uniqueness of the Russian culture.

The search for a national style led, ironically, to yet another parallel with European architecture—eclecticism. But in Russia the rejection

363

457. *Window detail, Catherine Palace. Tsarskoe Selo.*

of neoclassicism in the late nineteenth century meant more than a transition to the styles and building types of a new economic and industrial era—railway stations, shopping galleries, apartment blocks, eclectically decorated mansions for the new rich. The rejection also implied a weakening of the centralized, autocratic direction that had sustained imperial architecture. In literature, from Gogol to Andrey Bely, Petersburg was presented not as a city of harmony and reason, but as a disturbingly alien environment, strangely immaterial and dominated by a maze of bureaucracies supporting the state. The grandeur of Petersburg architecture, emblematic of the imperial will, acquired a set of connotations unintended by its enlightened builders. Not only oppressive and dehumanizing, the city seemed to possess a spectral quality. For the great Symbolist poet Alexander Blok, Petersburg is the point where Russia vanishes, where Russia is and is not. The opening of Andrey Bely's novel *Petersburg* makes a similar point— parodistically reducing the city to a point on the map, from which emanate bureaucratic circulars.[9]

Petersburg and post-Petrine architecture had not always been thus interpreted. In the eighteenth and early nineteenth centuries the beauty of the city and the work of its architects were frequently eulogized by major poets such as Mikhail Lomonosov and Gavriil Derzhavin. To a certain extent this was court poetry, praising in formulaic flourishes the achievements of Peter the Great and Catherine the Great; but the enthusiasm is there nonetheless. As late as 1820, the poet Konstantin Batyushkov, a fervent admirer of Peter the Great as the importer of progress to Russia, wrote of the capital: 'What unity, how all its parts do resonate with the whole; what beauty in the buildings, what taste, and above all what variety in the play of water and buildings.'[10]

The pivotal figure in the literary perception of Petersburg is, appropriately, Russia's greatest poet, Alexander Pushkin. Like his predecessors and contemporaries, Pushkin sang of Petersburg's comeliness; but in his narrative poem 'The Bronze Horseman' (1833) he also alluded to the great cost of Peter's creation. The poem is a 'sorrowful tale' of a government clerk driven mad by personal loss during the great Petersburg flood of 1824; prefaced by a majestic invocation to the city (few writers have equaled Pushkin's sense of the setting and architecture of Petersburg), the poem links the misery of an insignificant man to the ruthless will expressed in Étienne Falconet's monument to Peter the Great—the 'Bronze Horseman.' In this poem Pushkin can be said to have created the Petersburg myth, with its underlying themes of suspect beauty, madness, and suffering—a myth that appeared at the end of the era of imperial architecture.

For the rest of the century, the recurrent lament on the state of Russian architecture—from Gogol and Dostoevsky to the architect Konstantin Bykovsky—can be reduced to the lack of a unifying idea. For those who complained of the soulessness of Petersburg's monuments, Moscow became a counterexample, redolent of the past, 'organic' in its clutter of styles and buildings dating back as far as the fourteenth century.[11] But the Moscow revival styles provided only a superficial attempt to regain, or create, continuity with the architecture of the seventeenth century. Petersburg neoclassicism, neglected during the same period for its bureaucratic associations, seemed to its revivalists at the beginning of the twentieth century to offer a coherent solution to the problem of architectural direction; for others, the international *style moderne* provided the conveniences of modern design and materials combined with the possibility for distinctive decorative effects. But despite the developments during these decades in planning and technology, none of the above movements satisfactorily addressed the need for housing in Russia's major cities at the beginning of the twentieth century.

After the Revolution, the conditions for a unifying idea seemed once again at hand: centralized planning, a dedication to the development of new building methods, the idealism of a new social order, and a cooperation between the state and a group of talented architects, trained in classical architectural principles but unconstrained by the eclectic or revival fashions. Like the grand designs of the imperial period, the new architecture demonstrated a familiarity with contemporary European work; and like them, it was intended to be applied on an extensive scale (few of the gargantuan projects from the drawing boards of the 1920s were, however, realized). And despite the apparent break with the Russian past, the works of the functionalist-constructivist movement often bore a resemblance to the geometric laconism of early medieval Russian architecture, particularly as developed in Novgorod and Pskov. (Cf. Novgorod's twelfth-century Cathedral of Saint Antony with the Zuev Club in Moscow.)

The collapse of the new movements can be attributed to many factors, including architectural rivalries and envy on the part of those who felt excluded from the groups of architects whose ideas were far in advance of their time. Radical proposals for communal living arrangements and some of the more abstract designs made convenient targets for those interested in a safe career in eclectic architecture based on structures designed at the beginning of the twentieth century. Finally, infighting among factions in the modernist camp, while not a cause of the repression, was symptomatic of the failure of all segments of the intelligentsia accurately to perceive the threat posed by Stalinism.

The decision in Stalinist architecture to revert to models of the late-imperial period might seem ironic, but only if we fail to understand that Stalin and his associates had a greater sympathy for tsarist culture than for the innovative, rationalist cosmopolitan thought of the 1920s—loud in its debates and obviously a hotbed of deviationism. Even more significant is the reversion to neo-Muscovite forms in the periods immediately preceding and following the Second World War. Apart from obvious nationalistic overtones, this move provided a link with the architecture of such strong rulers as Ivan the Terrible, whom Stalin admired. Although Ivan's architects built better than Stalin's, both rulers built for grandiose effect. (Ivan's magnificent tower churches —and that of his predecessor, Basil III, at Kolomenskoe—were built as votive offerings and displays of princely wealth, rather than as places of worship. *Mutatis mutandis*, the same could be said of the buildings for Stalin's administrative apparatus; he was, it must be remembered, educated in a seminary.)

Indeed, the architecture of Russia frequently exemplifies the principle, elucidated by the Czech semiotician Jan Mukařovský, of substitution for vanished functions.[12] The usual functional considerations of the design and use of a structure are displaced by symbolic functions, denoting, in the case of Stalinist Russia, the power of the state, the glory of Muscovite culture, the central position of Moscow in the Communist world, and, by implication, the omnipotence of Stalin himself. Of course the symbolic also functioned in constructivist designs, but within a rational framework. It is telling that none of the grandiose constructivist projects intended to dominate Red Square was ever built; the Kremlin walls and Saint Basil's still preside over the area, in the popular imagination as well as in fact.

At present the notion of practicality has returned in full force to Russian architecture; but there is no clearly defined æsthetic that could be called 'international' or 'Russian.' In view of the extraordinary circumstances surrounding Russia's earlier periods of architectural distinction, one hesitates to predict the provenance of the next great idea. History demonstrates, however, that it is unlikely to come without some form of exchange with the architecture of the West. The Russian genius for importing architectural concepts is matched only by an ability to develop them in an unpredictable manner, one that reminds us of our own, Western, architectural traditions and yet seems so far removed. It is, as Gogol said, 'a distance of enormous measure.'

458. *Church of the Dormition, from the village of Kuritsko. 1595. Now at the Vitoslavlitsy Museum, Novgorod.*

APPENDIX A

RUSSIA'S WOODEN CHURCHES

Medieval Russian chronicles contain intriguing references to complex wooden churches, such as the first church of Saint Sophia in Novgorod, with thirteen 'tops'; and from archæological and historical data we know that wood was used for almost every type of structure in Russia until well into the eighteenth century. Russian carpenters were fully aware of the strengths of wood, which they exploited to remarkable effect; but fire and decay have taken their toll, and little has been preserved from before the eighteenth century. Apart from a few churches recently dated to the sixteenth century and some early photographs of others—churches that are now inaccessible or destroyed—there is almost no reliable information about pre–seventeenth-century wooden structures.[1] In studying the surviving churches, however, we can establish a classification based on existing types; for despite variations in decoration and silhouette, the basic forms are traditional, and in some cases probably predate by centuries any of the extant churches.

The simplest type of wooden church (for example, the Church of the Dormition from the village of Nikulino, built in 1599) resembles the peasant house, with its steeply pitched roof and rectangular 'cells' (*klet*). The plan is linear, on the traditional east-west axis, with one cell for the service and another, the *trapeza*, that accommodated the congregation before and after the service. These churches often have one or two additional units: an apse, on the east, and a bell tower attached to the *trapeza*, on the west. The richer churches, like the larger peasant houses, were frequently decorated with carved end boards and galleries.

Although the steeply pitched roof gave the larger cell churches an imposing silhouette, the vertical line is much more emphatic in the second type of wooden church, the 'tent' (*shatyor*), so named for the pyramidal shape of its central tower. The linear concept is here replaced by a centralized cross plan, whose square center space is surmounted by an octagonal structure supporting a tall eight-sided tower (an excellent example is the Church of the Dormition, 1595, from the village of Kuritsko). Galleries, an apse, and a *trapeza* were frequently attached to the central cube.

Patriarch Nikon's condemnation in 1653 of the *shatyor* as insufficiently Orthodox was adroitly circumvented by a third type of church, the tiered, or *yarusny*, structure, in which a pyramidal silhouette ascends in a series of diminishing octagons over the main part of the building. (See the Church of the Transfiguration, 1756, from the village of Kozlyatevo.) With its numerous levels, the tiered form engendered a proliferation of cupolas; but in contrast to the picturesque silhouette, the interior of these churches is quite modest: the ceilings are low, the windows small, and the walls are of untreated wood. The main decoration is the iconostasis.

Whatever the form (and the above typology ignores many variations), the time-honored methods of construction were basically the same. Logs were cut in the late fall after the final ring of the tree—usually pine or fir—had hardened, and they were left on the ground until the beginning of building season, in late spring. The logs were then taken to the construction site, where master carpenters trimmed, notched, and if necessary planed them. The most common tools were an ax and an adze, nails were rarely used, and the logs were left unsurfaced. (In the nineteenth century many of these churches were covered with plank siding, but this is now being removed in restoration projects.)

The carpenters used two forms of joining: the notch (*oblo s ostatkom*), for round logs, and the dovetail (*lapa*), for round or squared logs. In order to support a roof overhang for protection against moisture runoff, the logs used—laid horizontally on a stone foundation—were increasingly longer toward the top of the wall, creating a flare (*poval*) to buttress the extension. The roof was covered with planks, whose tips displayed carved points; and the tower surface consisted of vertical boards or patterned shingles. These shingles (*lemekhi* or *cheshui*—'fish scales') are among the most attractive and ingenious details of Russian wooden architecture. Typically, they were carved from ash wood, which ages from a golden hue to silver. The reflection under the winter sun is brilliant, metallic, and distinguishes the towers and cupolas from the darker logs of the main structure.

In pre-Revolutionary times, churches were frequently bought in one village and transported to another; a small church can be taken apart for reassembly in a few hours. Today, many of Russia's wooden churches are being dismantled and rebuilt at architectural preservation sites, such as the Vitoslavlitsy Museum of Wooden Architecture near Novgorod[2] and similar museums at Suzdal and Kizhi. Other churches still stand, in disrepair in remote locations; but unless measures are taken to preserve them, they will soon exist only in photographs. This would be a regrettable loss indeed, for Russia's wooden architecture is eloquent testimony to the integrity and beauty of folk traditions in the art of building.

459. *Church of the Dormition, from
Nikulino (now at the Vitoslavlitsy
Museum of Wooden Architecture near
Novgorod). 1599. A good example of
the simple 'cell' type of wooden
church, with three rooms along a
single axis. The gallery is on the
south side only.*

460. *Church of the Transfiguration of the Savior, from the village of Kozlyatevo. 1756. Now at the Museum of Wooden Architecture, Suzdal. A centralized tiered church.*

461. *Church of Saint Nicholas, from Ust-Volmo and, later, Tukholya (now at the Vitoslavlitsy Museum). 1600s. In the eighteenth century this church was moved from its original village to another one. In this version of the 'cell' church, the refectory chamber (*trapeza*) is larger than the main part of the church. Until the nineteenth century such chambers were frequently used for social gatherings.*

462. *Church of Saint Nicholas. West view.*

463. *Church of Saint Nicholas, from Myakishevo (now at the Vitoslavlitsy Museum). Latter half of the seventeenth century. This remarkable pine church has a cross-centered plan, with a rectangular two-tiered elevation over the central part. An enclosed gallery is attached to the church on the west and north sides.*

464. *Church of Saint Nicholas, from Myakishevo. Gable detail, with carved endboards.*

465. *Chapel from the village of Kashira
(now at the Vitoslavlitsy Museum).
Eighteenth century. An example of
dovetail construction, with a carved
railing (*balyasnik*) for the gallery.*

466. *Church of the Nativity, from Peredki. Roof detail.* [LEFT]

467. *Church of the Nativity, from Peredki.* Pomochi, *or extended logs, support the gallery.*

468. *Church of the Nativity of the Virgin, from Peredki (now at the Vitoslavlitsy Museum). Presumed to have been built shortly before 1539. One of the oldest extant wooden churches in the Soviet Union, the Nativity is in the form of a Greek cross, with an octagonal drum supporting the central tent tower (shatyor). The height of the building is approximately 100 feet.* [OPPOSITE]

469. *Church of the Dormition, from Kuritsko (now at the Vitoslavlitsy Museum). 1595. A simpler form of the tower church, this example has a greatly elongated* shatyor.

470. *Church of Saint Nicholas, from
Vysoky Ostrov or 'High Island' (now
at the Vitoslavlitsy Museum). 1757.
A fine example of a tiered structure
imposed on a cellular, linear plan.
Both notch and dovetail construction
are used to join the logs.*

471. *Church of Saint Nicholas, from Vysoky Ostrov. East view.*

472. *Church of Saint Nicholas, from
Glotovo (now at the Museum of
Wooden Architecture, Suzdal). 1766.*

473. *Church of the Resurrection, from Potakino (now at the Museum of Wooden Architecture, Suzdal). 1776.*

474. *Yekimovaya's house, from Ryshevo (now at the Vitoslavlitsy Museum). Probably the second half of the nineteenth century. This elaborately decorated two-story village house (izba) displays the traditional motifs of wood carving, but its window surrounds are taken directly from the Petersburg baroque—not surprisingly, as many of the carpenters in this area would have worked in the capital.*

475. *Windmill near Suzdal. Latter half of the nineteenth century(?).*

Appendix B

Illustrated Architectural Elements

The following illustrations identify selected Russian and European
architectural terms and three common types of cruciform church plans.

ELEVENTH CENTURY, KIEVAN RUS

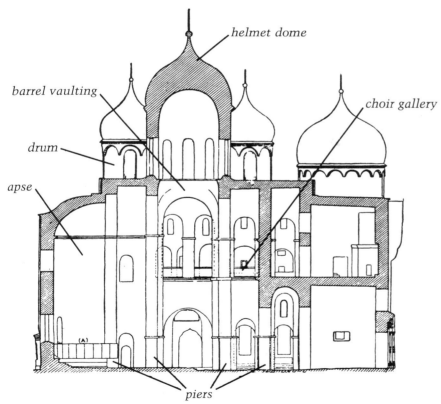

Cathedral of Saint Sophia. Novgorod. 1045–52. Section.

FOURTEENTH CENTURY, NOVGOROD

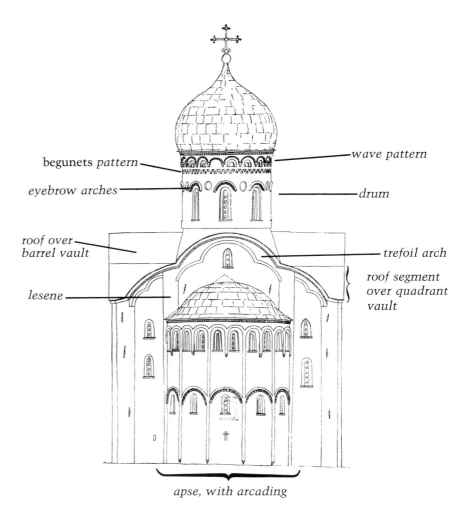

begunets *pattern*

wave pattern

eyebrow arches

drum

*roof over
barrel vault*

trefoil arch

*roof segment
over quadrant
vault*

lesene

apse, with arcading

Church of Saint Theodore Stratilites on the Brook. Novgorod. 1361.

FIFTEENTH CENTURY, MOSCOW

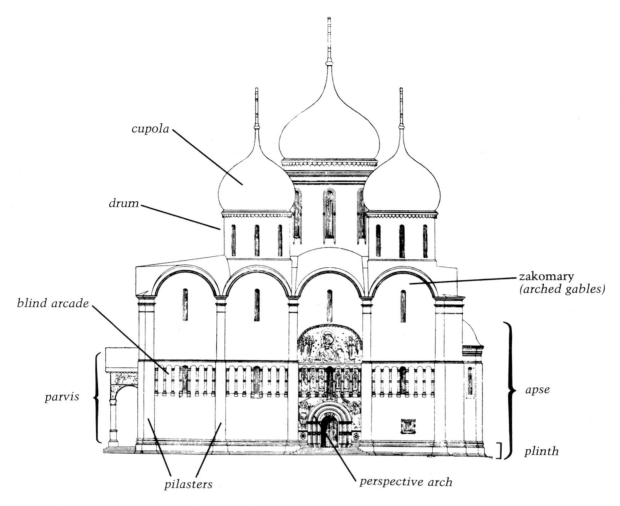

cupola

drum

zakomary
(arched gables)

blind arcade

parvis

apse

plinth

pilasters

perspective arch

Cathedral of the Dormition. The Kremlin, Moscow. 1475–79.
South elevation.

SIXTEENTH CENTURY, MOSCOW

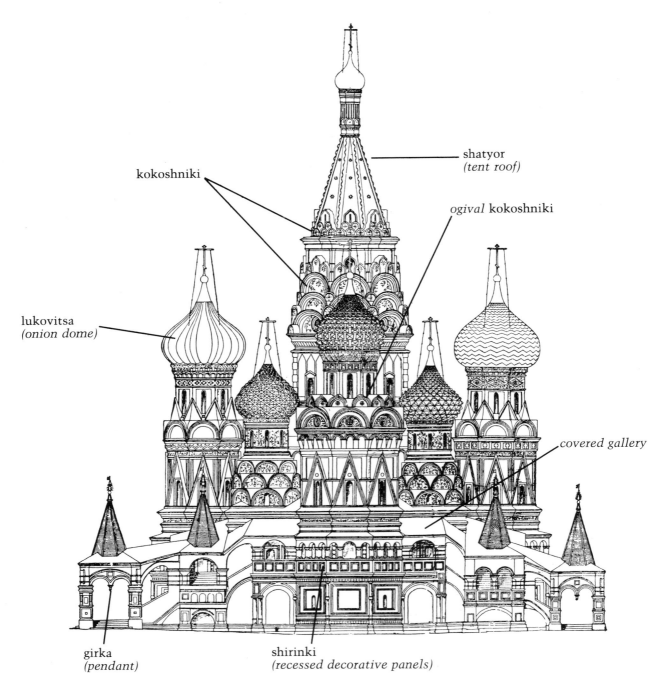

kokoshniki

shatyor
(tent roof)

ogival kokoshniki

lukovitsa
(onion dome)

covered gallery

girka
(pendant)

shirinki
(recessed decorative panels)

Cathedral of the Intercession (Saint Basil's). Moscow. 1555–60.

WOODEN CHURCH

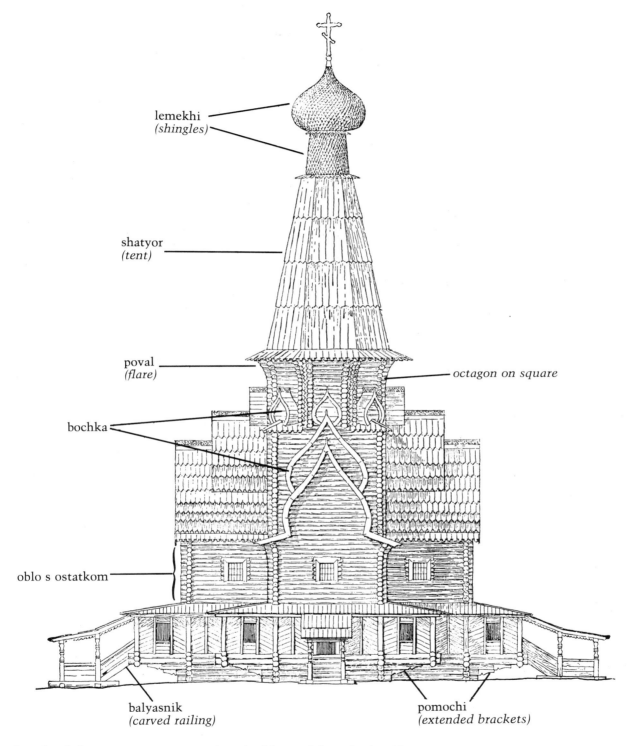

lemekhi
(shingles)

shatyor
(tent)

poval
(flare)

octagon on square

bochka

oblo s ostatkom

balyasnik
(carved railing)

pomochi
(extended brackets)

Church of the Presentation. Osinovo (Arkhangelsk region). 1684.

Cross-domed plan.
Cathedral of Saint Sophia.
Novgorod.

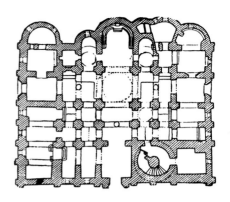

Inscribed cross (quincunx).
Cathedral of Saint Dmitri.
Vladimir.

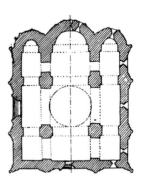

Latin cross.
Cathedral of the Trinity,
Alexander Nevsky Monastery.
Leningrad.

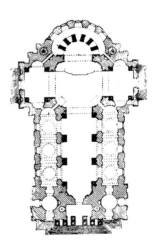

NOTES

PROLOGUE

1. *Plany drevne-russkikh khramov* (Plans of Old Russian churches) (Petrograd, 1915), p. 234.

2. B. Vipers [Vipper], *Baroque Art in Latvia* (Riga, 1939), pp. 8–9. A specialist in European art of the sixteenth and seventeenth centuries, Vipper was well qualified to assess the complexities of cross-cultural exchange. He was also a leading authority on the work of Bartolomeo Rastrelli. A discussion of Vipper's work and its reception in the Soviet Union is contained in James Cracraft's review of B. R. Vipper, *Arkhitektura russkogo barokko*, in *Kritika*, vol. 17 (1981), no. 1, pp. 18–28.

CHAPTER ONE

1. An English translation may be found in S. H. Cross, *The Russian Primary Chronicle*. For a brief, lucid summary of the controversy concerning the rise of the Kievan state, see N. V. Riasanovsky, *A History of Russia*, pp. 25–30. A more detailed examination is set forth in works such as G. Vernadsky's *Kievan Russia* and B. D. Grekov's *Kievskaya Rus*— also available in English. (For bibliographical citations of Riasonovsky, Vernadsky, and Grekov, see Bibliography: History.) The latter vigorously challenges the 'Normanist' theory, in which the Vikings are assigned a major role in the political and cultural development of the eastern Slavs.

2. There were, undoubtedly, a large number of buildings in Kiev—and other Russian settlements—before the advent of Byzantine influence; but by all evidence they were rudimentary in form and intended for the basic needs of housing, trade, and defense. For a description of the remains of a small pagan temple in Kiev, see P. P. Tolonchko and Ya. E. Borovsky, 'Yazichnitske kapishche v "gorodi" volodimira,' in *Arkheologiya Kieva*, ed. L. L. Vashchenko, pp. 3–10.

3. In his account of the spread of Christian architecture throughout the Roman Empire in the fourth and fifth centuries, Richard Krautheimer writes: 'Yet wherever evidence is available, it leads to the conclusion that the architects in charge of the new buildings had come from abroad, frequently in the suite of the court. On the other hand, masons, as a rule, were home-bred.' (*Early Christian and Byzantine Architecture*, p. 71.) Something of the same process may be said to have occurred in Kiev in the tenth century, although there masons, too, were probably imported at the earliest stages. Located on the periphery of the Byzantine cultural

sphere, Kievan Rus soon developed its own variant of Orthodox church architecture, a local flourishing of what is known as Middle Byzantine (ninth–twelfth centuries). The most thorough study of the relation between Byzantine architecture and that of Kiev is contained in A. I. Komech's 'Vizantiyskaya architektura IX–XII vekov i arkhitektura Kieva kontsa X–nachala XII stoletiy' (dissertation, Moscow State University, 1971).

4. An exhaustive account of the historical and archæological evidence concerning the Church of the Tithe is contained in Mikhail Karger's Drevny Kiev 2:9–59. For the composition of the walls and an inventory of decorative fragments, see pp. 49–59.

5. The development of the cross-domed church is discussed in Krautheimer, Early Christian and Byzantine Architecture, pp. 299–315. Whereas the term cross-domed is appropriate for large churches such as Saint Sophia in Kiev and Novgorod, and the destroyed Church of Saint Irene in Kiev (1037)—each with at least five aisles—some specialists have felt the need for a specific term to designate the more modest, compact plan typical of much Middle Byzantine and early Russian architecture. Called variously the inscribed cross, cross-in-square, or quincunx, this plan is defined as containing nine units—a central bay with drum and cupola, four barrel-vaulted extensions representing the arms of the cross, and four corner bays (sometimes with cupolas)—and is traditionally derived from the Nea Ekklesia in Constantinople (consecrated in 881; not extant), although an earlier derivation is considered possible. See Krautheimer, pp. 359–63. The use of these terms, however, has led to confusion in the description of Russian monuments: Krautheimer characterizes not only Saint Sophia in Kiev but also the Cathedral of the Transfiguration in Chernigov as 'cross-domed,' (pp. 309–10), but later states that the quincunx is 'almost universally accepted all over the sphere of Byzantine and dependent architecture, from the tenth century to the Fall of Constantinople, and surviving in Russia and the Balkans far beyond'

(p. 360). In addition, he considers untenable the hypothesis that derives the quincunx from the cross-dome type (pp. 360–61). Soviet scholarship tends to settle for the term Krestovo-kupolny (cross-domed), while Komech (note 3) simplifies matters still further by calling all Russian churches from the eleventh to the thirteenth centuries four-piered; that is, cross-domed structures that derive from a central bay whose drum and cupola rest on four piers.

6. There has been much controversy surrounding the dates of construction of Saint Sophia: the Novgorod chronicle gives 1017 as the date of the cathedral's founding, while the Kievan chronicle indicates 1037. For a summary of the various positions, see Karger, pp. 98–104. Karger, incidentally, accepts the latter date for the beginning of construction, which, in his opinion, was completed sometime in the 1040s. Andrzej Poppe, in an unpublished article, also argues in favor of 1037, with a completion date in the 1050s. (Yaroslav the Wise was buried in the church in 1054).

7. The complex structure of Saint Sophia, with its strong vertical emphasis, has been analyzed by K. N. Afanasev in terms of an elaborate system of proportional relations. See Postroenie arkhitekturnoj formy drevnerusskimi zodchimi, pp. 58–60 (Bibliography: Art and Architecture). Komech has argued for a more pragmatic and less precise method of construction, in which the building's proportions were determined by the need to create an extensive choir gallery for the grand prince's family and retinue. See his 'Rol knjazheskogo zakaza v postroenii Sofijskogo soborz v Kieve,' in Drevnerusskoe iskusstvo: Khudozestvennaya kultura Domongol-skoy Rusi, ed. V. N. Lazarev, pp. 50–64; and 'Postroenie vertikalnoy kompozitsii Sofijskogo sobora v Kieva,' in Sovetskaya arkheologiya, no. 3 (1968), pp. 232–38. The literature on the Cathedral of Saint Sophia is copious, but very little is available in English. Among the fundamental works are N. I. Kresalny's Sofissky zapovidnik u Kiivi and Karger's Drevny Kiev (2:98–206), which contains extensive bibliographic references.

8. The frescoes and mosaics of Saint Sophia have been meticulously studied by V. N. Lazarev, whose book *Mozaiki Sofii Kievskoy* remains the fundamental work on the subject. For a survey of Russian mosaics and frescoes, see his *Drevnerusskie mozaiki i freski*.

9. For a survey of the history of the Kiev lavra, see S. K. Kilesso, *Kievo-Pecherskaya lavra*.

10. Recent research on the Cathedral of the Dormition is presented in M. V. Kholostenko's articles 'Uspensky sobor pecherskogo monastirya,' from the collection *Starodavnii Kiiv* (Kiev, 1975), pp. 107–70, and 'Novi doslidzhennya Ioanno-Predtechenskoy tserkvi ta rekonstruktsiya Uspenskogo soboru Kievo-Pecherskoy lavri,' in *Arkheologichni doslidzhennya starodavnogo Kieva* (Kiev, 1976), pp. 131–65. See also Karger, 2:345–69.

11. For a reconstruction and analysis of the original plan of the Cathedral of the Archangel Michael at Vydubetsky Monastery, see Karger, 2:287–310. For references to the other monuments listed in the text, see Karger, *passim*.

12. See Karger, 2:390–91, and Kilesso, p. 53, for a description of the masonry technique. In addition, Kilesso contains illustrations of the church's valuable twelfth- and seventeenth-century frescoes (figs. 34–45).

13. G. K. Vagner, *Belokamennaya rezba drevnego Suzdalya* (Moscow, 1975), pp. 15, 29 (Bibliography: Chapter Three).

14. For a description of tne renovation of Kiev's monuments in the seventeenth and eighteenth centuries, see Karger, *passim*. There have been modest attempts at regaining the original appearance of Kiev's early monuments: in particular, the stucco has been removed from fragments of eleventh- and twelfth-century walls. The most extensive project under way is the cleaning of the Cathedral of Archangel Michael at Vydubetsky Monastery, but because of topographical changes, only a portion of the structure can be restored.

15. A detailed analysis of the Cathedral of the Transfiguration of the Savior and its relation to Byzantine architecture is presented in Komech's article 'Spaso-Preobrazhensky sobor v Chernigove' (*Drevne-russkoe iskusstvo: Zarubezhnye svyazi*, ed. G. V. Popov). Additional descriptions of this and other monuments in Chernigov are contained in G. N. Logvin's *Chernigov, Novgorod-Seversky, Glukhov, Putivl* and in Yu. S. Aseev's articles on Kievan architecture in *Istoriya ukrainskogo mistetstva*, 1:135–223.

16. The date frequently given for the construction of the Cathedral of Saints Boris and Gleb, 1123, has been demonstrated to belong to an earlier church—on the same site—whose foundations have been partially excavated. See Karger, 2:480, and Aseev, *Istoriya ukrainskogo mistetstva*, 1:199–200. On the basis of stylistic features, Aseev and others now place the cathedral's construction at some point in the 1170s, but that is only an educated guess. Its postwar reconstruction, by N. Kholostenko, has elicited criticism, partly because of the placement of the capitals (their diameter does not correspond to that of the attached columns on which they rest), and partly because of the stucco, whose thick, smooth surface does not reproduce what is considered to be the original appearance—of a thin layer, scored to resemble ashlar. See Aseev, 1:199, and Logvin, *Chernigov*. For Kholostenko's opinions, see 'Neizvestnye pamyatniki monumentalnoy skulptury drevney Rusi. (Relefy Borisoglebskogo sobora v Chernigove),' *Iskusstvo*, no. 3 (1953), pp. 84–91.

CHAPTER TWO

1. For this and subsequent references from the Novgorod chronicle, see entries under the appropriate year in *The Chronicle of Novgorod*, trans. Robert Michell and Nevill Forbes.

2. A summary of the archæological data uncovered in Novgorod is presented in A. V. Artsikhovsky's article 'Novgorod Veliky po arkheologicheskim dannym,' from the miscellany *Novgorod: k 1100-letiyu goroda*, ed. M. N. Tikhomirov. For a more general survey, see A. L. Mongait, *Archeology in the U.S.S.R.* (Bibliography: Art and Architecture). Novgorod continues to

be one of the most productive sites for the archæological study of life in medieval Russia, and the material presented in the above works has been greatly supplemented by recent discoveries concerning both the topography of the ancient city and its culture. For an appreciation of the latter topic see D. S. Likhachev, *Novgorod Veliky: Ocherk istorii kultury Novgoroda X–XVII vv.*

3. There were, in fact, churches from the late twelfth and the thirteenth century that made extensive use of bricks in the construction of walls, but these buildings are attributed—for that very reason—to masons from other cities (cf. the Church of Saint Paraskeva-Pyatnitsa, 1207, and the Church of Saints Peter and Paul on Sinichya Hill, 1185–92). For a brief account of the variations in construction materials, see Mikhail Karger, *Novgorod: Pamyatniki arkhitektury XI–XVII vekov.*

4. Three churches with extensive frescoes were destroyed on the western edge of the city during the Second World War: the Church of the Savior on the Nereditsa, (cf. infra), the Church of the Savior at Kovalyova (whose exterior has now been restored), and the Church of the Dormition at Volotovo. The last is the subject of a splendidly illustrated book based on prewar photographs by L. A. Matsulevich and colored copies of the frescoes. The book's author, M. V. Alpatov, notes: 'The copies were executed in the 1920s, when the very idea of a possible destruction of the Novgorod relics would have seemed absurd.' (*Freski tserkvi Uspeniya no Volotovom pole,* with English and Russian texts). No attempt has yet been made to restore the exterior of the church.

5. Few of the cathedral's early frescoes (eleventh and twelfth centuries) have survived the various renovations of the building and the bomb damage of World War II. V. N. Lazarev summarizes the most interesting fragments in *Drevnerusskie mozaiki i freski,* plates 175–78 (Bibliography: Art and Architecture). For a discussion of the plan of Saint Sophia, with its extensive galleries, see Komech, 'Rol predelov v formirovanii obshchei

kompozitsii Sofiiskogo sobora v Novgorode,' in *Srednevekovaya Rus,* eds. G. K. Vagner and D. S. Likhachev.

6. For a tentative reconstruction of these churches, see G. M. Shtender, 'Arkhitektura domongolskogo perioda,' part of the survey 'Arkhitektura Novgoroda v svete poslednikh issledovany,' in *Novgorod k 1100-letiyu goroda,* ed. M. N. Tikhomirov, pp. 186–91.

7. See G. M. Shtender, 'Vosstanovlenie Nereditsy,' in *Novgorodsky istorichesky sbornik* (Novgorod, 1962), pp. 169–205; and 'Tserkov Spasa Nereditsy,' in *Novgorod k 1100-letiyu goroda,* ed. M. N. Tikhomirov, pp. 194–201. Originally part of a monastery endowed by Novgorod's princes, the Church of the Savior fell into neglect because of its remote location and the lack of support. After 1764 it was open only once a year, for the Feast of the Transfiguration of the Savior, and thus its frescoes escaped the extensive repainting that damaged so many works of art in more active churches. As with the Church of the Dormition at Volotovo, we are fortunate to have at least prewar photographs of the interior. For a survey of the Nereditsa frescoes, see Lazarev, *Drevnerusskie mozaiki,* plates 242–76 (Bibliography: Art and Architecture).

8. See G. M. Shtender, 'Arkhitektura domongolskogo perioda,' in *Novgorod k 1100-letiyu goroda,* ed. M. N. Tikhomirov, pp. 201–14.

9. See 'Pamyatniki smolenskoy arkhitekturnoy shkoly v drugikh russkikh zemlyakh,' in N. N. Voronin and P. A. Rappoport, *Zodchestvo Smolenska XII–XIII vv.,* pp. 348–53.

10. See L. M. Shulyak, 'Arkhitektura kontsa XIII–XV vv.,' in *Novgorod k 1100-letiyu goroda,* ed. M. N. Tikhomirov, p. 238, fn. 143. The same article also contains a useful survey of construction techniques utilized in one of the most prolific periods of Novgorod architecture—the second half of the fourteenth century and the beginning of the fifteenth (pp. 228–32). For his entry on the Church of Saint Theodore Stratilates, see pp. 232–34.

11. Theophanes is presumed to have arrived in Novgorod, from Constantinople, in the early 1370s.

(His frescoes at the Church of the Transfiguration date from 1378.) His work brings the ambience of the Paleologue Revival to Russian spirituality, so strikingly represented in his series of stylites and other ascetics. See Lazarev, *Drevnerusskie mozaiki i freski*, plates 303–24 (Bibliography: Art and Architecture).

12. The authors of the restoration of the Church of Saints Peter and Paul in Kozhevniki are G. M. Shtender and L. M. Shulyak. For a brief analysis of the church see Shulyak in *Novgorod k 1100-letiyu goroda*, ed. M. N. Tikhomirov, pp. 238–39.

13. The most detailed commentary on Novgorod architecture of the sixteenth century is offered by L. E. Krasnorechev and T. V. Gladenko in 'Arkhitektura XVI v' (*Novgorod k 1100-letiyu goroda*, ed. M. N. Tikhomirov, pp. 244–63).

14. A. I. Gertsen [Herzen], *Sobranie sochineniy v 30 tomakh* (Moscow, 1954), 2:47–48.

15. See Yu. P. Spegalsky, *Pskov: Khudozhestvennye pamyatniki*, pp. 20–22, and G. Alferova, 'Sobor Spaso-Mirozhskogo monastyrya,' *Arkitekturnoe nasledstvo*, 10(1958): pp. 3–32.

16. For a survey and schematic outline of the frescoes, see Lazarev, *Drevnerusskie mozaiki i freski*, plates 187–206 (Bibliography: Art and Architecture).

17. See Spegalsky, pp. 127–30. Although Spegalsky here gives the year of construction as 1413, he later considered it to date from the sixteenth century. (See 'Tserkov Vasiliya na Gorke v Pskove,' in *Arkhitekturnoe nasledstvo*, 12(1960): 42.

18. Spegalsky's book provides an excellent survey of the church, fortress, and civilian architecture of medieval Pskov. See also N. S. Khrabrovaya and B. S. Skobeltsyn, *Pskov*.

19. See N. V. Riasanovsky, *A History of Russia* (New York: Oxford University Press, 1963), pp. 137–38 (Bibliography: History).

20. For an English translation, see *Medieval Russia's Epics, Chronicles, and Tales*, ed. Serge A. Zenkovsky, pp. 277–88 (Bibliography: History).

21. For a discussion of the role of Pskov masters in the development of Muscovite architecture, see G. I. Vsdornov, 'Postroyki pskovskoy arteli zodchikh v Moskve,' and M. A. Ilin, 'Pskovskie zodchie v Moskve v kontse XV veka,' in *Drevnerusskoe iskusstvo: Khudozhestvennaya kultura Pskova*, ed. V. N. Lazarev et al.

CHAPTER THREE

1. From the *Primary Chronicle* (under A.M. 6532). For the English translation, see S. H. Cross, *The Russian Primary Chronicle* (Cambridge: Harvard University Press, 1930).

2. See I. B. Purishev, *Pereslavl-Zalessky*, pp. 9–11.

3. The Novgorod-chronicle account is contained under [A.M.] 6677 and 6678. For an English version, see *The Chronicle of Novgorod*, trans. Robert Michell and Nevill Forbes, pp. 26–27 (Bibliography: Chapter Two).

4. G. K. Vagner's *Skultura drevney Rusi XII v.: Vladimir-Bogolyubovo* contains a thorough description of the surviving fragments of the original carvings, pp. 95–124.

5. Ibid., pp. 125–49.

6. Ibid., p. 223.

7. See Nikolai Voronin, *Vladimir, Bogolyubovo, Suzdal, Yurev-Polsky* (in English), p. 145.

8. For the account in the Kievan chronicle, see *Drevnerusskie letopisi*, eds. V. Lebedev and V. Panov (Moscow and Leningrad, 1936), pp. 223–26 (under A.M. 6683).

9. Ibid., p. 223.

10. Ibid., p. 225.

11. See George Heard Hamilton, *The Art and Architecture of Russia*, pp. 39, 43 (Bibliography: Art and Architecture). Also: Vagner, *Skultura drevney Rusi*, pp. 390–415.

12. Vagner, *Skultura drevney Rusi*, pp. 244–93.

13. Ibid., pp. 250–53.

14. There is some confusion in thirteenth-century sources as to who actually built the first church on the site: Vladimir Monamakh or Yury Dolgoruky. In his recent book on the Cathedral of the Nativity, Georgy Vagner supports the view that Vladimir did indeed construct a church in Suzdal in 1108 (its foun-

dations have been uncovered), and that it quickly fell into ruin because of poor construction techniques and was replaced by Dolgoruky's cathedral, which, however, was shifted slightly to the north. The latter church was then rebuilt by Yury Vsevolodovich. Vagner's book contains his usual exhaustive analysis of the monument's stone carving and its other forms of thirteenth-century decoration. See *Belokamennaya rezba drevnego Suzdalya*, pp. 14–25.

15. The fundamental work on the cathedral at Yurev-Polsky is Georgy Vagner's *Skulptura Vladimiro-Suzdalskoy Rusi: G. Yurev-Polskoy*.

16. Novgorod chronicle (under A.M. 6732.) See Michell and Forbes, pp. 63–66 (Bibliography: Chapter Two).

17. See *Drevnerusskie letopisi*, eds. V. Lebedev and V. Panov, pp. 270–71.

18. 'On the Insignificance of Russian Literature' (1832), *Polnoe sobranie sočinenij* (The complete works in ten volumes) 7:307.

CHAPTER FOUR

1. There are a number of works that attempt to reconstruct the early stages of Moscow's development. One of the classic studies is I. E. Zabelin's *Istoriya goroda Moskvy*.

2. A survey of archæological and restorative projects in the Kremlin is presented in the bulletin *Sokhranenie arkhitekturnykh pamyatnikov moskovskogo kremlya* (Moscow, 1977). The fragments of a thirteenth-century limestone church were discovered in the course of work supervised by V. I. Fedorov and N. S. Shelyapina, under the auspices of the State Museum of the Moscow Kremlin (see above, p. 28). A summary of their findings was published in *Arkheologicheskie otkrytie 1968 goda* (Moscow, 1969), pp. 81–83. See also N. S. Shelyapina, 'K istorii izucheniya Uspenskogo sobora moskovskogo Kremlya,' *Sovetskaya arkheologiya*, 1 (1972): pp. 200–14.

3. From the vita of Sergius by Epifany the Wise. For an English translation of the vita, see *Medieval Russia's Epics, Chronicles, and Tales*, ed. Serge Zenkovsky,

pp. 208–36; in particular, p. 230 (Bibliography: History).

4. For a concise description of the church, see M. A. Ilin and T. V. Moiseeva, *Moskva i Podmoskovie*, p. 501. The vaulting of the church, which has no interior piers, rests on the reinforced corners of the structure, a device that has led some to compare it to the Balkan churches of the same period. For a more detailed analysis, see M. A. Ilin, 'Redky pamyatnik drevnerusskoy arkhitektury (khram sela Kamenskogo),' *Istoriya SSSR*, 3 (1969): pp. 150–55.

5. See T. V. Nikolaeva, *Drevny Zvenigorod*, p. 9 (contains thorough annotation).

6. See Nikolaeva, pp. 27, 37. Also M. A. Ilin, 'Dekorativnye reznye poyasa rannemoskovskogo kamennogo zodchestva,' in *Drevnerusskoe iskusstvo: Zarubezhnye svyazi*, ed. G. V. Popov, pp. 223–39 (concerning the possible sources for this ornamentalism). (Bibliography: Chapter One.)

7. For a detailed history of the architecture of the Holy Trinity lavra, see V. I. Baldin's entry 'Arkhitektura' in *Troitse-Sergieva lavra: Khudozhestvennye pamyatniki*, eds. N. N. Voronin and V. V. Kostochkin, pp. 15–71 (with copious annotation); and the same author's book *Arkhitekturny ansambl Troitse-Sergievoy lavry*.

8. Ilin and Moiseeva, p. 470.

9. An imaginative description of all this, as well as the cultural ambience of Ivan's court, is contained in V. Snegirev's *Aristotel Fioravanti i perestroika moskovskogo kremlya*.

10. A survey of the cathedral's history is provided in M. V. Alpatov's introduction to *Uspensky sobor* (English translation, pp. 11–16). Fioravanti's technical innovations are analyzed in the same book by Z. P. Chelyubeeva, pp. 27–30.

11. See A. S. Ramelli, 'Il Cremlino di Mosca, esempio di architettura militare,' in *Arte lombarda*, nos. 44–45 (Milan, 1976), pp. 130–38. This volume of *Arte lombarda* contains a number of articles, in Italian and French, concerning the influence of the Italian Renaissance on Muscovite architecture.

12. 'Venetsianskie istoki arkhitektury moskovskogo Arkhangelskogo sobora,' in *Drevnerusskoe iskusstvo: Zarubezhnye svyazi*, ed. G. V. Popov, pp. 253–86 (Bibliography: Chapter One).

13. There has been some question as to the date of construction of the Cathedral at Novodevichy Convent, but 1524–25 is now generally accepted. See Yu. M. Ovsyannikov, *Novo-Devichy monastyr*, pp. 16–20. Ovsyannikov notes the cathedral's resemblance not only to the Kremlin churches but also to the cathedral at the Pokorovsky (Intercession) Convent in Suzdal (1510–14), with which it is very closely related—historically as well as architecturally.

14. See M. A. Gra and B. B. Zhiromsky, *Kolomenskoe*, p. 110. A. I. Nekrasov, in his book *Drevnerusskoe zodchestvo XI–XVII veka* (Bibliography: Art and Architecture), supported the idea that Renaissance influence played a decisive role in the genesis of the Church of the Ascension, and sharply criticized the wooden-derivation theory as 'reactionary,' a remnant of 'monarchist ideology' (p. 244). Such views were not appreciated in the late thirties. There is little direct evidence for Nekrasov's position, presented within an odd, pseudo-Marxist framework that the Soviets now call 'vulgar sociologism'; yet the presence in sixteenth-century Moscow of Italian architects thoroughly familiar with brickwork as well as the presence of Italianate features in the church itself suggest more about the design of the church than the rather vague notion of a wooden prototype.

15. During restoration of the church, in 1977, workers uncovered the date 1533 engraved on capitals of some of the pilasters. The numerals were Arabic and the date conformed to the Western calendar—neither of which was accepted in Russia at that time. This indicates not only the presence of Western (Italian) masters, but also the fact that substantial work on the church continued after its consecration, in 1531. See Ilin and Moiseeva, p. 480.

16. Soon after the completion of the Cathedral of the Intercession, additional structures began to proliferate, including a chapel built over the burial place of Saint Basil (in 1588), and the present tent-shaped bell tower (no later than the 1670s). There is no precise evidence as to when the church began to be painted, but the earliest layers of color date from the seventeenth century, and the earliest reference to painting occurs in connection with a major renovation in 1682. See V. L. Snegirov, *Pamyatnik arkhitektury khram Vasiliya Blazhennogo*, pp. 85–86.

It should be noted that many of Moscow's brick monuments were painted in the seventeenth century—a fact that has presented contemporary restorers with a dilemma: to paint or whitewash? For example, both the Cathedral of the Archangel Michael and the Bell Tower of Ivan the Great were painted red and white in the seventeenth century, and there are specialists who suggest that they should be returned to these colors—in place of the whitewash that is currently applied. See M. P. Kudryavtsev, 'Problema tsveta pri restavratsii pamyatnikov arkhitektury,' in *Metodika i praktika sokhraneniya pamyatnikov arkhitektury* (Moscow, 1974), pp. 77–78. On the other side there are those who insist that the polychromatic Saint Basil's and the massive red walls of the Kremlin demand a large white grouping (the Kremlin cathedrals) in the center. (Yu. Raninsky, 'Ansambl i gorod,' in *Arkhitektura i stroitelstvo Moskvy*, 3 [1976]: p. 34.)

A related dispute has arisen over the recent coat of whitewash applied to the Church of the Ascension at Kolomenskoe: here critics state that the brick surface should have been left uncovered, in order to reveal the contrast between brick walls and white limestone detail. (P. Zinovev, 'Sporny eksperiment,' in *Arkhitektura i stroitelstvo Moskvy*, 7 [1979]: p. 32.) It has been argued—with good reason—that every seventeenth-century church in Moscow should be painted (not whitewashed, as many now are) in order to highlight the devices of Muscovite ornamentalism: since limestone was not extensively used in the decoration of smaller

churches from that period, the color
of brick ornamentation (window
surrounds and so on) should be distinguished from that of the walls.

17. The compound at Alexandrov
(later to become a monastery, in the
seventeenth century) is one of the
more interesting concentrations of
Muscovite architecture, from the
Intercession (now Trinity) Cathedral,
built by Basil III in 1515, to the
imposing bell tower–church, whose
present form dates from the 1570s.
Alexandrov benefited not only from
the traditional forms of tsarist largess,
but also from the spoils of Ivan's campaigns against Novgorod and Tver,
whose treasures he stored within—
and underneath—its churches. See
G. N. Bocharov and V. P. Vygolov,
Aleksandrovskaya sloboda.

18. For a more detailed analysis
of the characteristics of Godunov's
churches (with emphasis on the Old
Cathedral at Donskoy Monastery), see
Yu. I. Arenkova and G. I. Mekhova,
Donskoy monastyr, pp. 12–17.

19. See E. S. Ovchinnikova, *Tserkov
Troitsy v Nikitnikakh*, p. 16. Ovchinnikova's book contains reproductions
of the well-preserved seventeenth-
century frescoes at the Church of the
Trinity.

20. From V. Podklyuchnikov, *Tri
pamyatnika XVII stoletiya*, p. 20.
See also M. A. Ilin, *Zodchiy Yakov
Bukhvostov*, pp. 111–34.

21. See V. P. Vygolov, 'O razvitii
yarusnykh form v zodchestve kontsa
XVII veka,' in *Drevnerusskoe iskusstvo: XVII vek*, eds. V. N. Lazarev,
O. T. Podobedova, and V. V. Kostochkin, p. 248. The focus of Vygolov's
article is on early masonry examples
of the tiered church.

22. See F. F. Gornostaev, 'Barokko
Moskvy,' in *Istoriya russkogo is-
kusstva*, ed. I. E. Grabar, 2:430, 454
(Bibliography: Art and Architecture).

23. A detailed analysis (with drawings) of the Kadashi settlement and
its significance in the composition of
Moscow at the turn of the eighteenth
century is presented in T. N. Kud-
ryavtseva's article 'Kadashevskaya
sloboda v Moskve i ee razvitie v
kontse XVII–XVIII vv. (gradostroitelny
analiz),' in *Arkhitekturnoe nasledstvo*,
no. 27 (1979), pp. 38–48.

24. The Pashkov family archives
burned during the fire of 1812,
and there is no evidence confirming
Bazhenov as the architect. The case is
made largely on the basis of stylistic
affinities between the Pashkov house
and Bazhenov's project for the Great
Kremlin Palace. See V. L. Snegirev,
Zodchy Bashenov, pp. 162–67.

25. For a survey of Moscow's neoclassical monuments, see *Moskva:
Pamyatniki arkhitektury XVIII-
pervoy treti XIX veka* by M. A. Ilin
with photographs by A. Aleksandrov.

26. See *Kuskovo, Ostankino, Arkhangelskoe*, ed. I. M. Glozman.

The Moscow estates—their mansions, parks, and pavilions—compose the theme of what is perhaps the
most lavish art book ever produced
by the Soviet Union. Entitled . . . *v
okrestnostyakh Moskvy*, by M. A.
Anikst and V. S. Turchin, the work is
extremely weighty and should not be
placed on any but the sturdiest of
surfaces. (Includes a separate volume
with résumés in English, French, and
German, beautifully printed.)

27. For a listing of works attributed
to Grigorev, see *Arkhitektor A. G.
Grigorev*, ed. V. I. Baldin.

28. A. V. Ikonnikov, *Kamennaya
letopis Moskvy: Putevoditel*, p. 94.

29. For an exhaustive study—one
might almost call it an apology—
of nineteenth-century Russian eclecticism, see E. A. Borisova, *Russkaya
arkhitektura vtoroy poloviny XIX
veka*. E. I. Kirichenko covers much the
same material in the first part of her
admirable book *Russkaya arkhitektura 1830–1910-kh godov* (Moscow,
1978). Her primary interest, however,
appears to be the Russian variant of
art nouveau, '*style moderne*' (cf. infra).

CHAPTER FIVE

1. The standard Soviet history of
the city's early years is contained in
volume one of *Ocherki istorii Leningrada*, ed. M. P. Vyatkin. For a more
detailed account of the planning and
construction of Saint Petersburg in
its first decades, see S. P. Luppov, ed.,
*Istoriya stroitelstva Peterburga v per-
voy chetverti XVIII veka*. In English,

Christopher Marsden's *Palmyra of the North* (London: Faber and Faber, 1942) contains an entertaining, if frequently unreliable, account of Petersburg in the eighteenth century.

2. For a comprehensive account of the development of Vasilevsky Island (particularly its point, or *strelka*), see M. S. Bunin, *Strelka Vasilevskogo ostrova*. This book contains a magnificent photograph of the island and the Neva delta, taken from a balloon in 1886.

3. Igor Grabar, *Istoriya russkogo iskusstva* 3:10 (Bibliography: Art and Architecture).

4. Although the stylistic experimentation of Petersburg's early structures has been frequently noted, only recently has there been a thorough study of the evolution of architectural thought in Russia at the turn of the eighteenth century and in the following decades (in Moscow as well as Petersburg). In her book *Arkhitekturnaya teoriya v Rossii XVIII v.*, N. A. Yevsina demonstrates that the state did not simply invite foreign architects to Russia, but made a comprehensive effort to assimilate, to create a new architectural language. The role of foreign architects in the formation of Russian cadres is examined in E. A. Borisova's article '"Arkhitekturnye ucheniki" petrovskogo vremeni i ikh obuchenie v komandakh zodchikh-inostrantsev v Peterburge,' in the collection *Russkoe iskusstvo pervoy chetverti XVIII veka*, ed. T. V. Alekseeva, pp. 9–26.

5. Trezzini's party disembarked at Arkhangelskoe in July 1703 and proceeded first to Moscow, where all eight of his master craftsmen were to remain—apparently to create the baroque interiors of such churches as the Archangel Gabriel (Menshikov's Tower) and the Sign at Dubrovitsy. See Irina Lisaevich's colorful biography of Trezzini, *Pervy arkhitektor Peterburga*, pp. 5–14.

6. Although there is no information on Rastrelli's travel in Europe (after his departure from France in 1715), Hamilton notes an affinity between his work and the late-baroque monuments of Austria and northern Europe. Hamilton further suggests that the theatricality of Rastrelli's style may be related to the set designs and architectural engravings of Ferdinando and Giuseppe Galli da Bibiena. (George Heard Hamilton, *The Art and Architecture of Russia*, pp. 196, 305, fns. 12, 13.) (Bibliography: Art and Architecture.) For a survey of Rastrelli's sketches, see Yu. M. Denisov and A. N. Petrov, *Zodchy Rastrelli*.

7. Rastrelli's interior at Peterhof is as luxuriant as that of his other palaces; and although most of it was destroyed during the Second World War, much has since been restored on the basis of drawings and photographs. A detailed history of work on the interior, first by Rastrelli, then, in the 1770s, by Georg Veldten, is contained in N. I. Arkhipov and A. G. Raskin, *Petrodvorets*, pp. 47–51.

8. Quoted in D. Arkin, *Rastrelli*, p. 105.

9. *Zapiski Imperatritsy Ekateriny Vtoroy* [Notes of the Empress Catherine II] (Saint Petersburg, 1907), pp. 120–21. For an account of the earlier stages of work, including the designs of Andrey Kvasov and Savva Chevakinsky, see A. N. Petrov, *Pushkin: Dvortsy i parki*, pp. 28–32.

10. William Coxe, *Travels into Poland, Russia, Sweden, and Denmark* (London, T. Cadell, 1785) 1:477.

11. Grabar, op. cit., p. 223 (Bibliography: Art and Architecture).

12. For a chronicle of the various redecorations of the Winter Palace, see Levinson-Lessing's *Ermitazh: Istoriya i arkhitektura zdaniy*. Copiously illustrated.

13. Grabar, p. 223. S. B. Alekseeva makes an impressive attempt to analyze the various sculptural elements of the Winter Palace, in terms not only of the plasticity of the facade, but also of their domination of the extensive space within which the palace is set. See her 'Arkhitektura i dekorativnaya plastika Zimnego dvortsa,' in *Russkoe iskusstvo barokko*, ed. T. V. Alekseeva, pp. 128–58. In his survey of the design of the facade in the Russian baroque, V. I. Pluzhnikov states: 'The facades of the baroque, perhaps to a greater degree than those of any other architectural style, are distinguished by their theatricality, imposing a dynamic on stable elements of the

structure and creating a rhythmic complexity unrequired in a functional sense, and sometimes in opposition to it' ('Organizatsiya fasada v arkhitekture russkogo barokko,' in *Russkoe iskusstvo barokko*, p. 88). Russian architecture has witnessed earlier examples of a dichotomy between the resolution of the facade and the structure of a building (particularly in the seventeenth century), but not until the imperial era had the demands of architectural rhetoric been imposed on so large a mass, intended to project authority, wealth, and the control of a vast space.

14. For an analysis of the adaptation of the traditional pentacupolar design in Russian baroque church architecture, see T. P. Fedotova, 'K probleme pyatiglaviya v arkhitekture barokko pervoy poloviny XVIII v.,' in *Russkoe iskusstvo barokko*, ed. T. V. Alekseeva, pp. 70–87. In view of the Italian origins of so many of Russia's baroque architects, it is logical to assume, as Fedotova does, that Italy's seventeenth-century churches (especially the work of Borromini) were influential in the Russian integration of baroque decoration with the concept of the central dome and surrounding towers.

15. *Sbornik Imperatorskogo Russkogo istoricheskogo obshcestva* [Collection of the Imperial Russian Historical Society], 23: 'Pisma Imperatritsy Ekateriny II k Grimmu' [Letters of Empress Catherine II to Grimm] (text in French; Petersburg, 1885), p. 157.

16. Hugh Honour, *Neo-classicism*, p. 18 (Bibliography: Art and Architecture).

17. A brief biography of Rinaldi (of whom very little is known) is contained in D. A. Kyuchariants's monograph *Antonio Rinaldi*, pp. 7–14; see also G. G. Grimm's article on Rinaldi in *Istoriya russkogo iskusstva*, eds. I. E. Grabar et al., 6:68–76. A detailed analysis of his work at Gatchina is provided by V. K. Makarov and A. N. Petrov in their book *Gatchina*; Rinaldi's palaces and pavilions at Oranienbaum—closed to foreigners, unfortunately—are described in A. G. Raskin's *Gorod Lomonosov: Dvortsova-parkovye ansambli XVIII veka*.

18. For an investigation of Cameron's apparently spurious claim, see Tamara Talbot Rice's 'Charles Cameron, Architect to the Imperial Russian Court,' in the catalogue *Charles Cameron* (London: The Arts Council, 1967), pp. 8–10.

19. Hamilton, p. 307, fn. 24 (Bibliography: Art and Architecture).

20. The case for Brown is made by Isobel Rae in her book *Charles Cameron: Architect to the Court of Russia*, p. 70.

21. Views of Quarenghi's nonextant English Palace are available in M. F. Korshunova's *Dzhakomo Kvarengi*, pp. 31–35, and in *Disegni di Giacomo Quarenghi: Catalogo della mostra*. The latter contains a comprehensive selection of Quarenghi's architectural sketches.

22. Quoted in Grabar, op. cit., p. 466.

23. For a discussion of the possibility of a link between Bazhenov's work and Voronikhin's design for the Kazan Cathedral, see V. G. Lisovsky, *Andrey Voronikhin*, pp. 87–105. Lisovsky considers the evidence insufficient to establish a case of direct influence. It must be noted, however, that Voronikhin had studied with Bazhenov, and that both Russians had a first-hand acquaintance with the work of distinguished French neoclassicists such as de Wailly and Chalgrin.

24. The best study of Petersburg's system of open space and architectural ensemble is S. B. Alekseeva's 'Rol monumentalno-dekorativnoy skulptury v formirovanii ansamblya tsentralnkh ploshchadey Peterburga pervoy poloviny XIX v.,' in *Russkoe iskusstvo vtoroy poloviny XVIII–pervoy poloviny XIX v.*, pp. 38–68.

25. Quoted in M. Z. Taranovskaya, *Karl Rossi*, p. 27.

26. Dostoevsky, *The Diary of a Writer*, trans. Boris Brasol (New York: Octagon Books, 1973), p. 121.

27. For a history, with excellent illustrations, of the architectural trends fashionable in Petersburg at the turn of the century, see E. I. Kirichenko's *Russkaya arkhitektura 1830–1910-kh godov*.

28. The watercolors are reproduced in *Vidy Peterburga i ego okrestnostey*

serediny XVIII veka, with text by G. N. Komelova; the photographs are contained in I. N. Bozheryanov's bicentennial album *Nevsky Prospekt, 1703–1903*.

CHAPTER SIX

1. Originally published in Austria in 1930 as *Russland, Die Rekonstruktion der Architektur in der Sowjetunion*, Lissitzky's essay was republished, with supplementary material, in 1965 in Germany as *Russland: Architektur für eine Weltrevolution*. Eric Dluhosch's English translation, published by the MIT Press in 1970, draws its title from the German edition.

2. Quoted in Ye. I. Kirichenko, *Russkaya arkhitektura 1830–1910-kh godov*, p. 170.

3. In her sympathetic study of *style moderne*, Kirichenko admits that the style is frequently trivial, yet argues that this is the result of social conditions and should not affect our understanding of the 'model' of the style: by 'model' she means an emphasis on the organic structure, developed 'from within,' and an attempt to unite the useful and the beautiful. But there is little actual distinction between the real and the ideal in *moderne*, this most commercial of styles. Ibid., p. 326.

4. For photographs and a discussion of Shekhtel's work, see Ye. I. Kirichenko, *Fyodor Shekhtel*, pp. 49–51.

5. At the turn of the century, Russian architectural publications frequently proposed a 'rationalist' approach to the relation between new building materials (particularly iron or steel) and the design and appearance of large commercial structures. For example, V. P. Apyshkov, in his *Ratsionalnoe v noveyshey arkhitekture*, discussed by Kirichenko in *Russkaya arkhitektura 1830–1910-kh godov*, pp. 219–25.

6. For a survey of this movement, see Ye. A. Borisova and T. P. Kazhdan, *Russkaya arkhitektura kontsa XIX–nachala XX veka*, pp. 167–219. At the risk of thoroughly confusing matters, it must be noted that Russian art historians use the term *klassitsism* to designate neoclassicism. The Russian term *neoklassitsism*, referring to the early-twentieth-century style, will be translated here as 'neoclassical revival.'

7. G. Lukomsky, *Sovremenny Petrograd*, p. 10. Quoted in Borisova and Kazhdan, p. 182.

8. Borisova and Kazhdan, pp. 188, 190.

9. See Kirichenko, *Russkaya arkhitektura 1830–1910-kh godov*, p. 366. O. R. Munts offered a general contemporary critique of the neoclassical revival in his article 'The Parthenon or Hagia Sophia' (in Russian), *Arkhitekturno-khudozhestvenny ezhegodnik*, no. 2, 1916. For excerpts, see Borisova and Kazhdan, pp. 217–18.

10. Surveys of the development of city planning and garden suburbs can be found in Borisova and Kazhdan, pp. 49–78, and S. Frederick Starr, 'The Revival and Schism of Russian Urbanism,' in *The Russian City in History*, ed. Michael Hamm, pp. 222 ff.

11. The Congress is described in Borisova and Kazhdan, pp. 37–38. For a survey of pre-Revolutionary modernist visions, see Ye. I. Kirichenko, *Moskva: Pamyatniki arkhitektury 1830–1910-kh godov* (with an English translation), pp. 94–104.

12. *Russia: An Architecture for World Revolution*, translated by Eric Dluhosch, p. 27.

13. See Lissitzky, pp. 28–34. An English survey of these developments is contained in Camilla Gray, *The Russian Experiment in Art: 1863–1922*, pp. 240–41 and *passim*.

14. See V. E. Khazanova, *Sovetskaya arkhitektura pervykh let oktyabrya*, p. 204.

15. See V. E. Khazanova, *Iz istorii sovetskoy arkhitektury 1926–1932 gg.*, pp. 39–41.

16. See Kazimir Malevich, *The Nonobjective World*, pp. 27–102 (with illustrations). See also V. E. Khazanova, *Sovetskaya arkhitektura pervykh let oktyabrya*, pp. 24–26.

17. Ibid., pp. 18, 39 (fn. 28), 203.

18. Ibid., p. 38 (fn. 25).

19. For material on the Union of Architects-Urbanists (ARU), see V. E. Khazanova, *Iz istorii sovetskoy arkhitektury 1926–1932 gg.*, pp. 123–46. The innovative views of Nikolay Milyutin on city planning and the

linear city are developed in his book of 1930, *Sotsgorod: The Problem of Building Socialist Cities*, translated into English by Arthur Sprague, with notes and introduction by George Collins and William Alex. See also Lissitzky, pp. 50–66. Soviet surveys of urban planning between 1918 and 1932 include: V. E. Khazanova, *Sovetskaya arkhitektura pervykh let oktyabrya*, pp. 43–100; V. E. Khazanova, *Iz istorii sovetskoy arkhitektury 1917–1925 gg.*, pp. 7–128 (includes documents and plans); and Selim Khan-Magomedov's chapter on city planning in *Arkhitektura sovetskoy Rossii*, ed. Yu. S. Yaralov.

20. For a brief history of the constructivists and their Union of Contemporary Architects (OSA), see V. E. Khazanova, *Iz istorii sovetskoy arkhitektury 1926–1932 gg.*, pp. 65–68.

21. I. Kokkinaki surveys the links between Soviet and Western architects of this period in 'K voprosu o vzaimosvyazyakh sovetskikh i zarubezhnykh arkhitektorov v 1920–1930-e gody' in the book *Voprosy sovetskogo izobrazitelnogo iskusstva i arkhitektury*, ed. I. M. Shmidt et al.

22. See relevant documents in V. E. Khazanova, *Iz istorii sovetskoy arkhitektury 1926–1932 gg.*, pp. 50–53, 43–44, 70–72.

23. See Lissitzky, pp. 43–45; S. Frederick Starr, *Konstantin Melnikov: Solo Architect in a Mass Society*, pp. 133–35; and Khan-Magomedov, 'Formirovanie novykh tipov obshchestvennykh zdaniy,' in *Arkhitektura sovetskoy Rossii*, ed. Yu. S. Yaralov, pp. 69–76.

24. For a discussion of the possible link between the design of the Rusakov Club and expressionism (à la Erich Mendelsohn), see Starr, ibid., pp. 135–37.

25. Starr suggests that the one structure that might have influenced the design of the Melnikov house is the American grain elevator. Ibid., p. 119.

26. Moisey Ginzburg, 'Funktsionalny metod i forma,' in *Sovremennaya arkhitektura*, 1926, no. 4, pp. 89–92. Included in V. E. Khazanova, *Iz istorii sovetskoy arkhitektury 1926–1932 gg.*, pp. 72–73.

27. According to A. V. Ikonnikov,

Kamennaya letopis Moskvy, p. 197.

28. G. Gorvits provides an interesting account of large project designs in Kharkov (capital of the Ukrainian S.S.R. until 1934) by architects from Leningrad—which had a surfeit of architects as a result of the shift of major construction to Moscow. In its years as the Ukrainian capital, Kharkov was the site of some of the most ambitious architectural complexes in the functionalist style. 'Iz istorii tvorcheskikh svyazey arkhitektorov Leningrada i pervoy stolitsy Ukrainy,' in *Voprosy sovetskogo izobrazitelnogo iskusstva i arkhitektury*, ed. I. M. Shmidt et al., pp. 311–49. For a survey of developments in other Soviet cities, see *Arkhitektura sovetskoy Rossii*, ed. Yu. S. Yaralov, pp. 5–31.

29. 'Forma i soderzhanie,' in *Arkhitekturnaya gazeta*, April 8, 1935. Quoted in M. A. Ilin, *Vesniny*, p. 111.

30. See V. P. Belov, *Monolitny zhelezobeton* (poured ferro-concrete), Moscow, 1977.

31. See, for example, *Arkhitektura S.S.S.R.*, 1980, no. 8, pp. 32–38.

EPILOGUE

1. 'Ob arkhitekture nyneshnego vremeni,' in N. V. Gogol, *Sobranie sochineniy v shesti tomakh* [N. V. Gogol, collected works in six volumes] (Moscow, 1959), 6:59.

2. 'Rech ob arkhitekture v Rossii do XVIII stoletiya' [Discourse on Russian architecture until the eighteenth century], quoted in Ye. I. Kirichenko, *Russkaya arkhitektura 1830–1910-kh godov*, pp. 57–58.

3. *Khudozhestvennaya gazeta*, SPb, 1838, no. 12, pp. 393–94. Quoted in Ye. A. Borisova, *Russkaya arkhitektura vtoroy poloviny XIX veka*, p. 92.

4. See Kirichenko, Ibid., p. 57.

5. *Zhizn khudozhnika: Vospominaniya* [The life of an artist: reminiscences] (New York: Chekhov Publishing House, 1955), p. 70.

6. As examined in Erwin Panofsky, *Gothic Architecture and Scholasticism* (New York: Meridien Books, 1957).

7. Borisova, Ibid., p. 98.

8. See B. Vipers (Vipper), *Baroque*

Art in Latvia (Riga, 1939), pp. 8–9.

9. See *Petersburg*, translated, annotated, and introduced by Robert Maguire and John Malmstad (Bloomington: Indiana University Press, 1978), p. 2.

10. 'Progulka v akademiyu khudozhestv' [A stroll to the Academy of Arts], in *Sochineniya K. N. Batyushkova* [Works of K. N. Batyushkov], three vols., edited by P. N. Batyushkov (Saint Petersburg, 1885), 2:97.

11. For a sampling of opinion on Moscow, see Borisova, Ibid., pp. 134–39.

12. See 'On the Problem of Functions in Architecture,' in *Structure, Sign, and Function: Selected Essays by Jan Mukařovský*, translated and edited by John Burbank and Peter Steiner (New Haven: Yale University Press, 1978), pp. 236–50, specifically p. 245.

APPENDIX A

1. The best photographs of many of these remote churches and information on their dates are contained in volume one of Igor Grabar's *Istoriya russkogo iskusstva* (Moscow, 1910–15).

2. A thorough description, in Russian, of the Vitoslavlitsy Museum is to be found in Lyudmila Filipova's *Vitoslavlitsy: Muzey derevyannogo zodchestva* (Leningrad, 1979).

bibliography

The following is not a comprehensive bibliography on Russian architecture. It is, rather, a list of books that I have found to be of value in the preparation of this work. Included are collections of articles, but not references to specific articles; these are in the footnotes.

Russian works marked by an asterisk contain either a full translation or a summary in English, French, or German. Translations of the Russian titles are in brackets; those that are also within quotation marks are by Soviet translators.

General Reference Works

HISTORY

Billington, James H. *The Icon and the Axe: An Interpretive History of Russian Culture.* New York: Alfred A. Knopf, 1966.

Fedetov, Georgii Petrovich. *The Russian Religious Mind: Kievan Christianity, the Tenth to the Thirteenth Centuries.* Cambridge: Harvard University Press, 1966.

Grekov, Boris Dmitrevich. *Kievskaya Rus.* Moscow, 1953.

Hamm, Michael, ed. *The Russian City in History.* Lexington: University of Kentucky Press, 1976.

Miliukov, Paul. *Outline of Russian Culture.* Edited by Michael Karpovich. New York: Barnes, 1960.

Riasanovsky, Nicholas V. *A History of Russia.* New York: Oxford University Press, 1963.

Vernadsky, George. *A History of Russia.* 5th rev. ed. New Haven: Yale University Press, 1961.

Zenkovsky, Serge A., ed. *Medieval Russia's Epics, Chronicles, and Tales.* New York: E. P. Dutton, 1963.

ART AND ARCHITECTURE

Afanasev, K. N. *Postroenie arkhitekturnoy formy drevnerusskimi zodchimi* [The conception of architectural form by early Russians]. Moscow, 1961.

Brunov, N. I., et al. *Istoriya russkoy arkhitektury* [A history of Russian architecture]. 2nd rev. ed. Moscow, 1956.

Encyclopedia of World Art (entries under 'Union of Soviet Socialist Republics' and 'Slavic Art'). New York: McGraw-Hill, 1967.

Faensen, Hubert, and Ivanov, Vladimir. *Early Russian Architecture.* London: Paul Elek, 1975.

Fleming, John; Honour, Hugh; and Pevsner, Nikolaus. *A Dictionary of Architecture.* Baltimore: Penguin Books, 1974.

Grabar, Igor Emmanuilovich, ed. *Istoriya russkogo iskusstva* [History of Russian art]. Moscow, 1910–15.

Grabar, I. E., Lazarev, V. N., and Kemenov, S. S., eds. *Istoriya russkogo iskusstva,* 13 vols. Moscow, 1953–68.

Hamilton, George Heard. *The Art and Architecture of Russia,* 2nd rev. ed. Baltimore: Penguin Books, 1975.

Honour, Hugh. *Neo-Classicism.* Baltimore: Penguin Books, 1968.

Lazarev, V. N. *Drevnerusskie mozaiki i freski* [Old Russian mosaics and frescoes]. Moscow, 1971.

Milchik, M. I. and Ushakov, Yu. S. *Derevyannaya arkhitektura russkogo severa. Stranitsy istorii* [Wooden architecture of the Russian north. Pages of history]. Leningrad, 1981.

Mongait, A. L. *Architecture in the USSR,* translated by M. W. Thompson. Baltimore: Penguin Books, 1961.

Nekrasov, A. I. *Drevnerusskoe zodchestvo* [Old Russian art]. Moscow, 1936.

Opolovnikov, A. V. *Russky sever* [The Russian north]. Moscow, 1977.

Rice, Tamara Talbot. *A Concise History of Russian Art.* New York: Praeger, 1963.

Zabello, S., Ivanov, V., and Maksimov, P. *Russkoe derevyannoe zodchestvo* [Russian wooden architecture]. Moscow, 1942.

Chapter One: Kiev and Chernigov

Aseev, Yu. S., et al., eds. *Istoriya ukrainskogo mistetstva* [History of Ukrainian art (in Ukrainian)], vol. 1. Kiev, 1966.

Aseev, Yu. S. *Mystetstvo starodavn' oho Kyieva* [Architecture of old Kiev (in Ukrainian)]. Kiev, 1969.

Cross, S. H., trans. *The Russian Primary Chronicle.* Cambridge: Harvard University Press, 1930.

———. *Medieval Russian Churches.* Cambridge: The Medieval Academy of America, 1949.

Karger, M. K. *Drevny Kiev* [Old Kiev], vol. 2. Moscow and Leningrad, 1961.

*Kilesso, S. K. *Kievo-Pecherskaya lavra* [Kiev monastery of the caves]. Moscow, 1975.

Krasovsky, Mikhail. *Plany drevnerusskikh khramov* [Plans of Old Russian churches]. Petrograd, 1915.

Krautheimer, Richard. *Early Christian and Byzantine Architecture.* New York: Penguin Books, 1979.

Kresalny, N. I. *Sofiissky zapovidnik u Kiivi* [The Saint Sophia historical site in Kiev]. Kiev, 1960.

Lazarev, V. N., ed. *Drevnerusskoe iskusstvo: Khudozhestvennaya kultura domongolskoy Rusi* [Old Russian art: The artistic culture of pre-Mongol Rus]. Moscow, 1971.

———. *Mozaika Sofii Kievskoy* [The mosaics of the Saint Sophia Cathedral in Kiev]. Moscow, 1960.

Logvin, G. N. *Kievo-Pecherskaya lavra* [Kievan monastery of the caves]. Moscow, 1958.

———. *Chernigov, Novgorod-Seversky, Glukhov, Putivl.* Moscow, 1965.

———. *Kiev.* Moscow, 1967.

———. *Po Ukraini: Starodavni mystets'ki pam'iatky* [Around the Ukraine: old architectural monuments (in Ukrainian)]. Kiev, 1968.

Popov, G. V., ed. *Drevnerusskoe iskusstvo: Zarubezhnye svyazi* [Old Russian art: Foreign ties]. Moscow, 1975.

Tsapenko, M. P. *Arkhitektura levoberezhnoy Ukrainy XVII–XVIII vekoy* [Architecture of left-bank Ukraine, seventeenth to eighteenth centuries]. Moscow, 1967.

Vashchenko, L. L., ed. *Arkheologiya Kieva* [The archæology of Kiev]. Kiev, 1979.

Chapter Two: Novgorod and Pskov

*Alpatov, M. V. *Freski tserkvi Uspeniya na Volotovom pole* [The frescoes of the Church of the Dormition at Volotov Field]. Moscow, 1977.

Dietze, Joachim. *Die Erste Novgoroder Chronik.* Leipzig, 1971.

Filippova, Lyudmila. *Vitislavlitsy: Muzey derevyannogo zodchestva* [Vitaslavlitsy: museum of wooden architecture]. Leningrad, 1979.

Karger, M. K. *Novgorod the Great.* Moscow, 1973.

———. *˙Novgorod: Pamyatniki arkhitektury, XI–XVII vekov* ['Novgorod: Architectural Monuments: Eleventh to Seventeenth Centuries']. Leningrad, 1975.

Khrabovaya, N. S., and Skobeltsyn, B. S. *Pskov.* Leningrad, 1967.

Lazarev, V. N. *Iskusstvo Novgorod* [The art of Novgorod]. Moscow, 1947.

Lazarev, V. N., Podobedova, O. I., and Kostochkin, V. V., eds. *Drevnerusskoe iskusstvo: Khudozhestvennaya kultura Novgoroda* [Early Russian art: The artistic culture of Novgorod]. Moscow, 1968.

———. *Drevnerusskoe iskusstvo: Khudozhestvennaya kultura Pskova* [Early Russian art: the artistic culture of Pskov]. Moscow, 1968.

Likhachev, D. S. *Novgorod Veliky: Ocherk istorii kultury Novgoroda XI–XVII vv.* [Novgorod the Great: A study in the history of the culture of Novgorod]. Moscow, 1959.

Michell, Robert, and Forbes, Nevill, trans. *The Chronicle of Novgorod.* London: Royal Historical Society, 1914.

Onasch, Konrad. *Gross Novgorod: Aufstieg und Niedergang einer russischer Stadtrepublik.* Vienna and Munich: Anton Schroll, 1969.

Spegalsky, Yu. P. *Pskov: Khudozhestvennye pamyatniki* [Pskov: Monuments of art]. Leningrad, 1972.

Tikhomirov, M. N, ed. *Novgorod: K 1100-letiyu goroda* [Novgorod: On the 1100th anniversary of the city]. Moscow, 1964.

Vagner, G. K., and Likhachev, D. S., eds. *Srednevekovaya Rus* [Medieval Russia]. Moscow, 1976.

Voronin, N. N., and Rappoport, P. A.. *Zodchestvo Smolenska XII–XIII vv.* [The architecture of Smolensk, twelfth to thirteenth centuries]. Leningrad, 1979.

˙Vzdornov, G. I. *Freski Feofana Greka v tserkvi Spasa Preobrazheniya v Novgorode* [The frescoes of Theophanes the Greek at the Church of the Transfiguration of the Savior in Novgorod]. Moscow, 1976.

Chapter Three: Vladimir and Suzdal

˙Purishchev, I. B. *Pereslavl-Zalessky.* Moscow, 1970.

Rapov, M. *Kamennye skazki: Sokrovishcha drevney russkoy arkhitektury Yaroslavskoy oblasti* [Tales in stone: Treasures of old Russian architecture in the Yaroslavl area]. Yaroslavl, 1965.

Vagner, G. K. *Skulptura Vladimiro-Suzdalskoy Rusi: G. Yurev-Polskoy* [The sculpture of Vladimir-Suzdal Rus: The town of Yurev-Polskoy]. Moscow, 1964.

———. *Skultura drevney Rusi XII v.: Vladimir-Bogolyubovo* [The sculpture of Old Russia, twelfth century: Vladimir and Bogolyubovo]. Moscow, 1969.

———. *Belokamennaya rezba drevnego Suzdalya* [The limestone carving of Old Suzdal]. Moscow, 1975.

Varganov, A. D. *Suzdal.* Yaroslavl, 1971.

Voronin, N. N. *Zodchestvo severovostochnoy Rusi XII–XV vekov* [The architecture of northeastern Rus: twelfth to fifteenth centuries], 2 vols. Moscow, 1961.

———. *Vladimir, Bogolyubovo, Suzdal, Yurev-Polskoi: Old Russian Towns.* Moscow, 1971.

Chapter Four: Moscow

˙Alpatov, M. V., and Chelyubeeva, Z. P. *Uspensky sobor* [The Cathedral of the Dormition]. Moscow, 1971.

˙Anikst, M. A., and Turchin, V. S. *'. . . v okrestnostyakh Moskvy: Iz istorii russkoy usadebnoy kultury XVII–XIX vekov'* ['Country Estates around Moscow: From the History of Russian Estate Culture of the Seventeenth, Eighteenth and Nineteenth Centuries'].

˙Arenkova, Yu. I., and Mekhova, G. I. *Donskoy monastyr* [Donskoy Monastery]. Moscow, 1970.

Baldin, V. I., ed. *Arkhitektor D. V. Ukhtomsky.* Moscow, 1973.

———. *Arkhitektor A. G. Grigorev.* Moscow, 1976.

————. *Arkhitekturny ansambl Troitse-Sergievoy lavry [The architectural ensemble of the Trinity–St. Sergius Lavra]. Moscow, 1976.

Berton, Kathleen. *Muscovite Architectural History.* New York: St. Martin's Press, 1978.

*Bocharov, G. N., and Vygolov, V. P. *Aleksandrovskaya sloboda* [The Aleksandrov Compound]. Moscow, 1970.

Borisova, E. A. *Russkaya arkhitektura vtoroy poloviny XIX veka* [Russian architecture of the second half of the nineteenth century]. Moscow, 1979.

Fennel, J. L. I. *The Emergence of Moscow: 1304–1359.* Berkeley and Los Angeles: University of California Press, 1968.

Fletcher, Giles. *Of the Russe Commonwealth.* Introduction by Richard Pipes. Cambridge: Harvard University Press, 1966.

Glozman, I. M., ed. *Kuskovo, Ostankino, Arkhangelskoe.* Moscow, 1976.

*Gra, M. A., and Zhiromsky, B. B. *Kolomenskoe.* Moscow, 1971.

Gray, Camilla. *The Russian Experiment in Art: 1863–1922.* New York: Harry N. Abrams, 1970.

Ikonnikov, A. V. *Kammennaya letopis Moskvy: Putevoditel* [Moscow's chronicle in stone]. Moscow, 1978.

Ilin, M. A. *Zodchy Yakov Bukhvostov* [The architect Yakov Bukhvostov]. Moscow, 1959.

————. *Moskva: Pamyatniki arkhitektury XIV–XVII vekov* ['Moscow: Monuments of Architecture of the Fourteenth to Seventeenth Centuries']. Moscow, 1973.

————. *Moskva: Pamyatniki arkhitektury XVIII–pervoy treti XIX veka* ['Moscow: Monuments of architecture Eighteenth–the first third of the Nineteenth Century']. Moscow, 1975.

Ilin, M. A., and Moiseeva, T. V. *Moskva i Podmoskove* [Moscow and environs]. Moscow, 1979.

Ilyin, M. *Moscow: Architecture and Monuments.* Moscow, 1968.

Kirichenko, E. I. *Moskva: Pamyatniki arkhitektury 1830–1910-kh godov* ['Moscow: Architectural Monuments of the 1830–1910s']. Moscow, 1977.

————. *Russkaya arkhitektura 1830–1910-kh godov* [Russian architecture of the 1830s to the 1910s]. Moscow, 1978.

Lazarev, V. N., Podobedova, O. I., and Kostochkin, V. V., eds. *Drevnerusskoe iskusstvo: XV–nachala XVI vekov* [Old Russian art: fifteenth to beginning of the sixteenth centuries]. Moscow, 1963.

————. *Drevnerusskoe iskusstvo: XVII vek* [Old Russian art: seventeenth century]. Moscow, 1964.

*Nikolaeva, T. V.. *Drevny Zvenigorod* [Old Zvenigorod]. Moscow, 1978.

*Ovchinnikova, E. S. *Tserkov Troitsy v Nikitnikakh* [The Church of the Trinity in Nikitniki]. Moscow, 1970.

*Ovsyannikov, Yu. M. *Novo-Devichy monastyr* [The New Maiden Convent]. Moscow, 1968.

Podklyuchnikov, V. N. *Tri pamyatnika XVII stoletiya: Tserkov v Filyakh, Tserkov v Uborakh, Tserkov v Troitskom Lykove* [Three seventeenth-century monuments: The church at Fili, the Church at Ubory, the Church at Troitskoe-Lykovo]. In the series *Pamyatniki russkoy arkhitektury*, V. Moscow, 1945.

Podyapolskaya, E. N. *Pamyatniki arkhitektury moskovskoy oblasti* [Architectural monuments of the Moscow region], 2 vols. Moscow, 1975.

Snegirev, V. L. *Aristotel Fioravanti i perestroika moskovskogo kremlya* ['Aristotile Fioravanti and the reconstruction of the Moscow Kremlin']. Moscow, 1935.

————. *Pamyatnik arkhitektury khram Vasiliya Blazhennogo* [Saint Basil's: Architectural monument]. Moscow, 1953.

————. *Zodchy Bazhenov* [The architect Bazhenov]. Moscow, 1962.

Sytin, P. V. *Istoriya planirovki i zastroiki Moskvy* [History of the planning and construction of Moscow], 2 vols. Moscow, 1950–54.

————. *Iz istorii moskovskikh ulits* [From the history of Moscow's streets], 3rd rev. ed. Moscow, 1958.

Teltevsky, P. A. *Zodchy Bukhvostov [The architect Bukhvostov].* Moscow, 1960.

Vagner, G. K. *Ryazan.* Moscow, 1971.

*Voronin, N. N., and Kostochkin, V. V., eds. *Troitse-Sergieva lavra: Khudozhestvennye pamyatniki* [The Trinity-St. Sergius monastery: artistic monuments]. Moscow, 1968.

Zabelin, I. E. *Istoriya goroda Moskvy* [The history of the City of Moscow]. Moscow, 1902.

Chapter Five: Petersburg

Alekseeva, T. V., ed. *Russkoe iskusstvo XVIII veka* [Russian art of the eighteenth century]. Moscow, 1968.

———. *Russkoe iskusstvo pervoy chetverti XVIII veka* [Russian art of the first quarter of the eighteenth century]. Moscow, 1974.

———. *Russkoe iskusstvo barokko* [Russian art of the baroque]. Moscow, 1977.

———. *Russkoe iskusstvo vtoroy poloviny XVIII–pervoy poloviny XIX v* [Russian art of the second half of the eighteenth century and the first half of the nineteenth]. Moscow, 1979.

Antsiferov, N. P. *Dusha Peterburga* [The spirit of Petersburg]. Petersburg [*sic*], 1922.

Ardikutsa, V. E. *Petrodvorets.* Leningrad, 1968.

Arkhipov, N. I., and Raskin, A. G. *Petrodvorets.* Leningrad and Moscow, 1961.

———. *Bartolomeo Karlo Rastrelli: 1675–1744.* Leningrad and Moscow, 1964.

Arkin, David. *Rastrelli.* Moscow, 1954.

Belekov, N., and Petrov, A. *Ivan Starov.* Moscow, 1950.

Bogdanov, Andrey. *Istoricheskoe, geograficheskoe, topograficheskoe opisanie Sanktpeterburga* [Historical, geographic, and topographic description of Saint Petersburg]. (Completed in 1750; published, with a foreword, by Vasily Rubanov.) Saint Petersburg, 1779.

Bozheryanov, I. N. *Nevsky Prospekt: 1703–1903.* Saint Petersburg, 1903.

Bunin, M. S. *Strelka Vasilevskogo ostrova* [The tip of Vasilevsky Island]. Moscow and Leningrad, 1957.

Denisov, Yu. M., and Petrov, A. N. *Zodchy Rastrelli: Materialy k izucheniyu tvorchestva* [The architect Rastrelli: materials for a study of his work]. Leningrad, 1963.

Disegni di Giacomo Quarenghi: Catalogo della Mostra. Venice: Neri Pozza Editore, 1967.

Dokusov, A. M., ed. *Literaturnye pamyatnye mesta Leningrada* [Places of literary interest in Leningrad]. Leningrad, 1968.

Iogansen, M. V.. *Mikhail Zemtsov.* Leningrad, 1975.

Kaganovich, A. L. *'Medny vsadnik': Istoriya sozdaniya monumenta* [The 'Bronze Horseman': The history of the monument's creation]. Leningrad, 1975.

Kamensky, V. A., ed. *Pamyatniki arkhitektury Leningrada* [Architectural monuments of Leningrad]. Leningrad, 1972.

Kennett, Audrey. *The Palaces of Leningrad.* London: Thames and Hudson, 1973.

*Kirichenko, E. I. *Russkaya arkhitektura 1830–1910-kh godov* [Russian architecture from the 1830s to the 1910s]. Moscow, 1978.

Komelova, G. N. *Vidy Peterburga i ego okrestnostey serediny XVIII veka* [Views of Petersburg and environs from the middle of the eighteenth century]. Leningrad, 1968.

Komelova, G. N., ed. *Kultura i iskusstvo petrovskogo vremeni* [Culture and art of the Petrine era]. Leningrad, 1977.

Korshunova, M. F. *Dzhakomo Kvarengi.* Leningrad, 1977.

Kozmyan, G. K. *F. B. Rastrelli.* Leningrad, 1976.

Kurbatov, V. *Peterburg.* Saint Petersburg, 1913.

Kyuchariants, D. A. *Antonio Rinaldi.* Leningrad, 1976.

*Levinson-Lessing, V. F. *Ermitazh: Istoriya i arkhitektura zdaniy* [The Hermitage: The history and architecture of the buildings]. Leningrad, 1974.

Lisaevich, I. *Pervy arkhitektor
Peterburga* [The first architect
of Petersburg] (monograph on
Domenico Tressini). Leningrad,
1971.

Lisovsky, V. G. *Andrey Voronikhin.*
Leningrad, 1971.

Lo Gatto, Ettore. *Il mito di Pietro-
burgo: Storia, leggenda, poesia.*
Milan: Feltrinelli Editore, 1960.

Lukomsky, G. K. *Stary Peterburg*
[Old Petersburg]. Petrograd, 1917.

Luppov, S. P., ed. *Istoriya stroitelstva Peterburga v pervoy chetverti
XVIII veka* [The history of the
building of Petersburg in the first
quarter of the eighteenth century].
Moscow, 1957.

Marsden, Christopher. *Palmyra of
the North.* London: Faber and
Faber, 1942.

Matveev, A. *Rastrelli.*
Moscow, 1938.

*Makarov, V. K., and Petrov, A. N.
Gatchina. Leningrad, 1974.

*Petrov, A. N. *Pushkin: Dvortsy i
parki* [Pushkin: The palaces and
parks]. Leningrad, 1969.

Pilyavsky, V. I. *Zodchy Rossi*
[The architect Rossi]. Moscow and
Leningrad, 1951.

———. *Zodchy Vasily Petrovich
Stasov: 1769–1848* [The architect
Vasily Petrovich Stasov]. Leningrad,
1970.

Rae, Isobel. *Charles Cameron:
Architect to the Court of Russia.*
London: Elek Books, 1971.

*Raskin, A. G. *Gorod Lomonosov:
Dvortsovo-parkovye ansambli
XVIII veka* [The City of Lomonosov: The eighteenth-century palace
and park ensembles]. Leningrad,
1979.

Somina, R. A. *Nevsky prospekt:
istorichesky ocherk* [Nevsky Prospekt: a historical sketch]. Leningrad, 1959.

Stolpyansky, P. N. *Peterburg.*
Petrograd, 1918.

Vipper, B. R. *Arkhitektura russkogo
barokko* [The architecture of the
Russian baroque]. Moscow, 1978.

Vlasyuk, A. I., et al. *Kazakov.*
Moscow, 1957.

Vyatkin, M. P., ed. *Ocherki istorii
Leningrada* [Studies in the history
of Leningrad], vol. 1. Moscow and
Leningrad, 1955.

Yegorov, I. A. *The Architectural
Planning of Saint Petersburg:
Its Development in the 18th and
19th Centuries.* Translated by Eric
Dluhosch. Athens: Ohio University
Press, 1969.

Yevsina, N. A. *Arkhitekturnaya
teoriya v Rossii XVIII v* [Architec-
tural theory in eighteenth-century
Russia]. Moscow, 1975.

Chapter Six:
The Twentieth Century

Aleksandrov, P. A., and Khan-
Magomedov, S. O. *Arkhitektor
Ivan Leonidov.* Moscow, 1971.

Apyshkov, V. *Ratsionalnoe v novoy
arkhitekture* [The rational in new
architecture]. Saint Petersburg,
1905.

Banham, Reyner. *Theory and Design
in the First Machine Age*, second
edition. Cambridge: MIT Press,
1980.

Borisova, Ye. A., and Kazhdan, T. P.
*Russkaya arkhitektura kontsa
XIX–nachala XX veka* [Russian
architecture from the end of the
nineteenth to the beginning of the
twentieth century]. Moscow, 1971.

Chiniakov, A. G. *Bratya Vesniny*
[The Vesnin brothers]. Moscow,
1970.

D'Andrea, Jeanne, and West, Stephen,
eds. *The Avant-Garde in Russia,
1910–1930: New Perspectives.*
Cambridge: MIT Press, 1980.

Frampton, Kenneth. *Modern Architecture: A Critical History.* New
York: Oxford University Press,
1980.

Ginzburg, M. Ya. *Stil i epokha*
[Style and epoch]. Moscow, 1924.

Gray, Camilla. *The Russian Experiment in Art: 1863–1922.* New
York: Harry N. Abrams, 1970.

Ikonnikov, A. V. *Kamennaya letopis
Moskvy* [Moscow's chronicle in
stone]. Moscow, 1978.

Ilin, M. A. *Vesniny* [The Vesnins].
Moscow, 1960.

Khan-Magomedov, S. O. *M. Ya.
Ginzburg.* Moscow, 1972.

Khazanova, V. E., comp. *Iz istorii
sovetskoy arkhitektury 1917–1925
gg.: Dokumenty i materialy* [From
the history of Soviet architecture,

1917–25: Documents and materials]. Moscow, 1963.

———. *Iz istorii sovetskoy arkhitektury 1926–1932 gg.: Dokumenty i materialy* [From the history of Soviet architecture, 1926–32: Documents and materials]. Moscow, 1970.

———. *Sovetskaya arkhitektura pervykh let oktyabrya 1917–1925 gg* [Soviet architecture in the first years after the October Revolution, 1917–25]. Moscow, 1970.

Kirichenko, Ye. I. *Fyodor Shekhtel.* Moscow, 1973.

*———. *Moskva: Pamyatniki arkhitektury 1830–1910-kh godov* [Moscow: Architectural monuments of the 1830s to the 1910s]. Moscow, 1977.

*———. *Russkaya arkhitektura 1830–1910-kh godov* [Russian architecture of the 1830s to the 1910s]. Moscow, 1978.

———. *Sovetskaya arkhitektura pervoy pyatiletki: Problemy goroda budushchego* [Soviet architecture of the first five-year plan: Problems of the city of the future]. Moscow, 1980.

Le Corbusier (Charles-Édouard Jeanneret). *The Radiant City.* New York: Orion Press, 1967.

Lissitzky, El. *Russia: An Architecture for World Revolution,* translated by Eric Dluhosch. Cambridge: MIT Press, 1970.

Malevich, Kasimir. *The Nonobjective World,* translated by Howard Dearstyne. Chicago: P. Theobald, 1959.

Miliutin, Nikolay. *Sotsgorod: The Problem of Building Socialist Cities,* translated by Arthur Sprague. Cambridge: MIT Press, 1974.

Quilici, Vieri. *L'architettura del construttivismo.* Bari: Editori Laterza, 1969.

Senkevitch, Anatole. *Soviet Architecture, 1917–1956: A Bibliographical Guide to Source Material.* Charlottesville: University Press of Virginia, 1974.

Shmidt, I. M., ed. *Voprosy sovetskogo izobrazitelnogo iskusstva i arkhitektury* [Issues in Soviet visual art and architecture]. Moscow, 1976.

Shvidkovsky, O. A., ed. *Building in the USSR, 1917–1932.* New York: Praeger, 1971.

Starr, S. Frederick. *Melnikov: Solo Architect in a Mass Society.* Princeton: Princeton University Press, 1978.

———. *Il padiglione di Melnikov a Parigi,* translated by Teresa Fiori. Rome: Officina Edizioni, 1979.

Teige, Karel, and Kroha, Jiří. *Avantgardni architektura.* Prague, 1969. (Originally published in 1936; republished with an afterword by Josef Císařovský.)

Yaralov, Yu. S., ed. *Arkhitektura sovetskoy Rossii* [The architecture of Soviet Russia]. Moscow, 1975.

INDEX

Numbers in roman type indicate page references for the text and captions; numbers in italics denote pages on which illustrations appear. When available, dates of birth and death are given in brackets for architects active in Russia.

GOLD IN AZURE

has been designed by Richard Hendel and Jean LeGwin and set into type by Roy McCoy, Cambridge, Massachusetts. The text of the book has been set in a film version of Trump Medieval, a typeface designed by Professor Georg Trump in the mid-1950s and cast by the C. E. Weber Typefoundry of Stuttgart, West Germany. The roman letter forms of Trump Medieval are based on classical prototypes, but have been interpreted by Professor Trump in a distinctly modern style. The italic letter forms are more of a sloped roman than a true italic in design, a characteristic shared by many contemporary typefaces.

The result is a modern and distinguished type, notable for its legibility and versatility. The display type is Solemnis, set by Sans and Serif, Boston, Massachusetts.

Map of European Russia drawn by Jacqueline Sakwa.

The separations, printing, and binding
by South China Printing Co., Hong Kong.